SPHERES OF INFLUENCE
IN INTERNATIONAL RELATIONS

Spheres of Influence in International Relations

History, Theory and Politics

SUSANNA HAST

Visiting Postdoctoral Fellow, Graduate Institute of International and Development Studies, Geneva, Switzerland
Research Associate, Centre on Conflict, Development and Peacebuilding (CCDP) of the Graduate Institute
Partner, the Finnish Centre of Excellence: Choices of Russian Modernisation, Aleksanteri Institute, Finland

ASHGATE

Published by
Ashgate Publishing Limited
Wey Court East
Union Road
Farnham
Surrey, GU9 7PT
England

Ashgate Publishing Company
110 Cherry Street
Suite 3-1
Burlington, VT 05401-3818
USA

www.ashgate.com

British Library Cataloguing in Publication Data
A catalogue record for this book is available from the British Library

The Library of Congress has cataloged the printed edition as follows:
Hast, Susanna.
Spheres of influence in international relations : history, theory and politics / By Susanna Hast.
    pages cm
  Includes bibliographical references and index.
  ISBN 978-1-4724-2154-8 (hardback) – ISBN 978-1-4724-2155-5 (ebook) – ISBN 978-1-4724-2156-2 (epub) 1. International relations–History. 2. Spheres of influence. 3. Russia–Foreign relations. I. Title.
  JZ1305.H377 2014
  327.1'14–dc23

                                                                        2013031418

ISBN 9781472421548 (hbk)
ISBN 9781472421555 (ebk – PDF)
ISBN 9781472421562 (ebk – ePUB)

Printed in the United Kingdom by Henry Ling Limited,
at the Dorset Press, Dorchester, DT1 1HD

Contents

Preface

Spheres of influence and understanding about them remain part of international politics and for better or worse will continue to be (Keal 1983, 225).

Ever since the most distant lands were discovered and international relations became global in scale, the challenge of humanity has been to organise the political map of the world. It has never been possible to make the world one, and few have even wanted this. In the end, the division of people by borders of nation-states took place. However, the state is not a perpetual and stable unit of the international system, but one that has been challenged from the day it was introduced – by the states themselves with asserted hierarchies and great power management. Spheres of influence are part and parcel of this world of states and their hierarchical relations. *Sphere of influence* is an idea which takes a stance on the very core question of International Relations[1] (henceforth IR): how is the world divided politically?

This study is a critical analysis and reassessment of the concept of sphere of influence with an interest in normative and theoretical questions arising from the past and the present. The concept is characterised by a conflict between the lack of theoretical interest in it in IR and, at the same time, the frequent use of it in political discourse.[2] *Sphere of influence* is a contested concept which has awaited theoretical reassessment from a historical perspective for too long. The problem with spheres of influence is that there is no debate on the meaning of the concept. It simply *is* in its simultaneous vagueness and familiarity. Indeed, the term is very well known, frequently deployed, especially when describing Russian foreign policy. Its recurrent use in language testifies to its being part of our political imagination. This imagination is founded upon past experiences, namely, the spheres of influence of the Cold War. Regardless of whether we see the Cold War as a thing of the past, or as something still visible as a mentality of division and difference, international relations have entered a new era. In this new era, we still find the concept of sphere of influence attesting to the need to contest the concept itself.

What then is it that makes a sphere of influence 'special'; what separates it from other ideas on influence? It is the concept's pejorative connotation, that is, the notion that it is a form of influence which implies contempt and disapproval.

---

1   'International Relations' refers to the discipline, 'international relations' to relations among international actors.

2   This is not to say that influence beyond borders has not been studied in theoretical terms within IR, but only that there is no interest in contesting the concept.

More specifically, it often means contempt for and disapproval of Russia's foreign policy. Much as no theoretical work has been done on spheres of influence within the discipline for some 30 years, neither has the pejorative nature of the concept been discerned. This prompts the questions: where do the pejorative uses of the term *sphere of influence* come from? Has the concept of sphere of influence always had pejorative associations? Is there any tradition of justifying spheres of influence in international theory? Moreover is it useful to rely on the old political imagination of spheres of influence when discussing Russia's relations with the post-Soviet states? These are the research questions that I will examine in the following pages.

I believe it is time to begin elaborating the theories on spheres of influence again, and to become critical about the language we use to judge or approve of international influence. It is time to renew our political imagination on spheres of influence. The concept of sphere of influence belongs to the jargon of IR and to political parlance. Because of the strong pejorative connotation of the concept, the choice to use or not to use it is political. A sphere of influence signifies some form of influence beyond state borders, not just *any* influence. It means a particular form of influence, or even a particular form of *international order.* Some states are described as having or striving for a sphere of influence, but not all. Since not all international influence is referred to as emanating from a sphere-of-influence policy, there must be a clearly delimited space which is occupied by a sphere of influence. There must also be a reason for viewing some foreign policies as pursuing a sphere of influence and denying others that connotation.

Research must have its anchor in the realities of life; otherwise it is useless. There are three reasons why I consider a study on spheres of influence to be important and necessary. First, the concept deserves to be reassessed due to its persistence in political language. Second, the history of spheres of influence informs international theory by revealing knowledge which is not currently associated with the concept. Sphere of influence as a concept should be contested: its uses should be critically examined and its meanings theoretically explored. Third, *sphere of influence* has meanings beyond its pejorative senses; I will present these in order to sever the seemingly unavoidable link between (the pejorative pall of) *sphere of influence* and Russia. The aim is not to relieve Russia of its responsibility in its foreign policies, but to reflect on the value of using the notion of a sphere of influence as a means to judge and categorise Russian foreign policy.

In the spirit of Joseph Rotblat (2007), signatory to the Russell-Einstein Manifesto against nuclear weapons in 1955, I have tried to connect this research to the problems I have discovered in contemporary international relations. This explains the focus on the three interconnected themes of the concept of sphere of influence, its pejorative uses, and Russia. The purpose of this study is to address the questions and concerns related to the concept of sphere of influence in the past and within the contemporary political imagination. In order to open up new paths for understanding spheres of influence in the present, I detail a tradition of thought about spheres of influence – a history of ideas.

There is nothing more valuable than life. Life is supported and maintained in peace. Determination, optimism and idealism for the sake of peace is my driving force. It is thanks to friends, teachers, colleagues and family who have inspired me to pursue a courageous research agenda which is based on my own life philosophy. I am greatly indebted to University Lecturer Mika Luoma-aho (University of Lapland) and Professor Pami Aalto (University of Tampere) guiding me and showing me the way forward. I offer my sincerest gratitude to Professor (emeritus) Vilho Harle, Professor Christopher Browning (Warwick University) and Sinikukka Saari (The Finnish Institute for International Affairs) for valuable comments on the manuscript. Richard Foley and Helen Lambert did an amazing job with proofreading.

Colleagues at the University of Lapland deserve special thanks for support, especially Tiina Seppälä, Professor Julian Reid, Aini Linjakumpu and Petri Koikkalainen. This research was conducted while a doctoral candidate at the Aleksanteri Institute in Helsinki. I offer my appreciation to those countless wonderful colleagues in and around Aleksanteri, Director Markku Kivinen, Markku Kangaspuro, Katri Vallaste, Matti Jutila, Sari Autio-Sarasmo, Tuomas Forsberg, Hanna Smith, Anna-Maria Salmi, Hanna Ruutu and the rest of the staff. Katja Karelina and Kaori Uchida deserve special thanks for helping me with the Russian language.

I thank the Centre for Russian and East European Studies (CREES) in Birmingham and the Graduate Institute of International and Development Studies (IHEID) in Geneva for my visiting fellowships. Without the financial support of Aleksanteri Institute's Doctoral Programme, the Kone Foundation, Rector's grants of the University of Lapland and the 'Foundations' post doc pool' research grant from Alfred Kordelin Foundation this book would not have come to life. The research is also a part of the Finnish Centre of Excellence: Choices of Russian Modernisation, funded by the Academy of Finland.

Last but not least, I would like to thank my family for love and patience. Special thanks are due to my husband Juha, my parents, my children and rest of my family. I also want to extend my sincerest gratitude to all the friends who have been on my side in Geneva for three years now. I would also like to thank my mentor in life, Daisaku Ikeda, for a model of living a victorious life. Gratitude fills my heart.

Susanna Hast
December 2013
Geneva

List of Abbreviations

ECPR	The European Council on Foreign Relations
EU	European Union
IR	International Relations
RSCT	The regional security complex theory
SVOP	The Council on Foreign and Defence Policy
UN	United Nations

Chapter 1
Framing 'Sphere of Influence'

1.1   A Normative Concept

In 2004, when I first embarked on a study of 'Russia's sphere of influence', I thought it would require no more than finding out how Russia blackmails and oppresses its neighbours and violates their rights by meddling in their internal affairs and limiting their foreign policy options. But it did not take long before I discovered a problem: there was no literature discussing, defining and contesting the concept of sphere of influence. To my mind, it was not possible to study Russia's sphere of influence before first determining what *sphere of influence* meant. This observation has steered me towards an inquiry into the concept itself.

I began to look for theories on spheres of influence but, finding none, I began collecting the theoretically and historically relevant ideas that could help in defining the concept. I discovered that *sphere of influence* denotes not only a foreign policy tool but a complex of ideas on 1) international order and 2) acceptable and unacceptable influence. By 'international order' I refer to the rules and institutions that govern the functioning of the society of states. By 'acceptable and unacceptable influence' I refer to *sphere of influence* as a normative concept, one embodying certain assumptions about right and wrong. This focus on international order and the normative aspects of spheres of influence derives from what is known as the English School of International Relations and its potential in explaining the concept. The questions of order and justice directed my interest towards a group of theorists, active from the First World War until the aftermath of the Second World War, who were concerned with the demise of the state and the dangers of a world state. In addition to my interest in history, I became concerned with the contemporary use of the term *sphere of influence* in political language. I noticed that use and non-use of the term seemingly reflected that the referent was too straightforward to require a theory, too old for anyone to be interested in, or too common to pay attention to. This has resulted in the concept being denied its place in international theory. Most importantly, I came to realise that *sphere of influence* was a pejorative notion. As a foreign policy tool it was morally unacceptable, representing injustice. This last observation, the concept's pejorative connotation, greatly influenced the path that I would choose for writing a book about the concept. The work had to be concerned with history; it had to be critical; and it had to prove that we need to be interested in spheres of influence.

I began to see the way in which the concept of sphere of influence was used as an element of discursive power. I noticed that the pejorative sense of *sphere of influence* does not come out of nowhere: it comes from the injustice that the expression has always implied, not least when associated with the Cold War. *Sphere of influence* in its pejorative sense means not only disapproval of the practice of pursuing a sphere of influence but also avoiding a critical approach to the idea itself and, ultimately, avoiding use of the term. Yet, non-use renders the term *sphere of influence* as pejorative in tone as much as use does. For example, the fact that Russian scholars or politicians avoid the term does not help to create an image that Russia is not pursuing a sphere of influence. On the other hand, arguing why Russia is not pursuing a sphere of influence, and determining what exactly it is pursuing instead, might better explain Russia's interests to the outside world.

Spheres of influence constitute an issue that goes to the very core of international ethics. They are inseparable from the matter of justice, which we can define following Hedley Bull (2002, 75–6) as comprising moral ideas on actions that are right in themselves but which in world politics more often relate to the equal distribution of rights and privileges among states (see more in Chapter 3.5). Spheres of influence relate to yet another political concept bounded by normative considerations: power. For William Connolly (1993, 97), the position of exerting power over others indicates a position of responsibility and a need for justification. A sphere of influence denotes a relationship of power and as such it comes with responsibility and a need for justification even if those aspects are denied or concealed. Thus, there is something naturally normative about spheres of influence. By 'normative', I mean a norm in the legal and moral sense: that which is considered right or wrong and just or unjust. Historically, a sphere of influence has carried with it ideas on acceptable and non-acceptable codes of conduct and it has always necessitated justification. In the present, the pejorative use of the concept is manifested in criticism of Russia's foreign policy: where the country pursues a sphere of influence, this implies imperialism, oppression, pressure (military, economic or political) and a mentality of divisions, but not subsidies, support, protection, stability or peace. All this will be contested in the following pages by unravelling the normative history of the phenomenon. I wish to uncover that part of the concept which expresses the tension between acceptable and non-acceptable influence in international relations; to this end I will explore its normative scope in full. A theoretical and historical reassessment is very much in order given the failure to date of IR to discuss the pejorative nature of the concept and its being viewed instead as something self-evident and immutable.

As Robert Jackson (2000, 5) has put it, 'Normative discourse in international relations, as in any other sphere of human relations, operates by reference to certain assumptions and expectations concerning justified and unjustified conduct'. Throughout his book *The Global Covenant*, Jackson (2000) argues that world politics is normative, with an ethics of its own that is constructed by political leaders. Spheres of influence belong to this normative order. There is no international law on spheres of influence, but the principles of sovereignty and non-intervention establish the limits of international influence, and thus also the idea of a sphere of influence. Today there is no room for justifying the existence of a sphere of influence. Neither state leaders nor scholars will voice acceptance of an arrangement by that name. The only way to justify such a policy is to avoid any reference to the term or to formulate new expressions. Yet, the history of *sphere of influence* comprises more than attempts to condemn the policy it refers to. Spheres of influence have been explained as providing for *international order*, an argument completely lacking in our present political imagination (see Chapter 2 and 3). Spheres of influence also find justification as they are posited to illustrate the demise of state sovereignty and the fear of a world state (see Chapter 4).

I am proposing here that the injustice imputed to the pursuit of a sphere of influence, and thus the pejorative sense of the concept, are not writ in stone. Justifications of spheres of influence do exist in international political thought. On a more general level, justifications of injustices also exist. Jackson argues that the stability of international society and in particular the unity of the great powers are far more important than humanitarian protection or minority rights – if one has to choose between the two. He (2000, 291) asserts, 'War is the biggest threat to human rights. War between the great powers is the biggest humanitarian threat of all. Nothing else comes close'. This is the normative debate we try to avoid at present and this is exactly what I want to bring to light with regard to spheres of influence. I do this by presenting a history of the concept of sphere of influence in normative perspective.

I begin by explaining the pejorative associations of the concept and the purpose of the study, and continue towards theoretical/historical episodes that allow me to contest our present understanding of spheres of influence. First, I discuss *sphere of influence* as a social construct and my approach to contesting the concept. Next, I locate the concept in the contemporary political imagination by presenting different concepts of territorial influence. Finally, before the historical and conceptual journey begins, I present images of Russia's sphere-of-influence policy with references to that country's political thinking.

In Chapters 2 through 5, we find *sphere of influence* constructed as a normative idea on international influence in four settings: 1) the English School account of the history of the system of states, 2) the English School theory on the institutions of the society of states, 3) conceptualisations of regional constellations springing from the context of the First and Second World Wars and 4) Cold War spheres of influence.

The first chapter on the English School investigates the origins of the concept of sphere of influence in relation to the history of the states-system. Suzerainty, hegemony, colonialism and the Monroe Doctrine are discussed. The second chapter on the English School discusses balance of power, sovereignty, intervention, justice, international law, and influence as responsibility. The idea of a sphere of influence is fitted within the pluralist-solidarist debate on international order. Chapter 4 comprises an episode extending from the First World War until the aftermath of the Second World War (1915–1950), during which theorists formulated responses to the crisis of the states-system.[1] The solution these theorists offered to the problems caused by nationalism and the disintegration of the sovereign state was a system composed of regional constellations. Friedrich Naumann wrote about Mid-Europe, Carl Schmitt and E.H. Carr about *Großraum*, Walter Lippmann about the Good Neighbor Policy, and George Orwell about the fictional Oceania and Eastasia. Chapter 5 is an episode located in the Cold War setting, which reinvented the consolidation of spheres of influence as a central foreign policy practice of the time. I will explore not only the conceptualisations of the period but also the Cuban Missile Crisis (1962). I set out to prove that the Cold War spheres of influence should also be analysed by reinterpreting the dynamics of the *international society* of the time. In the concluding chapter, I encourage students of IR to take an interest in the concept of sphere of influence and I put forward thoughts on the relationship between spheres of influence, order and justice.

1.2 'Sphere of influence' is What We Make of It

It is with a focus on justice and order that I began the journey to reassess the concept of sphere of influence in terms of its past and present. My approach to the history of the concept is constructivist, in the belief that a great proportion of political action consists of speech acts. I claim that spheres of influence are constructed in inter-subjective interaction. Spheres of influence do not live lives of their own separate from political actors and the discursive constructions of those actors. If Alexander Wendt (1992) says that anarchy is what states make of it, then I say a sphere of influence is what states make of it. A sphere of influence is not a permanent structure in the international system but is instead shaped and re-shaped in the interactions and discourses among human beings across state borders. According to R.B.J. Walker (1995, 6), 'Theories of international relations are more interesting as aspects of contemporary world politics that need to be explained than as explanations of contemporary world politics'. The ideas, theories and conceptualisations of spheres of influence should not be seen as mere explanations of world politics, but as constitutive of the practices of international relations. References to spheres of influence enable certain political imaginations while limiting others. The concept of sphere of influence needs to be explained before it can be used to explain anything.

Jackson (2000, 10) writes that world politics is to a great extent a realm of discourse and dialogue which now operate on a global scale. Spheres of influence are constructed in discourses, and ones that have a rather prominent role in international relations. If developing a theory on spheres of influence has aroused little interest in researchers, the analysis of *discourses* on spheres of influence – the use of the term *sphere of influence* in speech – has prompted even less. Jackson

---

1   Most of the material is related to the Second World War. Only Friedrich Naumann's writings were published during the First World War (1915).

puts discourses in the centre of political activity by stating that the most significant facet of international human relations is discourse and dialogue on what actions are acceptable, desirable and justified:

> In politics, talk is not trivial; on the contrary, it is fundamental. Written or verbal discourse is the main vehicle of political activity. Without discourse there could be no politics in the ordinary meaning of the word. Without international discourse there could be no international relations. (Jackson 2000, 37)

According to Connolly (1993, 3), '[…] to share a language is to share a range of judgements and commitments embodied in it'. Connolly writes about the 'terms of political discourse', which refer to a certain vocabulary that sets frames for political reflection. More specifically, the terms of political discourse refer to a set of criteria that must be met before an event or an act falls within the definition of a concept. Moreover, with those criteria comes a judgement (2). Connolly continues, 'Since the discourse of politics helps to set the terms within which that politics proceeds, one who seeks to understand and to assess the structure of political life must deliberately probe the conventions governing these concepts' (3). For Connolly, the language of politics channels political thought and action into certain directions and '[t]hose who simply use established concepts to get to the facts of political life, those who act unreflectively within the confines of established concepts, actually have the perceptions and modes of conduct available to them limited in subtle and undetected ways' (1).

In the same spirit, Iver Neumann (2008, 62) declares, 'It [discourse] constrains what is thought of at all, what is thought as possible, and what is thought of as the "natural thing" to do in a given situation'. The terms of political discourse are what confine the concept of sphere of influence to a certain established framework, which I assert must be contested. A sphere of influence is not a fact of political life that can go without being critically examined first and foremost as *an idea*. If it remains uncontested and unrevised, the concept of sphere of influence will offer no more than a limited perception of international politics and will potentially reinforce established practices. Yet even if its referent were transparent, *sphere of influence* would not lead to a blithe liberty in the use of language. All concepts include some uncertainty: all are used and understood differently depending on the language, culture, time or even on the individual in question. Likewise, no concept can be totally 'purified' or made 'perfect'. But to let concepts live lives of their own without stopping to enquire what they mean and how they are used limits not only thought but also action.

Sphere of influence is a concept which encompasses Connolly's terms of political discourse: the vocabulary of influence, criteria informing a judgement and the potential to channel political thought and action. Contesting the concept of sphere of influence, one of my purposes here, means recognising that the language describing our political imagination is a means of power. A sphere of influence belongs to the world of language as much as to the world of deeds, and language is what I am interested in here. The term is endowed with power in language use: a state can be accused of pursuing a sphere of influence and a state can deny an interest in establishing one. The term *sphere of influence* is interpreted, used and misused – or omitted – in discourse as a means of power.

1.3   An Orbit Metaphor from the Cold War

By now the reader might be eager to see a definition of *sphere of influence*. We must begin somewhere in order to find the concept in the history of ideas and place it in the context of the contemporary political imagination. For scholars in political science, *sphere of influence* is a term used in international relations. The uses of the term are imbued with emotion and hostility stemming from the imagination of the Cold War. We simply have no other point of reference for the term, that is, no other historical or conceptual knowledge directing our thinking than the images of superpower rivalry and the oppression it caused. Hence, the definitions from two analysts of the period, Edy Kaufman[2] and Paul Keal, provide a suitable beginning for contesting the concept, although its actual historical origins lie elsewhere:

> A 'sphere of influence' can be best described then, as a geographic region characterised by the high penetration of one superpower to the exclusion of other powers and particularly of the rival superpower (Kaufman 1976, 11).

> A sphere of influence is a determinate region within which a single external power exerts a predominant influence, which limits the independence or freedom of action of political entities within it (Keal 1983, 15).

Kaufman's definition emphasises the relationship between superpowers: there is *penetration* into a region which *excludes* other powers from that region. Keal deals more with the relationship between the influencing and influenced powers: the sovereignty of those influenced is restricted. We can discern two features ascribed to a sphere of influence from these two definitions: exclusion of other powers and limitation of the independence or sovereignty of the influenced states. The rivalry between great powers and its repercussions for sovereignty are the underlying tenets of the present discourses as well, even though they are not discussed explicitly.

The notion of a sphere of influence extends beyond international relations. Wikipedia refers to the sphere of influence of Microsoft, for example. Even though

---

2   Kaufman's book *The Superpowers and Their Spheres of Influence* (1976) is, in addition to Keal's, one of the few explicit accounts of spheres of influence. Kaufman however deals with the concept and its meanings less than the name of the book would suggest, and he is not part of the English School, which is why I do not emphasise the significance of his work as I do Keal's. Nevertheless, Kaufman provides many important insights which correspond much to Keal's reasoning, and are presented especially in chapters 2.4 and 2.5.

one can find references to spheres of influence in fields ranging from sports to medical science, it is quite well established as a concept in IR. But it is not well established enough to have prompted a debate on its meaning. In comparison, the concept of security has attracted the attention of a large number of researchers indeed, resulting in a deluge of studies which redefine 'security' such that it encompasses forms of threats other than merely military ones and subjects other than only states. This interest in developing the concept of security is in striking contrast with the disinterest the discipline has shown when it comes to redefining the concept of sphere of influence.

One reason for the lack of interest in conceptualising spheres of influence and debating the uses of the term after the Cold War is that *sphere of influence* represents more of a metaphor than an analytical model to scholars in IR.[3] *Sphere of influence,* in its present use, is a metaphorical expression which takes the form of a figure of speech, just like Richard Little (2007, 21–3) argues is the case with *the balance of power.* As a metaphor, *sphere of influence* attempts to explain a power relation which involves the influencing and the influenced powers, as well as the territories they occupy. Little argues that a 'set of scales', or alternatively 'arch/body' is the source of the metaphor of the balance of power (see Chapter 6). The source of *sphere of influence* as a metaphor is an orbit, with the term 'orbit' referring to the influence of the United States, Russia and even the EU (see Brzezinski 1998; Hedenskog 2005, 132; Lippmann 1945, 65; Lo 2002, 77, 121; Routledge 1998, 246; Tsygankov 2010, 237). Dmitri Trenin (2002, 69), a well-known Russian scholar and director of the Carnegie Moscow Center, has written, 'Russia's economic success, should it eventually come, would not only draw Belarus and Ukraine into Moscow's *orbit*: Russia's *gravitational pull* would have an impact on the behavior and orientation of the Transcaucasian and Central Asian states' (emphasis added). Here 'orbit' is the 'sphere' and 'gravitational pull' is 'influence'.

Friedrich Naumann (1917, 180–83) illustrates this astronomical sphere of influence as a solar system composed of 'the sun' and the surrounding 'planet states'/'satellite nations'. The sun is the central power in whose orbit the planet-nations are situated. Naumann (1917, 180) describes how satellite nations or planet states (he uses the terms interchangeably) have a life of their own but no longer follow their own laws. Satellites only add strength to the guiding group to which they belong. Around the satellite states there exists a mass of unorganised national material: asteroids or comets – neutrals – which do not belong to any 'sun' but rather can be swept away into a satellite relationship with the Great Sovereignties (181). For Herbert Butterfield the order of the European states-system was 'a kind of terrestrial counterpart of the Newtonian system of astronomy'. For Butterfield all the bodies, the great and small powers, were tied together by a gravitational pull proportionate to their size and their distance from

---

3   See Little (2007, 19–50) for a discussion on the meaning and significance of metaphors.

others. Butterfield continues, that without counteracting forces (the balance of power) the greater powers will swallow the smaller ones close-by, 'just as the moon would fall into the earth' (Butterfield 1966, 132). Just as Naumann uses the sun and its planetary system to depict spheres of influence, Butterfield benefits from the metaphors of planets and their moons in order to explain international order with its balances and influences.

The way in which the orbit comes alive as the source of the metaphor is through circles or ellipses drawn on a map to represent the territories that are under the influence of a great power.[4] Spheres of influence are also seen as composed of concentric circles, with influence extending from the centre towards the periphery such that the closer the influenced state is to the core, the stronger the influence. One such example comes from James Burnham (1947, 104), who drew a picture of circles of influence, 'concentric rings around an inner circle', which the Soviet Union would attempt to implement. Burnham's rings illustrate the global domination pattern with circles of *absorption* (such as Baltic States, East Poland, Mongolia), *domination* (such as Finland, Germany, Balkans, Middle East etc.), *orienting influence* (such as Latin America, France, Central and Southern China) and finally *infiltration and demoralization* (United States and England) (105).

Burnham's circles imply borders. They suggests influence beyond the influencing state's territory, extending over the territory of the influenced states. This takes us to the significance of the metaphorical image: a sphere encompassing a territory delineated on a map and consisting of states. These spheres exist as something as evident as anything else drawn on a map, like a geographical or at least a political fact. They can be refuted in order to draw the circles differently, just like borders of states are sometimes re-drawn, but the existence of these spheres is refuted as infrequently as the existence of states themselves. Borders also make *sphere of influence* a pejorative concept, as it expresses a violation of or disrespect for a line drawn on a map. The violation of state borders means a violation of sovereignty and thus spheres of influence pertain to the question of *justice in international relations*. Moreover, the source of the metaphor – orbit – should be considered as an indication of the significance of *international order* for the conceptualisation of a sphere of influence. A system whose entities have orbits and are subject to the gravitational pull of the centre functions based on an order of things.

As I have noted, I wish to contest the concept and the idea of a sphere of influence through a historical and theoretical investigation. I argue that even though one should be critical of the uses of the concept of sphere of influence in shaming and condemning action, it does not mean that foreign policies should not be criticised. I also suggest that the mindset of Cold War spheres of influence can help to maintain established practices of thinking, speaking and acting. As a metaphor, *sphere of influence* provides an image of a map and maintains the aspect of disapproval, but it does not explain what a sphere of influence is or why one exists.

---

4   Astronomically orbits are elliptic.

I would contend that the metaphor as it stands leads to oversimplification of foreign policies and motives. For example, in order to condemn injustice by reference to a sphere of influence, one should first address the relationship between justice and the concept of sphere of influence. The pejorative connotation of the concept is a hidden agenda, and I propose we embrace transparency when using the concept to shame states. It should also be acknowledged that historically *sphere of influence* is a normative concept which has not been interpreted solely in pejorative terms. I will develop this argument in the chapters to come.

1.4 Contemporary Concepts of Influence

One explanation for the lack of interest in conceptualising spheres of influence is that there are already plenty of other concepts describing international influence. But if other concepts described international relations better, would not researchers and commentators then use those and leave *sphere of influence* in the past? My argument is that contemporary concepts describing influence beyond state borders do not replace *sphere of influence*, because the political language proves otherwise and because *sphere of influence* maintains its uniqueness due to its pejorative connotation. I will demonstrate this by introducing the concepts of regional security complex, empire lite, regionalism and soft power.

The regional security complex theory (RSCT) proposed by Barry Buzan and Ole Waever (2003) helps to explain the post-Cold War order and the relationship between globalising and regionalising trends. The RSCT claims that security interdependencies have become increasingly regional since the end of Cold War bipolarity, resulting in local powers having more room to manoeuvre and great powers having less incentive and desire to intervene in security affairs outside their own regions (3). Even though the RSCT is concerned with security dependencies, that is, power relations, the theory does not consider questions of justice, which are core issues in the case of a sphere of influence.

Buzan and Waever (2003, 55–6) identify different forms of security complexes by pointing to the centre of influence: 1) a standard RSC with a Westphalian, anarchic structure and no unipolar power at its centre, 2) a centred RSC led by a great or super power and 3) a region integrated by institutions. An RSC is a useful umbrella concept, or theory, for security relations, including influence beyond borders; in this framework, a sphere of influence could be compared to a 'centred RSC'. Even so, an RSC does not replace a sphere of influence; the two are not identical. First of all, even though spheres of influence are most often defined as regions (see for example Keal's and Kaufman's definitions above), historically they have not always been confined to a single region. If we look at the Cold War, the spheres of influence of the time do not fully adhere to the metaphor of an orbit depicted on the map, because influence was spread all over the globe. If we go even further back, the concept of sphere of influence first emerges in the literature on colonialism, where it is also quite different from an RSC. In fact, *sphere of influence* is such an old concept that comparing it to contemporary concepts such as RSC is of little help in contesting the former. Moreover, if we look at political discourses, the term *regional security complex*, unlike *sphere of influence*, is nowhere to be found. No other term has replaced *sphere of influence*, RSC included. *Sphere of influence* is a familiar term, easy to resort to, and has its purpose in the language we use.

Empire lite is another contemporary concept addressing influence beyond borders with potential relevance for the concept of sphere of influence. For the Canadian historian Michael Ignatieff, empire lite is the new American Empire:

> True, there are no American colonies and American corporations do not need their governments to acquire territory by force in order to acquire markets. So the new empire is not like those of times past, built on colonies and conquest. It is an empire lite, hegemony without colonies, *a global sphere of influence* without the burden of direct administration and the risk of daily policing. It is an imperialism led by people who remember that their country secured its independence by revolt against an empire, and who have often thought of their country as the friend of anti-imperial struggles everywhere (Ignatieff 2003, 89; emphasis added).

Ignatieff refers to the concept of sphere of influence yet prefers the concept of empire. Both have their pejorative ring, but, I would suggest, the Cold War image of a sphere of influence dominates so strongly as to explain Ignatieff's preference for the term 'empire'. Empire lite as the new model of American foreign policy has been cleansed of associations with colonialism – yet another pejorative idea for the Americans. Instead, empire lite is imperial tutelage on nation-building, seen in places such as Afghanistan, Bosnia and Kosovo, for the sake of global hegemony and ensuring stability in regions essential to the security of the United States and its allies (Ignatieff 2003, 89–90). Empire lite is a conception of influence which takes the United States closest to the idea of a power with a (global) sphere of influence, not least because its pejorative associations easily evoke questions of justice. Imperialism and empire (lite) are clearly closely connected to the idea of a sphere of influence and I will get back to this in Chapters 1.5.1 and 2.4.

Ignatieff brings up questions of justice relating to interventionism in the case of empire lite. The notion of a sphere of influence fits squarely in the midst of any debate on the justification of intervention by an empire lite or a great power, even though Ignatieff chooses not to use the term *sphere of influence*. I argue that when we go looking for a theoretical conceptualisation of what a sphere of influence is, we will find a debate on the role of the state. In other words, spheres of influence not only draw our attention to matters of justice in interstate relations but also highlight the fate of the state itself and the dangers of a world state. The uniqueness of the concept of sphere of influence is that its evident normative nature allows us to connect the questions of justice and international order. Thus, I find *sphere of influence* situated between the discourses on justice and order in a way that no other concept is – and the reason lies precisely in our present use of the concept in shaming another state's practices. The shaming of another state relates to the increasing concerns for justice (interstate and human) in international relations. Within this context, references to spheres of influence serve the purpose of pointing out injustice. But as a discursive tool, shaming can work as a means for identity-building and seeking political support from other states in a conflict with the Other. Western states have a long history in *othering* 'the East' – and Russia especially – for the sake of identity construction (see Harle 2000, Neumann 1999, Wolff 1994). This adds another interesting facet, and an ignored one, to *sphere of influence*: as a concept that is emotionally loaded, historically burdened and epitomised by considerations of injustice, it has the power to mobilise resistance and fuel resentment.

What about the concept of regionalism, then? Could that not replace *sphere of influence* in the contemporary international situation? Regionalism, especially when conceived of as *regional solidarism*, comes remarkably close to denoting a sphere of influence. The difference between the two lies in the pejorative connotation of the latter. Andrew Hurrell's (2007) discussion on *regional states-systems* or *regional international societies* is a good case in point. Hurrell presents a division comprising identity-based solidarist regions, regions as poles and regions centred on powerful states. Regarding regions centred on powerful states Hurrell explains that there is a regional state so overwhelmingly dominant that it can impose its will by creating consensual hegemony. This hegemony is enforced by providing economic benefits, ensuring regional security or defining a certain worldview or set of values (140–41). Finally, Hurrell mentions sphere of influence:

> Despite these difficulties over the longer run, it is important to hold open the possibility of a world order made up of large 'region-states' which might have a variety of internal forms of political organization – including perhaps *old-style spheres of influence*, hegemonically centered institutionalism and unequal forms of federal union (Hurrell, 2007, 141, emphasis added).

Hurrell envisions a regionalism led by a powerful state. This can take different forms, one being a sphere of influence, which belongs to the past ('old-style') but can still be incorporated in the new regionalism. I will discuss primacy, hegemony and dominance later (Chapter 2.3), arguing that the theoretical conceptualisation of spheres of influence begins with separating different forms of influence and solidarist tendencies. The point is that there is no reason to be shy in discussing the meanings of *sphere of influence* and searching for meaningful connections to other concepts, for as long as the term *sphere of influence* persists in the language of the discipline, IR needs to address the phenomenon. Regionalism (or an RSC) is one possible manifestation of a sphere of influence – although a sphere of influence is not always confined within regional boundaries – and within regionalism a sphere of influence can express a particular form of political organisation.

Clearly, the concept of sphere of influence has its place in general discussions on acceptable or justified influence, but the problem is that it is not explicitly included in these debates. Felix Ciută (2006) argues that the debate over American hegemony revolves around the ideas of 'the good state' or 'responsible hegemon'. Ciută (2006, 183) writes, 'However hidden, the definition of 'the responsible state' permeates all the debates about unipolarity, hegemony or imperialism, whether they are for, or against specific policies'. I ask, is Russian hegemony debated in the framework of responsibility? In a way, yes, but only in conjunction with the idea of 'irresponsible powers', where Russia as a 'sphere-of-influence power' is the antithesis of a 'responsible power'. Ciută (2006, 187) is right to argue that debates on the meaning of 'empire' inevitably – but almost always only implicitly – fall back on a deeply normative understanding of the state, hegemony and empire. We are on the right track here, acknowledging the normative aspects of hegemony or empire, but we are missing spheres of influence. In the present uses of the concept, pursuing a sphere of influence represents irresponsible conduct, and bringing spheres of influence within the debates on the nature of states, responsibility and 'the good state' would not only inform international theory but make it possible to contest the concept and assess its uses critically.

I will introduce the idea of responsible great powers in the English School context in Chapter 3.6, but also the distinction between hard and soft power in the contemporary debates potentially captures something about spheres of influence. Joseph Nye (2004, x) developed the idea of soft power as the ability to get what one wants by attraction rather than coercion and payments. Nye writes, 'When you can get others to admire your ideals and to want what you want, you do not have to spend as much on sticks and carrots to move them in your direction' (x). Hard power, by contrast, indicates economic and military might (5). The distinction between soft and hard power can be a distinction between more and less acceptable influence and in this respect relates to the pejorative nature ascribed to spheres of influence. Nicu Popescu (2006) writes that the European Union has seen itself as a soft power but recently Russia, too, has begun investing more in means of soft power in order to better justify and legitimise its influence in neighbouring states. This raises the question of whether hard power is what makes a sphere-of-influence policy and, if so, whether Russia is stepping out of its traditional sphere-of-influence policy if it is resorting to soft rather than hard means. Nevertheless, as I will demonstrate in the following chapter, Popescu still uses the term *sphere of influence* in characterising Russia's foreign policy, even in its softer form. The relevance of the distinction between soft and hard power lies in its capacity to distinguish influence which is more acceptable: soft influence could be a contemporary approximation of a sphere of influence but without the pejorative connotation. Even so, we are still faced with the fact that not even the soft-hard distinction has replaced the concept of sphere of influence in political parlance.

Even though comparing *sphere of influence* to other contemporary concepts of influence is meaningful, I am more interested in the history of the concept. The process of contesting the concept must start from an inquiry into its past meanings and origins. If we ignored the historicity of *sphere of influence*, we would end up burying a valuable body of knowledge. Empire lite and RSC, regionalism, integration and soft/hard power have their place in the IR jargon, just like *sphere of influence* does. Yet, I explore other concepts, such as colonialism, intervention and *Großraum*, and I argue that the meaning of sphere of influence becomes obvious precisely when it is juxtaposed with related conceptions such as these. In fact, an assessment of sphere of influence needs other concepts around it to connect the concept to international theory, away from metaphorical or emotional uses. But my view is historical, a voyage of discovery into the past meanings of sphere of influence.

Moreover, the terminology invented in IR after the Cold War is not very well suited to explaining the concept of sphere of influence, because the concept at hand is a much older one than regionalism, integration, empire lite or other more recent ideas. In fact, one should enquire why post-Cold War theoretical thinking on regional orders is not explicitly connected to the concept of sphere of influence, which has a long and significant history. Even if more recent conceptualisations of regional order and international influence have succeeded in explaining present developments better, it is spheres of influence that people talk about. Politicians do not speak of regional security complexes or of empire lites; they speak about spheres of influence. The term *sphere of influence* permeates even popular discourses and embodies a shared, unspoken knowledge of its meaning. I argue that there are not many concepts depicting regional order which can claim such a status. The special nature of the concept of sphere of influence comes from its interlinkage with normative questions as well as its long history and centrality in political parlance. Thus, this is a study on what has made *sphere of influence* a pejorative term and how has influence beyond state borders been justified and justification debated.

The reason why I see *sphere of influence* as a concept that needs a theoretical elaboration is the potential it holds for addressing normative questions. Sphere of influence as an idea indicates that 1) there is a matter of justice in interstate relations (justice is not confined to state borders) and 2) there is an exercise of influence which represents injustice. This is where I find the uniqueness of the idea of a sphere of influence. Of course, *sphere of influence* is not the only concept to capture injustice and influence: hegemony, imperialism, interventionism or 'export of democracy', for instance, are all somewhat pejorative in tone, but even so *sphere of influence* has persisted. Why? I suggest the reason is the power of the metaphor: the image of a map with a centre extending its power beyond its borders. More concretely, it endures because the Cold War map has not left our memories. *Sphere of influence* has taken on the function of describing Russia's continuing Cold War mentality or imperial legacy (see Lo 2002). No other concept has such a strong association with the unjust influence policies of the Cold War. Thus, regardless of their usefulness, other concepts have not superseded *sphere of influence* in describing influence and justice. But there is more than just the question of justice: 3) spheres of influence shine as a form of international order. It is no coincidence that during the turmoil of the world wars numerous ideas relating to spheres of influence were produced, Schmitt's *Großraum* being perhaps the most captivating. Political theorists reacted to the need to find solutions to the problems of international relations of their time. Accordingly, by combining the two aspects of justice and order, we can begin building a meaning for *sphere of influence* beyond its pejorative uses. Julie Wilhelmsen and Geir Flikke, from the Norwegian Institute of International Affairs, write that 'words, rhetoric and concepts *do* matter'. Norms, both positive and negative, spread within the international community, altering the way states act and interact (Wilhelmsen and Flikke 2005, 389). The way we speak of spheres of influence matters.

1.5   Russia's Sphere of Influence

The twenty-first-century discourses on spheres of influence are stories which represent and uphold spheres of influence as much as the actual practices of states. The notion of a sphere of influence emerges as an explanation for Russia's foreign policy motives in its relationship with the post-Soviet space. Finding a research paper (written by a non-Russian) which would either problematise the idea of a sphere of influence or prove explicitly that Russia is not constructing a sphere of influence is difficult, if not impossible. The use of the concept of sphere of influence in describing Russian foreign policy is frequent enough to raise concern over the lack of critical approaches to the concept. As there almost seems to be an unspoken agreement among European and American scholars that Russia is attempting to construct or maintain a sphere of influence, it becomes difficult to challenge this view. *Sphere of influence* is almost like a mantra, which when repeated often enough becomes a self-fulfilling prophesy. However, critical research should be able to challenge established knowledges; indeed this is the very purpose of my research. I do not argue that Russia is not seeking to establish influence beyond its borders, but suggest that the term *sphere of influence* – in its current pejorative and vague use – might not serve as an accurate description of Russia's foreign policy motives.

When the concept of sphere of influence is used in describing Russian foreign policy, it represents something self-evident, undisputed and unproblematic. Given that IR has forgotten to theorise sphere of influence, it is quite understandable that foreign policy researchers refer to the term without questioning its meaning. Moreover, it is not possible to define every single concept that one happens to use in a given piece of research. As Jens Bartelson (1995, 43) states, 'as soon as one decides to investigate something, one has to take other things for granted'. But debating a concept or an idea has tremendous influence on its use. Consider *identity politics*. The term carries a very different meaning depending on whether identity is understood as innate rather than as a social relation. Racism thrives on the idea of natural characteristics belonging to a particular nation or people. This notion has been contested within the discipline by claiming that a national – or in fact any – identity is socially constructed and can change and be manipulated. If IR is rich in theorising about identity and other concepts, theoretical conceptualisations of sphere of influence are conspicuous by their absence. The lack of theoretical debate leads to use of the concept without pondering its meaning and its effects. It is important to be aware that using the concept of sphere of influence to describe Russian foreign policy evokes pejorative associations and images of the Cold War.

In what follows, I offer some examples of the uses of the term *sphere of influence* in contemporary IR. Western analysts produce a view of spheres of influence that shows they are not conscious of the intellectual history underlying the concept. The problem is the indifference within IR towards the concept, which leaves Russian foreign policy analysts without the necessary disciplinary debate that would give them tools for identifying different forms of influence and their normative aspects. Moreover, Western scholars use the concept as a means to highlight the alienness of Russian foreign policy vis-à-vis that of the Western (specifically, European) states. In order to further challenge the assumptions about Russia's sphere-of-influence policy, I present some Russian discourses on the topic which demonstrate that *sphere of influence* has as pejorative a ring to many Russian analysts as it has to any others.

1.5.1   Blind Spots

It is not particularly difficult to prove that there is an image of Russia trying to consolidate a sphere of influence within the post-Soviet space. There are certain events that are referred to as if they form the body of criteria for identifying a sphere-of-influence policy. These include energy blackmail, interference in elections, military presence and military intervention. Moreover, Russian visions of regional integration are interpreted as a means to establish domination and control, and the influence of Russian culture and language and the protection of Russian minorities are also viewed as means to consolidate a sphere of influence. This influence is not just any influence; it is seen as a continuation of the Soviet era, an unwillingness on the part of Russia to 'let go'.

Russia is associated with the practice of pursuing a sphere of influence more than any other state. Curiously, Russia appears to be the only great power that is a captive of its tradition of influence. The former imperialist states of Europe, even though they still have influence in their former colonies and elsewhere, are viewed more as peace-builders than as states with sphere-of-influence ambitions. More interestingly, although denouncing imperialism, the United States also has a long history of international influence, which has only become stronger and wider. Despite the country's history as a great power with extensive international influence ever since the Monroe Doctrine (1823), in contemporary analysis the image of the United States is not tainted by a policy of establishing spheres of influence. Wilhelmsen and Flikke explain how during the Bush administration, after September 11, United States' foreign policy was founded upon its status as the world's sole remaining superpower, whose mission was to promote regime change in an anarchic international environment. They (2005, 387) note, 'This also involves the calculus that while rallying support from the international community and international law, the USA will reserve for itself the right to act unilaterally on the basis of imminent danger or even the suspicion that some states may have long term ambitions of inflicting damage on the USA'. Then why is this not a sphere-of-influence policy? The question is especially relevant when comparing the number of open attacks on and occupations of other states by Russia and the United States. Russia simply has not had the necessary financial and military means, or even an interest, to pursue an aggressive sphere-of-influence policy, unlike the United States. One explanation for the disassociation of the concept of sphere of influence from the United States is that the United States operates in a global arena; its foreign policy does not translate into pursuing a sphere of influence, which is often envisioned as a clearly delineated region on a map. Another, even more convincing explanation is the pejorative ring of the concept of sphere of influence. Even though the United States is often admonished for its enthusiasm for military solutions, its motives are seen as rooted in defending human rights and promoting democracy. When there is a need to express criticism of the United States' policy, it is done by reference to such ideas as empire (lite), hegemony, or world police. Imagining both the United States and Russia as states longing for spheres of influence would mean equating the policies and interests of the two. In order to keep the two states in different categories and in order to use *sphere of influence* as a pejorative expression, only Russian policy is currently described using the term.

The United States and the Soviet Union were seen as the two superpowers with spheres of influence during the Cold War. After the disintegration of the Soviet Union, the United States rid itself of the bad reputation of having a sphere-of-influence policy, whereas Russia was stuck with it. But it was not enough that Russia had to carry the image of a Cold War lust for influence: its sphere-of-influence policy, especially in the media, is often associated with imperialism, affirming the pejorative ring of the concept. Indeed, Bobo Lo (2002), a well-known expert on Russia, describes Russia's foreign policy as a reflection of an 'imperial syndrome' whereby Russia is both aware of its old empire and feels that the country has an imperial mission in the future. The territory of the old empire is now seen as Russia's sphere of influence (48). Lo adds that this does not mean a rebuilding of the Soviet Union, but a state of mind based on the attempt to increase influence (52). Lo continues that since the break-up of the Soviet Union, the idea of a sphere of influence has thrived and that in the background one can find a wish to preserve what remains of the Cold War status quo (114–16). In this respect, for Lo, the history of Tsarist Russia and the Soviet Union are visible in the current foreign policy thinking in Russia.

There is no denying that Russia is interested in international influence. But what kind of influence? For Lo it is a mixture of an imperial mission and Cold War spheres of influence. There are two shortcomings in Lo's account: 1) knowing that Russia's present ambitions have something to do with its past status and influence does not contribute to defining what Russia's present idea of a sphere of influence is, and 2) asserting the continuation of an 'imperial mission' and a 'Cold War sphere of influence' leaves no room for any other interpretation of Russia's sphere of influence than a negative one. This is not to say that Lo wants to contribute to the pejorative meaning of sphere of influence. However, by not saying what he means by the expression or, rather, by implying that it means imperial influence, he reinforces the negative image of influence. This evokes contempt and disapproval that are not openly discussed and argued for, but that come with the choice of expression.

The way Western analysts see it, Russia's involvement in regime change in another state, unilateral action within foreign territory and protecting national interests are nothing other than consolidation of the country's sphere of influence. Wilhelmsen and Flikke write:

> Even though the structural position of today's Russian Federation in international relations is not as strong as formerly that of the Soviet Union, Russian unilateral military action against terrorist bases in Georgian territory and Russia's more assertive policies in Central Asia all reveal that Russia has not given up on preventing the geopolitical space of the Commonwealth of Independent States (CIS) from eroding, or on preserving the post-Soviet space as a sphere of influence (Wilhelmsen and Flikke 2005, 388).

For Wilhelmsen and Flikke, Russia's influence is based on military action, assertive policies and 'holding on to a geopolitical space'. 'Geopolitical' implies power deriving from territory, which is why the concept of sphere of influence is invoked to explain Russia's actions and motivations. The problem with this kind of logic is that there is no set of criteria allowing one to determine that Russia's unilateral action in Georgian territory and assertive policies in Central Asia signify a sphere-of-influence policy. There is no list of actions to determine whether certain conduct belongs to the category 'sphere-of-influence policy' or not. If there were such a list, then we should also have a list of actions that do not constitute such a policy but would fall into the category 'influence of some other kind'. We do not know if Wilhelmsen and Flikke would, as a rule, deem any unilateral military action (that is, intervention) to be part of a sphere-of-influence policy, or perhaps would do so only when such an action is disapproved of by the international community. Would they see Russian humanitarian intervention as 'preserving the post-Soviet space as a sphere of influence'? Moreover, we do not know if they consider influence approved of by the influenced states to be a manifestation of a sphere-of-influence policy. Some post-Soviet states might in fact view their relationship with Russia as beneficial, despite their being under some form of Russian influence. Does the consent of the influenced mean that the relationship between the influencing and the influenced states is integration, cooperation or alliance instead of a sphere of influence? In fact, one justification for establishing a sphere of influence is that such a policy involves influence which respects the rights of the influenced states and benefits them as well. Later, I present the suzerain treaty as an example of such an arrangement (Chapter 2.2) and discuss Naumann's and Lippmann's ideas as representing a vision of mutually beneficial influence (Chapter 4).

As I have argued, IR has neglected contesting the concept of sphere of influence. Yet, there is an exception: an article titled 'Russia's Spheres of Interest, not Influence' by Dmitri Trenin (2009). Trenin implies that he is about to unravel the meaning of 'sphere of influence' and 'interests': 'Thus, a question arose: what is the difference, if any, between the sphere of interests proclaimed by the current Russian leadership, and the more traditional sphere of influence condemned by international public opinion?' (4) and 'More specifically, is the current usage of the spheres of "privileged interests" instead of "spheres of influence" significant or is it a mere window dressing?' (5). Trenin nevertheless fails to provide the answers to these questions. On the difference between influence and interest, he writes:

> The current policy of Russia's spheres of interest dates back from the mindset of the mid-2000s. Compared to the Soviet Union's, the Russian Federation's sphere is not only much smaller, but also much 'lighter' – 'interests' after all are not as compelling as 'influence'. In Russia, and throughout the former Soviet Union, ideology has been replaced by pervasive pragmatism. There is no hint of political control by Moscow either'. […] Unlike 'influence' which tends to be both all-inclusive and exclusive, 'interests' are more specific and identifiable. Rather than whole countries, they include these various politico-military, economic and financial, and cultural areas within them (Trenin 2009, 12–13).

According to Trenin, a sphere of interests is smaller in geographic terms and can consist of parts of states instead of whole states; it is 'lighter' and more specific, without ideological and political control. I find it problematic to dissociate influence and interest in terms of ideology and pragmatism. First, this kind of separation defines the concept of sphere of influence as a tool for advancing communist ideology in the Cold War setting. Second, one could say that an ideological struggle persists in the form of Russia resisting 'forceful imposition' by the West of its form of democracy. Attempts to draw a distinction between ideology and pragmatism also raise the question whether a sphere of influence that is defended for the sake of a balance of power is ideological or pragmatic. Are regional integration projects ideological or pragmatic? Moreover, what does Trenin really mean by ideology and pragmatism? When it comes to the claim that there is no hint of political control by Moscow, many Western analysts would disagree; they point to the energy disputes with Belarus and Ukraine, conflicts with Georgia, the bronze soldier dispute with Estonia in 2007 and other aspects of Russia's recent activity in the post-Soviet space. Thus, establishing the idea of a sphere of interests *without* political control, as distinct from a sphere of influence *with* political control, would necessitate agreement on what constitutes 'political control'. For Trenin, 'political control' has a pejorative connotation, while 'interests' are purified of all that makes influence unacceptable; but this does not explain the difference between influence and interests in practical terms. Here we come back to the question of what constitutes a sphere-of-influence policy, and we have not, in fact, got very far in distinguishing interests and influence. What also remains unclear is whether influence can include interests and interests can include influence.

Replacing the word 'influence' with 'interest' also entails a risk of simply inventing a new term to justify influence by claiming that is fundamentally different, as if to avoid the moral judgment that influence carries with it. Rather than replace one term with another, it is necessary to go to the root of the referent, to look at the discourses on spheres of influence as well as the meanings given to the concept and to reflect on the structures of the international system that underpin the practice. When we know what notions the old concept incorporates, we can begin to develop a new concept to describe Russia's influence. I admire Trenin's attempt to put the question of sphere of influence on the table; it was a necessary act in itself. Unfortunately, his analysis does not offer us theoretical insights. It does not free Russia from the stigma of being a sphere-of-influence power as long as the concept is not questioned in greater depth.

In the introduction, I identified the core problems of the concept of sphere of influence at present: the first is the lack of interest in the concept itself; the second is the range of pejorative associations which the concept has acquired. When the two problems are put together – lack of explanatory power and pejorative connotations – use of the concept can result in simplifications. Evoking the idea of a sphere of influence, without a robust conceptualisation to underpin it, reduces Russia's interests and influence to lines on a map. It imputes negative designs to the policy and ignores how spheres of influence are conceptualised in Russia, how spheres of influence relate to international order and how they are or can be justified (if they can). We need to debate the meaning of *sphere of influence* and to do so with reference to international theory. *Sphere of influence* is not just an expression of disapproval but a concept which tries to explain something about international relations. If we acknowledge these two factors – that *sphere of influence* is used pejoratively and that the purpose of the concept is to explain and not only to condemn something – we can approach it as a contested concept. Once we become conscious of our own uses of the concept, we can begin to discern Russian views on spheres of influence. And once we have become critical about the concept and its uses, we can become critical of policies based on pursuing spheres of influence.

1.5.2   What Say the Russians?

Typical examples of the uses of the term *sphere of influence* are found in materials produced by think-tanks such as the European Council on Foreign Relations (ECFR). One of the papers by the ECFR on Russia is 'A Power Audit of EU-Russia Relations' by Mark Leonard and Nicu Popescu, published in 2007.[5] Another

---

5   The paper is 'an audit of the power that the Union wields over its most important neighbour, Russia' conducted by a team of researchers from all 27 EU member states (Leonard and Popescu 2007, i).

paper by the same institution is titled 'The Limits of Enlargement-Lite: European and Russian Power in the Troubled Neighbourhood', published in 2009 by Nicu Popescu and Andrew Wilson and dealing directly with spheres of influence. The ECFR reports present a sphere-of-influence policy as something uniquely Russian. Popescu and Wilson (2009, 29) write, 'Moscow has been trying to establish a sphere of influence in its "near abroad" since the break-up of the Soviet Union'. What enables the pejorative interpretation of Russia's influence is the discourse on the more positive form of influence exercised by the European Union, creating a dichotomy of bad and good influence. Bad influence means 'an activist Russia that aims to bring countries into its sphere of influence' and good influence means 'an EU that wants to spread democracy, stability and the rule of law' (5). Leonard and Popescu go deeper into the differences between the two types of influence:

> Whereas the EU stands for an idea of order based on consensus, interdependence and the rule of law, Russian foreign policy is motivated by a quest for power, independence and control. The EU's main concern is to ensure that its neighbourhood is peaceful and well-governed. Russia wants to expand its sphere of influence and achieve control of economic interests and energy assets in neighbouring countries and the EU. (Leonard and Popescu 2007, 8)

In this account, the influence of the European Union, aimed at bringing about a peaceful neighbourhood and conducted with respect for the rule of law, stands in sharp contradiction to Russia's influence, which is based on economic interests and power ambitions (a sphere of influence). This can also be conceived of as a dichotomy between 'positive value-based influence' such as the promotion of democracy, and 'negative territorial/historical influence', which uses both political and economic means and can be called a 'near abroad' policy. But does this mean that the EU member states have no economic interests or need for additional energy assets elsewhere and that the EU is not moved by power? And that Russia has no interest in contributing to a peaceful neighbourhood, but acts on its power and economic ambitions? I argue that the influence of Russia and of the EU is a more complex issue. All international actors pursue self-serving interests; even the smallest countries. It is true that Russian politicians and researchers have made the argument for national interests an art form: the right to pursue national interests is seen as countering exclusion and 'containment' by the international community and rules dictated from the outside. The discourse on Russia's national interests is aimed against those who try to dismiss the country's voice or try to manage world affairs without it. 'National interests' is a sort of realist voice in Russia's foreign policy discourse and Russian decision-makers do not share the utopian dream of a common humanity, but they certainly have an interest in a well-governed and peaceful neighbourhood. The question is how to bring this about and what a well-governed neighbourhood looks like. For Russia, 'well-governed' means operating according to the same kind of managed democracy as its own, with democracy imported from abroad seen as a source of instability rather than of peace and prosperity. Second, economic interests motivate all countries and regional integration projects in the world, without exception. I believe a dichotomy of good and bad influence of the sort suggested above serves the purpose of an identity project by excluding the alien Other. In order to demonstrate that there is reason to question the language of spheres of influence, which, in my opinion, promotes the logic of exclusion, I present here some Russian visions which run counter to the ECPR reports.

Alexander Lukin (2008) from the Moscow State Institute of International Relations (MGIMO) writes, 'Every country has a natural desire to see friendly regimes in neighboring countries'. Yet, meddling in the internal affairs of another state, for example, by trying to influence elections, would be interpreted as a sphere-of-influence policy in the present – at least if it were Russia perpetrating such an act. Even Russians are suspicious of such interference, whatever the motives. Dmitry Furman (2006), from the Russian Academy of Sciences, does not discuss spheres of influence as such, but argues that influencing the regimes of neighbouring countries is a matter of survival for Russia, because all states want to be surrounded by regimes which are similar to their own. For Russia, being surrounded by managed democracies protects the managed democracy of Russia itself. Furman (2006) is not shy about admitting that Russia was 'gathering the lands together' after the collapse of the Soviet Union; however, he laments the fact that because there can be no open goal of promoting managed democracy, there can be no well-thought-out strategy for promoting that goal either.

There is an important lesson in Furman's thinking: the interest in influencing regimes of other states is not a Russian sin. The reason why we condemn such a policy is that we think Russia is imposing the wrong type of regime. It is easy to judge the influence of a country which is not built on pure Western democracy and respect for human rights. The influence of a country which is not the *Same* but the *Other* simply cannot be supported. The West, instead, promotes democracy, which we view as the best model of government. As the West represents that which is good and pure, its influence is not only accepted but preferred. But what Furman points out is that, in the end, we are still talking about influence that serves national interests and stability – from *our* perspective. The question then is who gets to judge what influence is right and what is wrong. In this sense, influence is not anything peculiar or extraordinary; it is part of international politics for better or for worse. But a sphere of influence is peculiar, because of its unspoken negative function.

Many Russian analysts refer to the concept of sphere of influence in a pejorative tone, whereas influence (without the sphere) is free from such disapproval (for example, Roundtable discussion 2010, 107–8). Influence, unless it is defined specifically as military or ideological, is something abstract. It has the potential to be neutral or even good, whereas the addition of 'sphere' often implies a bad, or at least suspicious, form of influence. Thus, one does not easily find Russian authors writing about 'Russia's sphere of influence' as opposed to the more common 'Russia's influence' (for example, Kremeniuk 2008, 47). Foreign Minister Sergei

Lavrov (2009, 14) writes that there can be no return to the former 'spheres of influence' and continues:

> Yet this does not give anyone the right to deny, let alone undermine, the natural mutual gravitation of nations toward each other generated by historical and other objective factors and based on mutual interests. Speaking of our closest neighbors, Russia wants them to be friendly, stable, and dynamically developing states. This approach is consistent with the plans of these states and cannot contradict anyone's interests.

Thus, in Lavrov's view, even though the Cold War spheres of influence are not celebrated, the 'gravitation' of nations towards others and an interest in a peaceful neighbourhood are only natural and should not offend anyone's interests. There is an assumption within IR that great power and influence go hand in hand. This is also the conclusion the English School came to. Discourses on great powers are inseparable from discourses on influence for this very reason. Where one finds a great power, one finds influence. If this connection appears evident, it is altogether a different matter to say that great powers necessarily have or aspire to establish spheres of influence. The reason for this is that adding 'sphere' is a statement in its own right: influence loses its innocence and becomes enveloped in pejorative associations. What then is the difference between exerting influence and establishing a sphere of influence? A sphere of influence in its present use implies territorial control that can even lead to annexation. 'Sphere' is the geopolitical element of influence; and this is the legacy that geostrategy and geopolitics have left us with (see also Chapter 4.1). I believe that use of the term 'influence' without 'sphere' is an attempt to eliminate the geopolitical elements from international influence. A separation of 'influence' from 'sphere of influence' also implies an attempt to cleanse 'influence' of its pejorative associations. It is part of neutralising speech which renders influence natural, normal and therefor no reason for alarmism (see below). Influence is a normal part of international relations, but spheres of influence involve geostrategy, a great game or an ideological struggle.

Even though Trenin (2009) did not go deep enough in his conceptual discussion, his attempt to separate influence from interest is important in the light of Russian discourses. Just as a distinction emerges between influence with or without a sphere, one appears between influence and interests. Many Russian foreign policy experts favour the word 'interest', and it works to neutralise the meaning of influence just like leaving 'sphere' out of 'sphere of influence' does. The experts try to dissociate the country's foreign policy from the idea of negative influence, and the notion of interest serves this purpose by making Russian foreign policy look like something reasonable and depoliticised. Several variations can be found: Russia's strategic/privileged/special/vital and legitimate interests (see Bordachev 2008; Minaev 2010; Markedonov 2007, 2008; Nikolaev 2009, 27). Interests are also defended against bloc politics or the universalist threat (Lavrov 2007), in which 'influence' is defined as the policy of the United States and 'interest' that of

Russia. For example, Sergei Karaganov (2010) from the Council on Foreign and Defense Policy (SVOP) posits an opposition between Russia's security interests and the United States' influence or domination:

> The real irritant of Russian-U.S. relations is America's unwillingness to acknowledge Russia's right to a zone of its own security interests. It nearly resulted in direct confrontation in August 2008, when Georgia attacked South Ossetia and Russian peacekeepers, and Moscow gave a tough response, aiming at the logic of NATO's endless expansion. This occurred amidst the constant expansion of the U.S. zone of not so much security interests as of influence – if not domination – in the military-political field, the most sensitive to Russia.

There is a concern over remilitarisation of international relations after the Cold War, which in this discourse refers to the interventionist policy of the United States, and constitutes the Russian understanding of influence in a pejorative meaning (see, for example, SVOP 2007). Konstantin Kosachev (2007), member of the State Duma, argues that Russia has no sphere of influence: no one is now compelled to join new structures and the economic dependence card is not played in order to consolidate what might be construed as a sphere of influence. The Russian analysts discussed here do not deny that Russia has interests in the post-Soviet space, but they perceive a need to explain the motives for pursuing those interests and make explicit the soft-power means for solidifying the country's influence. In President Putin's words the aim is to develop a 'common humanitarian space'. Putin (2006, 4) further explains the purity of Russia's motives: 'Our responses are therefore based on the genuine aspirations of the peoples living in the CIS [Commonwealth of Independent States], and these aspirations are for cooperation and good-neighborly relations on an equal basis and for integration that brings greater practical benefits and impact'. Underlying the 'normality discourse' is the need to justify Russian foreign policy. Lavrov (2008) insists on the normality of Russian's foreign policy and wishes that this could be understood abroad:

> Unfortunately, the Cold War experience has distorted the consciousness of several generations of people, above all political elites, making them think that any global policy must be ideologized. And now, when Russia is guided in international affairs by understandable, pragmatic interests, void of any ideological motives whatsoever, not everyone is able to adequately take it. Some people say we have some 'grievances', 'hidden agendas', 'neo-imperial aspirations' and all that stuff.

The argument is geared not so much to proving that Russia's influence is *good*, but that it is *normal*. Often when Russian analysts explain the country's relations to the post-Soviet states in response to what is a hail of accusations from the West, they defend Russia's policy as something logical, rightful and a normal way to handle interstate relations. Sergey Chernyshev insists that instead of imperial ambitions Russia wants leadership and that the members of the CIS are beginning to see that. The post-Soviet space is logically a foreign policy priority for Russia, since the economies are closely interlinked and the problems are common to the region (Chernyshev 2010). According to Lavrov (2007), Russia is building non-politicised relations in the CIS space with the aim of stabilising the region. For Lavrov, non-political in this context means that Russia is not playing any power games in its economic relations with its neighbours.

It is not peculiar for Russia to want unity with the post-Soviet states in the hope of achieving integration, economic cooperation and protection for Russian minorities in the new states. This is what any country would wish for territories that once belonged to it. When I say that the authors do not promote spheres of influence, this is not to say that Russia wants to relinquish its influence in the region. Russia's leaders have expressed the country's great power ambitions, and Russia has demonstrated its capacity for military intervention. If the post-Soviet space were insignificant to Russia, the country's representatives would not steadfastly resist NATO enlargement or the United States' influence. Yet, the concept of sphere of influence as such indicates hard power and the Great Game, relics from the Cold War which for the Russians better describe the democratisation efforts and world police actions of the United States. Thus, given that the concept of sphere of influence is resented also in Russia, one might well ask if there is any use in continuing to use it as a shaming and blaming tool.

From the perspective of Russia, the problem is that in denouncing a sphere-of-influence policy, Russian analysts fail to explain how their vision of influence differs from that implied by a sphere of influence. In other words, the question arises of what the Russian alternative to spheres of influence is. This is what Furman (2006) refers to as the lack of an open goal of promoting managed democracy. The alternative needs to be expressed openly against the idea of a sphere of influence, a bit like Walter Lippmann did with the 'Good Neighbor Policy' (see Chapter 4.5); otherwise the message will go unnoticed in the West. It is not enough to criticise military interventions or to argue that Russia's influence is normal, natural, and has a stabilising effect on the region. In order to address the criticism of the West, Russian experts need to take the concept of sphere of influence and discuss the role and rights of small states in relation to it, because, as I will begin to demonstrate in the coming chapters, justice is at the heart of the matter. Only by addressing justice in relation to influence, can a path be opened for alternative visions of spheres of influence.

1.6   Subjugated Knowledges

> It seems clear that diplomacy's present plight cannot be understood, or even be
> described as such, unless some knowledge of its origins is available. In practical
> terms, if we are to know what diplomacy is, or where it might be heading, we
> must know how it came into being. (Der Derian 1987, 2)

Some words are in order about the choice of material and the underlying methodological tenets of this study. As Der Derian argues, in order to understand international practices such as diplomacy, we need to look into the past. In fact, we need a discussion between the 'present plight' and past knowledge. The present study is a discovery of different, competing or complementary truths that have not yet been discovered and would remain undiscovered without an interest in the history of the concept of sphere of influence. In simple terms, this study is a theoretical reassessment of *sphere of influence*, an inquiry that problematises that which is evident in the present by looking into the past. The purpose of the research is to discover what Foucault calls 'subjugated knowledges', which is 'historical contents that have been buried and disguised in a functionalist coherence or formal systemisation'. Subjugated knowledges for Foucault also mean 'a whole set of knowledges that have been disqualified as inadequate to their task or insufficiently elaborated: naïve knowledges located down on the hierarchy, beneath the required level of cognition or scientificity' (Foucault 1980, 81–2). It is from the insurrection of these subjugated knowledges that the history of *sphere of influence* as a concept emerges. I argue that *sphere of influence* is not only a Cold War concept, and it can have connotations other than pejorative ones. The material to be examined here, in which spheres of influence are constructed as a middle way between nation and world state, allows for a reinvention of spheres of influence as justified and desirable entities in international theory. Thus, as presented in international theory, spheres of influence reflect something more than a pejorative Cold War orbit metaphor.

Colin Gordon (1980, 233) asks, 'What kind of political relevance can enquiries into our past have in making intelligible the "objective conditions" of our social present, not only its visible crises and fissures but also the solidity of its unquestioned rationales?'. Gordon continues, 'If Foucault poses a philosophical challenge to history, it is not to question the reality of "the past" but to interrogate the rationality of "the present"' (242). This rationality of the present Gordon refers to as *regimes of truth*. *Sphere of influence* represents such a regime. It excuses its user from exploring the rationale of the concept itself, as well as its explanatory power, as long as the concept is taken for a granted, that is, regarded as a truth. In IR 'contested concepts' (such as *political, security, identity*) are the prevailing paradigm: they are more the rule than the exception. Why is *sphere of influence* not a contested concept then? It is because the term is used in a metaphorical rather than an analytical sense, which means that the subjugated knowledge that the concept incorporates is left intact. A sort of emotional use – the pejorative use – is taken as a regime of truth and the terms of political discourse (the criteria constituting the concept) are taken for granted – never to be questioned or discussed. And as long as *sphere of influence* is an uncontested concept, it can be used as a regime of truth.

In order to challenge the regime of truth where spheres of influence are concerned I set out to answer the question, what are the historical roots of the concept's pejorative associations and how can we explain them? The approach is one where *sphere of influence* is studied not only in terms of the history of the concept but as a history of related ideas – *Großraum*, Mid-Europe, Good Neighbor Policy, super-state – and of the ideas which help to frame the concept's pejorative connotations – sovereignty, intervention, great powers, the balance of power, and international law. The impetus for embracing this approach lies not only in the pejorative uses of the term but also in the present need for a theoretical conceptualisation that is broader in perspective than just a conceptual history. The choice of related concepts framing the idea of a sphere of influence is not arbitrary. If we go through the literature on the concept of sphere of influence, we find it enveloped in these concepts, even in cases where reference to the term *sphere of influence* itself might be lacking.

When I sought that which is meant by *sphere of influence*, I became less interested in all possible, even relevant, historical origins and I began a journey towards the body of theory which could explain the concept in the present. In the past, *sphere of influence* not only took on many different meanings but also assumed different names. The purpose is not, however, to cover all possible related concepts, but only those which address questions of justice and which relate to international order. I believe that the full scope of *sphere of influence* – the concept explaining a type of power-relation in international relations – would be hard to capture without reflections on international order and related concepts if its meaning is to be more than borders on a map. And as long as its use is pejorative, there is reason to believe that the concept is a political one. If it is a political concept, it is also a contested concept or, rather, should be. Attaching *sphere of influence* to selected concepts perhaps fixes its meaning to a certain framework, which is why I want to emphasise that my approach is not the only way to historically conceptualise the phenomenon. Mine is a theoretical conceptualisation which is conditioned by the present pejorative uses of the term. A new, different present may later require a new history of *sphere of influence*.

I have found the potential to contest the concept of sphere of influence and address the pejorative uses of the term in the literature of the English School (Chapters 2, 3, and 5). The English School encompasses a historical perspective on international relations in addition to the normative theory for which it is famous, and this enabled me to discover both the historical origins of *sphere of influence* as a term and discuss order and justice within the English School framework. The English School history and theory relating to spheres of influence deal with the society of states, in which states form a community with common rules and institutions. The rules and institutions of international society do not only help in defining the concept in relation to sovereignty, intervention, international law, the balance of power and great power management; but most importantly they work as the normative framework for assessing it, that is, contesting it in relation to considerations of justice

In addition to the theory of the English School, the relationship between spheres of influence, order and justice can be found in what I call 'the world war theories' (Chapter 4). There I find a place for sphere of influence in international theory as a concept casting doubt on the viability of a world state and as a defence of plurality. The world wars signified yet another period in history which caused intellectuals in the West to reconsider what the international order should look like in the post-war world. Something old was crumbling and something new was about to be built. All ideas spring from their political and cultural contexts, but the period of the world wars in particular has produced the most interesting and theoretically best developed visions of spheres of influence. As an alternative to universalism, a sphere of influence became not only a matter of international order, but a development path which was supported and defended; the concept lost its pejorative pall. Bartelson (2009) writes about the dilemma of the universal and the particular – the idea of a world community on the one hand, and the bounded community of a state, nation or people, on the other. A sphere of influence represents a bounded community, but one which settles in between the idea of a world community and of a nation-state. Contemporary IR has neglected the relevance of spheres of influence in the debates on the universal versus the particular. Despite its potential, the idea of a sphere of influence has not been explored on the theoretical level as a solution to the disintegration of the system of states and the problems of forming a world community. This potential is based on the history of international thought, which I will analyse in this study.

Finally I tackle the period in history known as the Cold War and analyse the Cuban Missile Crisis as an illustrative incident. The significance of this historical episode lies in the fact that, as the principal reference to the nature of spheres of influence, it has rendered the term the pejorative concept that it is today. What happened to *sphere of influence* during the Cold War was that the concept came to denote so powerfully the superpower rivalry of the United States and the Soviet Union that its broader meaning and history were forgotten. Even though the extreme circumstances of bipolarity made *sphere of influence* look like a Cold War concept, it has had a much longer history. Ignoring the idea of a sphere of influence in the history of international theory has reduced it to geostrategy: imagining spheres of influence as circles on a map without asking what 'a satellite' is or what makes 'a camp' and what 'bloc discipline' means for international order (see also Chapter 5.1). Even during the Cold War the theoretical interest in spheres of influence was minimal, being limited to occasional references by the English school, for example, Paul Keal's book from 1983 and Edy Kaufman's remarks from 1976. After the Cold War, a new era of confusion emerged and the idea of a sphere of influence was left unproblematised. During that era, the injustice of spheres of influence became so obvious that there was no reason to open up normative questions relating to the phenomenon. If there was a need to theorise the nature of regional developments or international influence, other concepts would come to the rescue and *sphere of influence* could be left as a reminder of Cold War practices, and the continuation of Russian foreign policy. Political leaders and analysts in the West soon observed that the idea of a sphere of influence was alive in the foreign policy of Russia, but they were not interested in addressing the import of the concept for discussing the new world order. But neither the idea of an international society nor its connection to spheres of influence was crushed under the Cold War's unique bipolarity. The need to problematise the concept of sphere of influence did not disappear, nor has it disappeared in the present.

The aim here is to look for those knowledges on spheres of influence which have remained overlooked and underestimated. In fact, when it comes to the concept of sphere of influence, the lack of historical and theoretical interest is so pervasive that nearly all sources represent essentially a sort of 'subjugated knowledge'. These are marginalised texts even though in many other contexts they represent nothing less than 'great texts', as in the case of the thinking of the English School and Schmitt's and Carr's works. The reason why I argue that *sphere of influence* exemplifies subjugated knowledge is that we have failed to recognise the intellectual history underlying the concept. There has been no attempt to look beyond the observed practice and connect the concept of sphere of influence to the institutions of international society. Somehow, spheres of influence have been seen to operate alongside the balance of power as normal conduct of the great powers, but without anyone exploring the relationship between the two at a conceptual level. Spheres of influence have not been examined in the texts that are concerned with the disintegration of the system of sovereign states. In fact, spheres of influence have not been examined in terms of any international theory whatsoever. Accordingly, the purpose of the following historical inquiry is to reveal the subjugated knowledges relating to the concept of sphere of influence, stretching the limits of our present knowledge further and deeper into history.

Chapter 2
The Origins of Spheres of Influence

In order to find a place for the concept of sphere of influence in international theory, I begin with a school of thought that can provide insights into questions of justice and international order: The English School of International Relations. What makes the English School the most promising source for contesting the concept of sphere of influence are 1) its focus on normative theory, 2) its interest in the rules and institutions which govern interstate relations, and 3) its study of history of the system of states. While interest in the English School has been increasing within IR, there has been no investigation of the use of the concept of sphere of influence in the literature of the School. Likewise in studies which use the English School toolkit for otherwise meritorious analysis of Russian foreign policy, discussion on spheres of influence remains non-existent or superficial (for example Astrov 2011, Neumann 2011, Papkova 2011, Prozorov 2011, Sakwa 2011). In keeping with the aim of this research this chapter undertakes to establish the link that is currently missing between the English School and the concept of sphere of influence. This connection is based on the capacity of the School to discuss matters of justice in a way which creates potential to theorise on the *normative* aspects of spheres of influence. Moreover, the only extensive theoretical study on spheres of influence, Keal's *Unspoken Rules and Superpower Dominance* (1983), is not only strongly associated with English School theory but directly linked to the thinking of Bull, under whom Keal did his doctorate, and also John Vincent's ideas on intervention.[1] Since Keal's work builds on nothing but the idea of an international society, his work becomes the piece of the puzzle where the concept of sphere of influence gains its rightful place in the English School theory.

Excluding Keal's work, the uses of the concept of sphere of influence are mostly (but not wholly) limited to Bull's scholarship. This does not necessarily make the English School any less relevant as a source of theorising on spheres of influence. The knowledge of the English School on the concept is subjugated as much to the writers themselves as it is to those who attempt to make sense of their writings. The neglect of the concept by the English School is already an important finding, because it attests to the mysterious simultaneity of familiarity and unfamiliarity with it. The realist accounts of anarchy and the system of states might appear as a more natural source of the history of spheres of influence, but in my opinion the English School addresses the present problematique of the

---

1   Hidemi Suganami (2010, 16) includes Keal in a group of those people on whom 'the founding figures had exerted a formative influence directly or indirectly'.

concept's pejorative meaning more comprehensively and thus better enables the discovery of subjugated knowledge. Moreover, a focus on the English school does not exclude realist voices as such; it only excludes the idea of spheres of influence in a realist world without international society – a world without the driving force of shared rules and norms. Thus, the choice of sources has been made with a preference for the work of the English School for the very reason that the concept of sphere of influence is theoretically located within international institutions, not outside of them.

Next, some words on the English School itself are in order.

2.1   The British Committee on the Theory of International Politics

Excellent accounts and analyses have been written on the English School by Tim Dunne (1998), Brunello Vigezzi (2005), Andrew Linklater and Hidemi Suganami (2006) and Barry Buzan (2004a). I content myself here with a brief account of the School without the debates that the English School theory and methodology have increasingly aroused. As a school of thought, the English School emerged from the British Committee on the Theory of International Politics. The first formal meeting of the Committee was held in January 1959 by a group of scholars who set out to investigate questions of international theory (Dunne 1998, xi). Herbert Butterfield and Martin Wight were the organisers of the Committee, which would come to include Hedley Bull, Adam Watson, R.J. Vincent and others. In total, the members, guests and contributors comprised some 50 people with varying backgrounds (Vigezzi 2005, vii). According to Dunne, during the 'formative years' of the Committee (1959–62), *Diplomatic Investigations* (1966) was written, which elaborated the conception of *international society*. The period from 1964 onwards Dunne calls 'the second phase' of the Committee's work, which was characterised by growing interest in methodology and a comparative sociology of the historical states-system. No collaborative publication came out of these studies, but the phase did see two significant works, Wight's *Systems of States* (1977) and Watson's *Evolution of International Society* (1992). The culmination of the Committee's work was a volume edited by Bull and Watson titled *The Expansion of International Society* in 1984 (Dunne 1998, xiii–xiv).

The most important sources emanating from the English School in establishing the connection between spheres of influence and international society are Bull's *The Anarchical Society*, and Wight's *Power Politics* and *Systems of States*, all published in the 1970s.[2] I found elements of the concept of sphere of influence in Bull's institutions of international society and in Wight's ideas on the system

---

2   *Power Politics* was first published as pamphlets by the Royal Institute of International Affairs in 1946 and in 1978 as a book after Wight had passed away (Wight 1995, 7–9).

of states and hierarchy. Watson's account of the history of the states-system and Vincent's work on intervention fine-tuned the theoretical conceptualisation of sphere of influence in the English School framework, while Paul Keal's work provided the foundation for theorising on and historically contextualising the concept. I do not adhere to the work of the original members of the School only but also use material from people who reflect or have done research on the School. These include Buzan, Little and Jackson, who have contributed (along with many others) to the re-emergence of the English School as one of the most significant and intriguing traditions in IR.

The contribution of the English School to the idea of a sphere of influence comes from the historical account of the emergence of not only the system of states but also, and in particular, the great power order. Within that history we can find the Congress of Vienna (1815), the Monroe Doctrine (1823) and the practice of colonialism. In the next chapter, I will illustrate the second important finding from the English School literature for conceptualising sphere of influence: the pluralist-solidarist debate, which emerged from a discussion on the institutions of international society. I argue that a sphere of influence is a conception of a territorial order in between pluralism (the system of states) and solidarism (often understood as a cosmopolitan world community). As Dunne (1998, 142) writes, Bull developed the pluralist and solidarist wings of the English School by exploring the normative possibilities of the society of states. These possibilities are precisely the ones which define the normative limits of spheres of influence.

Vincent played with the pluralist-solidarist division within the field of human rights, trying to build a bridge between the two (Dunne 1998, xiv). Wight and Watson inserted hegemonic order as the central tendency of international society – lying between the extremes of sovereignty and empire – while also reflecting on the pluralist-solidarist debate. Regardless of Paul Keal's work on sphere of influence and international order, the English School has not made spheres of influence part and parcel of the society of states. A sphere of influence is not an institution of international society to Bull (2002) and not even a derivative institution for Buzan (2004a). Even so, if we acknowledge that the referent of *sphere of influence* is not confined to a certain foreign policy tool but embraces a conception of international order as well, we can use international society as a point of departure for discussing the normative aspects of establishing and consolidating spheres of influence. A look at the theory on international society breathes life into the idea of a sphere of influence, giving it a dimension outside the pejorative and metaphorical uses of the term. The pluralist-solidarist debate makes the concept of sphere of influence part of the theorisation on international order even if the English School itself has failed to realise this. A sphere of influence becomes transformed from a metaphor of astronomy into an idea about the nature and form of international order *between nation and humanity.*

2.2   From Suzerain to Sovereign

The term *sphere of influence* appeared only after the emergence of the system of states; as such it describes relations among states. Nevertheless, if we look beyond the system of states we can find a model which bears a resemblance to the idea of a sphere of influence: the suzerain system. Although I focus on the idea of a sphere of influence as deeply rooted in the system of states, a wider historical perspective helps to locate sphere of influence in the framework of international order. This is where the work of Bull, Watson and Wight comes to my aid.

Common to Bull, Wight and Watson is an interest in suzerain systems and hegemony. Wight explains that a system of states means that states claim for themselves independence of any political superior and recognise the validity of like claims to independence by all others. This has been formulated in the doctrine of legal equality of states. But there is also something Wight calls suzerainty, where one among a group of states 'asserts unique claims which the others formally or tacitly accept'. 'This is the suzerain, the sole source of legitimate authority, conferring a status on the rest and exacting tribute or other marks of deference' (Wight 1977, 23). In the international states-system, the fundamental political principle is to maintain a balance of power, but in a suzerain state-system the policy is *divide et impera* (24). Bull explains Wight's suzerainty as a system of one state imposing supremacy over others; this is why it is a suzerain *state* system, not *states* system. Bull writes that there is a difference between hegemony in an international system and in a suzerain-state system. In a suzerain-state system, hegemony is permanent and unchallengeable, while in a system of states hegemony can pass from one power to another and can be disputed (Bull 2002, 10–11). This difference means that the only international system is a states-system, since under a suzerain system only one power can be sovereign.

In *The Expansion of International Society*, Bull and Watson (1985) use the concept of suzerainty to explain the international system before the emergence of sovereign states. They state that the European expansion began in the late fifteenth century, before which time the world consisted of several regional international systems with distinctive rules and institutions based on the dominant regional culture (1).[3] These systems were hegemonial or imperial with a suzerain supreme ruler at the centre who 'exercised direct authority over the Heartland; and around this empire extended a periphery of locally autonomous realms that acknowledged the suzerain's overlordship and paid him tribute'. Bull and Watson argue that within these systems there was no attempt to question the hegemonial nature of the system and thus the states in the periphery did not combine forces to overthrow the ruler. They assumed that there would always be someone who would lay down the rules and control the relations among the members of the system (3).

---

3   According to Bull and Watson (1985, 2) the most important systems were the Arab-Islamic system, the Indian subcontinent, the Mongol-Tartar dominion of the Eurasian steppes, and the Chinese system.

As an example of a suzerain system Wight (1977, 25) mentions the Hittite Empire in the Near East during the latter half of the second millennium B.C., which dominated over lesser powers. Michael Horton (2009) illustrates 'suzerainty treaties' with reference to the Hittite Empire in which a lesser king (vassal) in need of help entered into a covenant with the great king (suzerain), or the great king rescued the vassal from peril and thus considered it his right to annex the vassal's lands by covenant to his empire (24–5). The treaties stipulated as the duties of the vassals paying taxes to the great king, abstaining from alliances with other kings and abstaining from complaints against the king. In return, the suzerain pledged to guard his vassal, even though there were no obligations for the suzerain, who acted in absolute freedom (27). Horton argues that what distinguishes these suzerain treaties from modern analogues is that the suzerain was like a loved and revered father. The covenant was not merely a legal contract; it 'involved the deepest affections' (25). Horton's account of the Hittite Empire attests to the existence of a ruler who not only takes but also gives.

If we want to find the earliest sphere-of-influence agreements, the Hittite suzerain treaties could well fit the bill. What is curious about a suzerain treaty, however, are the ideas of protection, acceptance, legitimacy and the respect for the great king – all features lacking in our present understanding of spheres of influence. The present idea of a sphere of influence recognises neither the legitimacy of the influence involved nor goodwill on the part of the influencing power. But if we look at the origins of great power influence represented by the Hittite king, the relationship between the sovereign and the vassal is not necessarily one of injustice. Then why is a sphere of influence considered unjust by definition? Could it be that the norm of state sovereignty is so powerful as to always disapprove of international influence? The answer is 'yes' in the case of spheres of influence, but not all international influence is seen as negative by the analysts of international relations. The EU's international influence is often viewed positively even though it also has its opponents. Those who argue that there is a need for, or accept, humanitarian intervention, and uphold the principle of 'responsibility to protect' consider the protection of human rights to be more compelling than respect for state sovereignty. Influence in the form of developmental aid is sometimes criticised but more often it is seen as beneficial and necessary. Yet, a sphere of influence, with its pejorative connotations, is not associated with the fatherly influence of the suzerain, humanitarianism, aid or mutual cooperation in contemporary discourses. If we look at Keal's (1983, 15) definition, a sphere of influence 'limits the independence and freedom of action', thus violating sovereignty. This violation is what affirms the pejorative connotation of the concept of sphere of influence, and this mind-set makes it difficult to imagine a positive normative agenda on the part of the influencing power.

In the current popular use of the term *sphere of influence*, especially in the media, imperial domination is often cited as the pejorative element. The term 'imperial' evokes an image of a suzerain who deprives other states of their independence. The influencing power in the case of a sphere of influence is not

Horton's fatherly suzerain, but Bull's and Watson's Supreme Ruler. However, a sphere of influence does not necessarily entail a loss of independence by the influenced states. Falling under another power's sphere of influence might violate their sovereignty, but more often independence and sovereignty (or at least an illusion of them) are upheld within the relation (see Carr 2001, 213–17; Lippmann 1945, 77; Naumann 1917, 254–5; Schmitt 2003, 252). I argue that in international theory a sphere of influence rarely implies imperial authority. The suzerain and the vision of imperial authority reinforce the pejorative interpretation of spheres of influence and eclipse images of those spheres of influence that do not aim for total domination and absorption. Suzerainty, as an historical example, can work as a model of a sphere of influence, but we can find conceptualisations that are even better suited to situating spheres of influence in the framework of hegemony and hierarchy. This means locating spheres of influence in relation to sovereignty instead of suzerainty.

2.3   From Independence to Hegemony

> I, therefore, think that we should recognize the world, not as a hierarchy of states
> or a suzerain system, but as an international society managed to some extent by
> a group of Great Powers. This pattern is somewhat similar to the nineteenth-
> century concert in Europe. (Watson 2002, 150)

I agree with Watson that the battle for and against hegemony is at the centre of the international society. Hegemony must also be at the core of any conceptualisation of spheres of influence. The European international society of sovereign states emerged out of the fight against the hegemony of the universal church (Watson 1985a, 13–16; also Jackson 2007, 6–8). Nevertheless, the principle of sovereignty did not kill hegemony. Reading from Bull and Watson, we note first that even with the emergence of state sovereignty the European system consisted of a number of empires. Second, the idea that states were equal in rights emerged in the middle of the eighteenth century only to be reversed in the nineteenth when the five great powers formed the Concert of Europe, claiming special responsibilities for maintaining order and special rights that the small powers did not possess (Bull and Watson 1985, 6–7). Watson explains that within the development of the European society of states two principles became crucial: All member states were to be regarded as juridically equal and their sovereignty was absolute. Regardless of this, the European system of states did not disregard the great differences of power among its members. Lesser powers remained juridically sovereign but were to be accorded only a secondary role (Watson 1985a, 23–30). Thus, in a system of states inequality and differences of power have existed side by side with the principle of sovereignty. It is this simultaneity of sovereignty and hegemony which creates the conditions for spheres of influence to exist, and which provides us with a framework to theorise on the nature and position of spheres of influence within international society.

Like Wight, Watson (2007, 11) observes that the European system was a succession of hegemonies rather than a pure Westphalian system. In his later work, Watson establishes an idea which diverges from his earlier strict separation of systems of independent states, suzerain systems and empires. He proposes a spectrum ranging from absolute independence to absolute empire, these two extremes being theoretical absolutes, not practical realisations. Between *independence* and *empire* lie *hegemony* and *dominion*. '*Independent* states in a system indicates [sic] political entities that retain the ultimate ability to take external decisions as well as domestic ones' (19). When a hegemon emerges, it is able to 'lay down the law' on behalf of others concerning their relations, but leaves them domestically independent (20). For Watson, a suzerain's claims that he was entitled to decide on the rules and institutions of international society were backed up by legitimacy and an acknowledgement by others of the need for suzerainty – this legitimacy the hegemon lacks (18). Dominion means imperial authority which can determine how other communities are governed but allows them to retain their identity and some control over their affairs. For Watson empire means direct administration of different communities from an imperial centre. Watson sees this model as a pendulum with a gravitational pull away from the extremes towards the centre. What Watson wants to illustrate with the pendulum is 'the tension between the desire for order and the desire for independence' (21). The significance of the pendulum idea lies in its establishing hegemony and dominion as the equilibrium point of the pendulum – not necessarily the ideal state of affairs, but somehow one that is more natural than the extremes of independence and empire. If hegemony and dominion are where the international system tends to gravitate, this is the logical space also for spheres of influence, which will lie somewhere between the two. Before the states-system the pendulum did not exist, only the empire, that is, the suzerain system. With the introduction of states the independence extreme was born, creating the possibility of a pendulum movement. Within the sweep of the pendulum a sphere of influence is not quite a suzerain system but definitely does not belong to the independence extreme either. Thus, the establishment of a sphere of influence could be likened to hegemony and dominion, the former representing looser control of the influenced state than the latter.

But as Watson's hegemony and dominion do not quite capture the justice problematique of spheres of influence, we need a finer-grained view on the differences in how the greater members of the society of states use power. Bull explores this middle ground, which Watson considers the equilibrium position of the pendulum. According to Bull (2002, 200) great powers possess a managerial responsibility in the international system which signifies that they unilaterally exploit their local preponderance, agree on spheres of influence and act jointly in a great power concert. Bull identifies three forms of preponderance: *dominance*, *hegemony* and *primacy*. Dominance means habitual use of force by a great power against lesser states and disregard of universal norms such as sovereignty, equality and independence in relation to those states. This is not quite imperial sovereignty but treating small states as second-class members of international society. As an example, Bull cites the United States' policy of military interventions in Central America and the Caribbean from the late nineteenth century until the introduction of Franklin Roosevelt's Good Neighbor Policy in 1933 (207). For Bull what lies at the opposite extreme to dominance is primacy. Primacy is achieved without use or threat of use of force and with no more than an ordinary degree of disregard for sovereignty, equality and independence. Primacy manifests itself among states whose peoples display some signs of being a single political community. Bull cites the British Commonwealth, which was founded without coercion or systematic disregard for sovereignty. The position the United States holds in NATO is also a form of primacy (208).

According to Bull, between dominance and primacy lies hegemony. Hegemony involves occasional and reluctant resort to force and the threat of force. The great power involved does not disregard the principles of sovereignty, equality and independence but is ready to violate them if needed (Bull 2002, 209). For Bull, hegemony describes the relationship between the Soviet Union and Eastern Europe. According to Bull, the Soviet Union recognised the sovereignty, equality and independence of the Eastern European states but also limited these rights through the Brezhnev Doctrine of 1968, which treated any threat to a socialist country as a threat to the socialist community as a whole. Likewise, the relationship between the United States and Central America and the Caribbean (but not South America) is one of hegemony, where the United States resorts to force only in extreme cases. What Bull describes as Soviet or American hegemony is tantamount to a sphere of influence – but so are primacy and dominance too. Bull offers us a way to diversify the idea of a sphere of influence beyond the confines of its pejorative connotation. Bull's forms of preponderance are divided in rather vague terms in relation to violation of sovereignty and resort to force, but they do indicate a separation between more or less forceful and acceptable forms of influence. The three levels of preponderance do not settle the question of what constitutes a sphere of influence but they help to visualise spheres of influence that can take many forms and affect sovereignty differently.

If we do not assign *sphere of influence* to any of the three categories of preponderance but think of the concept as a fluid one that can signify varying degrees of control and resort to use of force, we have the possibility to analyse influence within the entire spectrum of dominance, hegemony and primacy. The normative effect of this would be to conclude that a sphere of influence exemplifying primacy is more acceptable than one involving influence, which is closer to dominance because the rights of the influenced are more seriously violated under dominance than primacy. Conceptualising different levels of influence as having different implications for sovereignty, independence and equality, leaves room to speculate whether a sphere of influence takes the form of one of the three or to which end of the spectrum it comes closest. In this manner, we can imagine influence without the dichotomy of good influence and bad influence. This would mean dissociating the concept of sphere of influence from any particular state (Russia) and also dissociating certain foreign policy practices (such as interfering in elections or raising energy prices) from sphere-of-influence policies. Instead, influence would be identified and evaluated on the basis of its implications for sovereignty, independence, equality, use of force and other relevant normative indicators.

2.4 Agreements on Spheres of Influence and Colonial Influence

> When first this phrase [sphere of influence] was employed in the language of diplomacy I do not know, but I doubt if a more momentous early use of it can be traced than that in the assurance given by Count Gortchakoff to Lord Clarendon in 1869, and often since repeated, that Afghanistan lay 'completely outside the sphere within which Russia might be called upon to exercise her influence'. (Curzon 1907, 42)

After the Cold War meaning of *sphere of influence*, the second most prominent use of the term is to denote the relationship between European powers and their colonies. The first historical idea resembling that of a sphere of influence after the suzerain system or suzerain treaty is the notion of empire or imperialism. However, in its present use – and in other historical uses, excluding colonialism – *sphere of influence* is more informal and less comprehensive. In terms of Watson's (2007) pendulum idea, an empire indicates direct influence while a sphere of influence belongs more to the equilibrium point of the pendulum (hegemony or dominion). Hardt and Negri (2001, xii) explain how European imperialism was an extension of sovereignty beyond the borders of the imperialist state. Contrary to imperialism, a sphere-of-influence policy rarely indicates absorption or conquest but rather an occasional violation of sovereignty or maintenance of at least some level of sovereignty even under domination. Not even the Cold War spheres of influence led to a complete loss of sovereignty. Moreover, the group of theorists I will later introduce all essentially defended the independence of the influenced states (see Chapter 4). The imperialist associations of the concept of sphere of influence reinforce its pejorative connotation and strip it of its potential to defend, if not the sovereignty of the nation-state, at least a plurality of bounded communities.

In the present, the empire analogy is problematic also because of the ambiguity of the concepts of empire and imperialism. I have already presented empire lite as a name for the new American foreign policy (Chapter 1.4). Hardt and Negri (2001) use 'Empire' to denote a new global form of sovereignty, a kind of global covenant that knows no territorial or temporal boundaries. Hardt and Negri in fact draw a clear line of demarcation between imperialism, founded on sovereign states, and Empire, which means the end of sovereign nation-states (xii). The essence of the concept of sphere of influence is deeply rooted in the international system predicated on plurality, which is not the case for the Empire in the sense used by Hardt and Negri. To be more precise, the Empire of Hardt and Negri is not the equivalent of a sphere of influence, but rather of the single sovereign, or 'universe'. In fact, it was to counterbalance the emergence of a world organisation in the form of an 'Empire' that visions of spheres of influence were developed during and after the two world wars (see Chapter 4).

Keal (1983) explores a whole group of concepts which needed to be distinguished from the concept of sphere of influence. He argues that separating 'spheres of influence' from 'spheres of interest' would be like splitting hairs, but that the latter is more acceptable than the former (25). Likewise, 'spheres of action', which were used in the scramble for Africa; spheres of preponderance, which signify superiority of power and influence; and 'zones of influence' all mean the same as sphere of influence (19–23). Keal also distinguishes a sphere of influence from a buffer zone, which can comprise independent or neutral states. A buffer zone can coincide with a sphere of influence but might include territories which do not fall within a sphere of influence. By the same token, a sphere of influence can comprise areas which are not buffer zones (26–7). Keal borrows the definition of buffer zone from Wight (1995, 160), for whom 'buffer state' means 'a weak power between two or more stronger ones, maintained or even created with the purpose of reducing conflict between them'.

For Keal (1983, 27) spheres of restraint are grey areas in which no one power is predominant. 'Frontiers' can involve relations between influencing states (two great powers) whereas spheres of influence cannot be understood without a reference to the relationship between the influencing state and the influenced state. Moreover, according to Keal, frontiers demarcate the interests, but not necessarily the influence, of great powers (30). I find these distinctions rather unclear in defining what a sphere of influence is for two reasons: First, they lack the type of analysis I have proposed in Chapter 2.3, which would see influence from the perspective of sovereignty and hegemony, that is, which would attach the types of influence to a discussion on the nature of the international society and its power structures. Second, Keal does not pay attention to the politics of language. In Keal's time, *sphere of influence* was less of a curse word and more of a simple fact of international life; thus, unlike today, the political uses of the term were not as relevant as an object of study. What I would like to embark on next, instead of dwelling on the aforementioned concepts, is a closer look at colonial influence, because at some level colonial practices can be considered historical predecessors of spheres of influence; they constitute an essentially similar, yet not identical, policy.

M.F. Lindley (1926), a source referred to by Bull (2002, 212–13) and Keal (1983, 16–17) alike, establishes the relationship between colonialism and spheres of influence. For Lindley, a sphere of influence has four uses: 1) It can entail a promise to abstain from acquisition of sovereign rights within a sphere allotted to the other. In this case the agreement is between colonising powers over an unorganised area. 2) It can mean recognition of special interests within a territory, which is sometimes called a sphere of interest. This is an agreement between colonising powers relating to the territory of a third state. 3) It can be an agreement regarding the territory of a third state made by agreement with that state. For example, a state can promise not to dispose of a part of its territory to any other than the interested power. 4) It can be 'inappropriate areas which adjoin, or are economically, politically, or strategically important to, territory already in the possession of a State'. In this case there is no international agreement (Lindley 1926, 207–8).

For not only Lindley but also Bull (2002, 212) the first sphere-of-influence agreements were the colonising activity of the Crowns of Castile and Portugal in the fifteenth century. The basis of those agreements were papal bulls, about which Lindley (1926, 124) writes, 'At the time of the great discoveries, the popes claimed the power to grant Christian monarchs the right to acquire territory in the possession of heathens and infidels'. Lindley continues that the modern era of spheres of influence began after the Berlin Conference (1884–1885), where it was formally recognised that a territory might be under the influence – as distinct from the protection or sovereignty – of a power (209). The term 'sphere of influence' had been used ten years earlier in Anglo-Russian negotiations on Central Asia, but was not yet formally recognised then (210).

Lindley's account is from the 1920s, when colonial influence was still the dominant form of international influence for the European powers, and at the time a sphere of influence could not carry any other meanings. It is fair to say that colonial influence is what gave birth to the concept of sphere of influence. Yet something also separates the present understanding of sphere of influence from its colonial past: a colonial relationship was actually an agreement between the colonising powers, and the relationship between the influencing and the influenced was not disputed. The influenced party was stripped of its rights – if it even had any to begin with. There was no need to debate inequality of power and the level of sovereignty accorded to the influenced, because the colonial powers were the only sovereign powers.

In 1907, Lord Curzon traced the history of the concept of sphere of influence by connecting it with the idea of protectorates. A sphere of influence represented an idea between the more developed form of influence, the protectorate, and the less developed sphere of interest (Curzon 1907, 42). Bull (2002, 215) had read Curzon and explained the scale as spanning 1) spheres of interest, which tend to become 2) spheres of influence, then 3) protectorates and finally 4) annexation. It seems that protectorates and annexation are the formal and more constraining forms of influence, with a sphere of interest then being something even less formal or less compelling than a sphere of influence. This is the idea Trenin (2009) tried to express by distinguishing between spheres of influence and spheres of interest (see Chapter 1.5.1). For Curzon (1907, 41), the concept of protectorate was more accurate in defining colonial influence than sphere of influence, which had become commonly used but which was less precise. What the concept of sphere of influence denotes for Curzon is influence by one power to the exclusion of others and to a degree chosen by that power based on its needs and preferences (42). Moreover, the local government is left as it is and its sovereignty can even be reaffirmed, but political influence and commercial exploitation are seen as the rights of the interested power (42–3). For Curzon, as I read his work, 'protectorate' is the appropriate term for a colonised status since a sphere of influence appears to be a more unofficial form of influence. A sphere of influence also gives more freedom to the influenced party, although Curzon does not explore in detail the difference between a protectorate and a sphere of influence in this respect.

Geddes W. Rutherford wrote an article in *The American Journal of International Law* in 1926 about spheres of influence as an aspect of semi-suzerainty in which he also explored the difference between a sphere of influence and a protectorate. Rutherford (1926, 317) writes that a protectorate requires or at least suggests recognition. 'Spheres of influence, whether affected by unilateral or bilateral arrangements, are not considered as binding on Powers not parties to such arrangements', whereas protectorates are recognised by third parties (304, 318). Moreover, for Rutherford, a sphere of influence does not imply responsibilities, unlike a protectorate does. Rutherford also explores negative and positive aspects of influence, but because he does not discuss the normativity of influence, there is really nothing in his work that defines positive and negative. In fact, control over foreign policy of the influenced state is both positive and negative for Rutherford and he only discusses the pervasiveness of that influence, not its justification. With a stance on normativity Rutherford could have discussed responsibility as positive influence, but he does not take a step in this direction either, because in his opinion responsibility is not an element relevant to spheres of influence. Although in many particulars Rutherford's analysis of spheres of influence makes them sound essentially like colonial relations, he attempts to draw a line between a sphere of influence as a more informal type of influence and a protectorate as a form of complete territorial control. This distinction is one between *political influence* and *direct authority* (Rutherford 1926, 316). In fact, it goes to the very core of the concept of sphere of influence and it deserves more attention.

Kaufman sought to separate spheres of influence from colonialism by introducing the term *sphere of direct influence*. Kaufman associates the concept of sphere of influence with the colonial period, but recognises a difference between the concepts representing a more formal type of domination – colonies and protectorates – and spheres of influence, which are less subject to the controlling power. Kaufman (1976, 10) explains how colonialism was *de jure* control of foreign territories but, at a later stage, when most geographic regions were distributed and the doctrines of nation-state and self-determination became widespread, *de facto* spheres of influence were introduced. For Keal (1983, 45), spheres of influence have been agreed upon on the basis of tacit understandings instead of formal agreements ever since non-European powers became influential in international politics and state sovereignty was established as a universal principle. Bull is sceptical about the existence of even tacit agreements on spheres of influence. He (2002, 213) urges us to separate the *fact* of a sphere of influence from the *right* to a sphere of influence. This means that even though a great power might recognise another's sphere of influence, recognition of legal or moral rights does not automatically follow (214). As an example, Bull argues, the European powers did not think that the proclamation of the Monroe Doctrine by the United States gave it a right to exclude them from the Western Hemisphere; rather, they saw it as an American policy that they should take into account (213). Bull observed that the spheres of influence of the United States and the Soviet Union were not based on agreement, but on understandings and a code of behaviour of the parties (214, 216). As such these understandings were established and terms altered not by discussion but through struggle (218). Thus, for Bull the Cold War spheres of influence represent 'negative sphere-of-influence agreements', which are more competitive than cooperative (217) (see Chapter 3.6).

For Kaufman and Keal, colonial influence and spheres of influence indicate separate levels of formality or legitimacy of influence. Colonies could be established based on formal agreements, whereas spheres of influence imply tacit agreements. Keal explains how the concept of sphere of influence was first used in connection with the partition of Africa, with the term implying territorial acquisition. According to Keal, when influence was exerted on states, diplomats avoided using the term 'sphere of influence', because it was no longer a question of acquiring *territorium nullius*. For Keal the origin of spheres of influence lay in the colonialist tradition, but they later lost the meaning of territorial acquisition and became political and economic influence in the affairs of another state (Keal 1983, 22–3). According to Keal, formal agreements on spheres of influence had become unacceptable in practice (45). Keal thus differentiates the more formal agreements on expansion (colonialism) and the more informal agreements on spheres of influence.

The concept of sphere of influence originated in the era of European expansion but its meaning later changed to signify unspoken agreements on influence. Finding the historical roots of the concept of sphere of influence in colonialism is only the beginning. We need to find additional sources that have contributed to our present political conception of the phenomenon. One of the most powerful images of what a sphere of influence comprises is the famous Monroe Doctrine.

2.5 The Monroe Doctrine

The Monroe Doctrine had its origin in President James Monroe's annual address to the United States Congress on 2 December 1823. For many it is the embodiment of a sphere-of-influence doctrine: It represents the beginning of a division of the world into spheres of influence, even a new international order. The Monroe Doctrine is also seen as explaining the vagaries of United States foreign policy: Sometimes it adheres to the Doctrine; sometimes it repudiates it. The Doctrine also appears to have had some universal meaning and it had considerable bearing on the principles of sovereignty and intervention. For these reasons, for the importance that the Monroe Doctrine is ascribed by those who theorise on spheres of influence, I have chosen to look in more detail at the discussion on the Doctrine.

In the Doctrine, President Monroe urges the European states to stay out of the Western Hemisphere. It is a declaration which forbad the European states to intervene on the American continent, where the United States was the sole guardian of hemispheric security. Explaining the background of the Doctrine, Watson writes that Washington and Jefferson argued that the Old and New Worlds were two separate spheres of political activity which should have as little to do with each other as possible. The Monroe administration feared Russia's activities in Alaska and was concerned that the Holy Alliance would restore the Spanish Crown in the Americas (Watson 1985b, 137). The doctrine states: '[T]he American continents, by the free and independent condition which they have assumed and maintain, are henceforth not to be considered as subjects for future colonisation by any European powers', repudiating European colonialism. The Doctrine also denied the European states the right to extend any influence in the Western Hemisphere: 'We owe it, therefore, to candor, and to the amicable relations existing between the United States and those powers, to declare that we should consider any attempt on their part to extend their system to any portion of this hemisphere as dangerous to our peace and safety' (Monroe 1823).

Vincent (1974, 111–12) reads the Monroe Doctrine as expounding both the right to intervention and the principle of non-intervention: The Doctrine embodied an isolationist principle, but if the United States had to use force to prevent European influence it would depart from the principle of non-intervention. In Vincent's estimation, after the Latin American colonies achieved their independence, the United States followed the principle of non-intervention; the interventionist interpretation of the Doctrine came much later. In his view, '[i]t was not until the end of the century that new interpretations of the Monroe Doctrine coincided with the growth of American power and turned the policy of non-intervention into one of intervention, and the threat to the independence of the Latin American states then seemed to come as much from the United States as from across the Atlantic' (119). The Roosevelt Corollary to the Monroe Doctrine, articulated by President Theodore Roosevelt (1904), continued and strengthened the thrust of the Monroe Doctrine, introducing the idea of the right to intervention:

> Chronic wrongdoing, or an impotence which results in a general loosening of the ties of civilized society, may in America, as elsewhere, ultimately require intervention by some civilized nation, and in the Western Hemisphere the adherence of the United States to the Monroe Doctrine may force the United States, however reluctantly, in flagrant cases of such wrongdoing or impotence, to the exercise of an international police power.

For Vincent, where the Monroe Doctrine denied the European states the right of interference in Latin America and the Caribbean, the Roosevelt Corollary justified the United States' interference in those areas. President William Howard Taft followed the foreign policy of intervention after Roosevelt and so did Woodrow Wilson after him (Vincent 1974, 135–6). The core issue in the case of the Monroe Doctrine is the legitimacy of intervention as a tool furthering a sphere-of-influence policy. The original intention of the Monroe Doctrine was non-interventionist. It meant only fending off the influence of other powers. As a declaration of a sphere of influence, it defended the rights of the influenced and was very restrained when it came to the United States' own influence. Later, the Doctrine became a declaration justifying intervention, either betraying its original meaning or only extending it to include the establishment of influence in addition to counteracting that of other states. In this light, the Monroe Doctrine raised the normative question of justification.

Kaufman also explains the relationship between the Monroe Doctrine, intervention and spheres of influence. According to Kaufman, the Doctrine was seen as the first step in declaring a right of the United States to spheres of influence, but it would be the turn away from isolationism to interventionism or imperialism that marked the emergence of the practice of pursuing spheres of influence. For Kaufman, the meaning of the Monroe Doctrine for the United States' influence in Latin America could not be overemphasised as it was a foreign policy principle that had been maintained for such a long period of time (Kaufman 1976, 178). Indeed, the meaning of the Doctrine was not confined to the hemisphere but was recognised by the League of Nations Charter in Article 54 as regional 'understanding' (Kaufman 1976, 179; also Keal 1983, 107–9).

The significance of the Monroe Doctrine for the present research lies in its exemplifying a 'sphere-of-influence doctrine'. When we get to Schmitt's work in Chapter 4, the Doctrine is ascribed yet another meaning: it (or its interventionist application) was viewed as a threat to the pluralist system of states (see Schmitt 2003, 281–3). For Carr (1965, 45) the Monroe Doctrine represents the space between nationalism and internationalism, not the threat of world domination Schmitt saw. When we study Franklin Roosevelt's Good Neighbor Policy, analysed in detail by Walter Lippmann, the Monroe Doctrine is again reflected against the principle of non-intervention and acceptable forms of influence within the international system (see Chapter 4.5). In light of the historical significance of the Doctrine to the conceptualisation of *sphere of influence* it is curious how spheres of influence are not very often connected at the present time with the Monroe Doctrine and United States foreign policy.

In 1916, *The New York Times* featured a long article on the Monroe Doctrine by Rear Admiral French E. Chadwick in which he suggested extending the principles of the Doctrine to include the world, abolishing spheres of influence and laying the road for peace. 'Spheres of Special Influence' for Chadwick meant the evil of imperialism. 'Man's inhumanity to man' could only be stopped under the Golden Rule, and that could happen by the application of the Monroe Doctrine to the entire world. 'We want no imperialism; we want only justice in the world', Chadwick (1916) wrote. Even though Chadwick did not want to call the Monroe Doctrine a sphere-of-influence policy, and even though he specifically defines a sphere of influence as a colonial policy, I believe that he is addressing exactly the point where colonialism is transmuted into a sphere-of-influence policy. They become two different forms of influence. The term *sphere of influence* denotes influence which is tacitly agreed upon at a time when colonial influence as a more formal and submissive form of influence becomes increasingly difficult to justify. The idea of a sphere of influence represents stability and instability alike; it is salvation as well as ruin. It brings states together but it also divides them. Spheres of influence thus become reflections of international theory – theory on international order, states and sovereignty. And the Monroe Doctrine emerges as a significant signpost which represents the advent of spheres of influence in international theorising.

2.6   Order and Spheres of Influence

The historical account of the emergence of the system of states and its development into a great power order makes it clear that spheres of influence have something to do with international order. In fact we cannot understand spheres of influence without understanding international order, because international order is what makes spheres of influence a facet of international theory. International order, and especially the pendulum movement within it, enables us to imagine where spheres of influence are situated within the political organisation of the world.

For spheres of influence, as well as the English School theory, international order signifies the political organisation of the world expressly as a system/society of states. Bull examines international order in *The Anarchical Society* (2002) first published in 1977. Keal follows in his footsteps to theorise on sphere of influence and order. For both Bull and Keal, it is important to notice that order has a purpose. Order is not promoted for its own sake, but for some purpose laid down by international society (Keal 1983, 194–5). Bull explains that order is something more than simply regular behaviour. Bull claims that states' behaviour in war and crisis, even though it would seem organised and orderly, is not an expression of order in social life. Order in social life has certain goals and values to promote and thus cannot encompass just any regular relations (Bull 2002, 3–4).

Then what is the purpose of international order? According to Bull international order is 'the pattern or disposition of activity that sustains the primary, elementary or universal goals of the society of states, or international society'. This is important for the idea of sphere of influence: international order sustains the goals of the society of states, which means that the components of that order are states. For Bull, the first goal is the preservation of the system and society of states as the prevailing form of universal political organisation. Bull refers to instances in history where this has been challenged by a dominant state trying to form a universal empire: the Habsburg Empire, Napoleon's France, the Third Reich, and, as Bull notes, 'perhaps post-1945 America'. The second goal of international order is maintaining the independence or external sovereignty of states (Bull 2002, 16). The preservation of the system nevertheless comes first, encouraging and tolerating such practices as agreements establishing spheres of influence. The third goal of international order is peace, which, like sovereignty, is again subordinate to the preservation of the system itself but also subordinate to the preservation of the sovereignty of independent states (17). Fourth, Bull lists the goals of 'limitation of violence resulting in death or bodily harm, the keeping of promises and the stabilization of possession by rules of property' (18). The emphasis Bull gives to the preservation of the system of states – over sovereignty and peace – as the main goal of international society becomes extremely relevant for spheres of influence because it helps to justify their existence. In Bull's theory, spheres of influence represent a practice of limiting sovereignty which is acceptable as long as it does not threaten the international order of states. In fact, spheres of influence could help to maintain political plurality against universalising tendencies, as Schmitt (2003) reasoned (see Chapter 4.3).

Keal discusses the relationship between order and spheres of influence in detail, and poses the question whether spheres of influence contribute to order. His (1983, 199) answer is that the contemporary international order relies on superpower relations, and, more specifically, order rests on the pillar of mutual acquiescence with regard to spheres of influence. According to Keal, spheres of influence contribute most importantly to stability of possessions, limitation of violence, and to the sanctity of contracts or stable expectations – all elements of the fourth goal of Bull's international order (204–7). This is so because a sphere of influence is removed from the disputes between the influencing powers (205). For Keal '[s]pheres of influence contribute to order between influencing powers, and hence to order in general, through tacit understanding which serves the goals of social coexistence, and by contributing to what influencing powers perceive as necessary to a balance of power' (209–10). The problem is, as Keal notes, that for spheres of influence to contribute to order static relations are required but social systems are constantly changing (211).

According to Keal, the defence of spheres of influence in general has been that they diminish the possibility of conflicts in the international system. Hierarchical relationships maintain order within a bloc and a sphere of influence removes the focal area from external challenges, thus contributing to order (Keal 1983, 199). Relations among the influenced states are kept in check by the influencing power, thus limiting conflicts (200). Keal describes how a relationship of dependence is also a synonym for a sphere of influence: 'Through aid, trade and investment and through the harmony of interest between the elites in both the influenced states and the influencing power, control has been established and can be maintained' (201). Keal goes on to argue that as a form of dependence a sphere of influence can lead to disorder by unjust distribution of wealth, which will prompt revolutionary action for economic and social justice. This might have consequences for the international system, especially if armed conflict breaks out between the influencing and the influenced and if an outside power intervenes (203).

For Keal (1983, 197–9), stability of possessions is safeguarded not only in sovereignty but also in spheres of influence. Thus, Keal does not contrast sovereignty and spheres of influence but sees both as contributing to the same goal of international order. As elements of international order spheres of influence remain squarely within the limits of the system of states. This means that spheres of influence at the same time support the system of states and violate its core principles (sovereignty and non-intervention). Bull takes essentially the same position on the order-producing mechanisms of inequality in the international society as Keal does when justifying the special status of great powers. For Bull the contribution of great powers to international order derives from the inequality of power within the states-system. As Bull (2002, 199) puts it, if all were equal in power, it would be hard to see how international conflicts could ever be settled. Bull explains how great powers contribute to international order when they manage relations with each other by preserving a balance of power, seeking to limit and avoid crises, conflict and war among themselves and imparting a central direction to the affairs of international society (200). Like Keal, Bull (2002, 199–206) reasons that spheres of influence (those of the United States and the Soviet Union) prevent, keep within bounds, help to resolve and contain conflicts – even if they can also deliberately manufacture crisis.

There are two conclusions to draw about the relationship between spheres of influence and international order:

1. *Spheres of influence are a reflection of international order within a system composed of sovereign states.* Both Keal and Bull are able to incorporate spheres of influence within the system of sovereign states; there is no fundamental conflict between influence and sovereignty. The system of states does not crumble because of spheres of influence. Enough plurality and sovereignty remain to provide the foundation of the states-system. What is more, spheres of influence even support the states-system as a means of great power management that prevents the emergence of a universal empire.

2. *Spheres of influence in Bull's and Keal's conceptualisation can contribute to international order.* We should not ignore or take for granted the relationship between spheres of influence and international order; this we do if spheres of influence are taken to signify only a self-serving foreign policy practice. Spheres of influence can still mean a power game, but this game affects international structures, which is why we should be interested in the effects of spheres of influence on the system, not only on its members. What we can conclude from Bull's and Keal's discussion is that there is room to debate the normative aspects of great power management and spheres of influence. For Keal, spheres of influence contribute to international order by stabilising relations among great powers, but the injustice that a sphere of influence entails can also become a source of conflict. Another hindrance to spheres of influence providing benefits for international order is that the stability and predictability which spheres of influence create are subject to constant change. As the distribution of power within the system changes, so do the spheres of influence. Bull, too, views spheres of influence, although they are based on inequality, as a practice which promotes order. Spheres of influence function as a part of great power management, which

is a necessity for settling conflicts among states. These are important perspectives in questioning the pejorative associations of the concept of sphere of influence in the present.

Chapter 3
International Society and the Normative Question

We now know that for Bull and Keal spheres of influence can contribute to international order, but there is more to be discovered on the English School theory by examining further the idea of *international society*. Bull's list of the rules and institutions of the society of states frame the concept of sphere of influence: it can be conceptualised by exploring the rules of sovereignty and non-intervention and examining the institutions of great power management, balance of power and international law. What binds the concept of sphere of influence to the rules and institutions of international society is the question of justice. It is necessary to discuss matters of justice in order to look beyond the pejorative uses of the term *sphere of influence*. Pejorative interpretations of the concept assume that spheres of influence violate international law by violating the principles of sovereignty and non-intervention. Yet, as a tool of great power management and for maintaining the balance of power, spheres of influence represent a component of international order.

3.1 The Rules and Institutions of International Society

According to Buzan (2004a, 161), the concept of institutions is central to the English School because it embodies the substantive content of international society and underpins what English School writers mean by 'international order'. The institutions of international society are defined in different ways by the scholars of the School (see Buzan 2004a). As this is not a study on the English School as such, I take the liberty to pass over much of the controversy that surrounds the subject and explore that which we need to know in order to ponder spheres of influence from a normative angle.[1] The foundations of English School thinking lie precisely where sphere of influence can be located: 1) international society as a community of states with rules and institutions and 2) the pendulum movement within this society between independence and empire or, in other words, between pluralism and solidarism.

I wrote earlier that for the English School international order is predicated on the system of states, but even more so on a society of states.[2] In a well-known

---

1 For a discussion on international society, see Little 2002, Buzan 2004a, Roberson 2002.

2 See Little (2007, 140–48) on the discussions of the usefulness of separating system from society.

quotation, Bull explains that '[a] society of states (or international society) exists when a group of states, conscious of certain common interests and common values, form a society in the sense that they conceive themselves to be bound by a common set of rules in their relations with one another, and share in the working of common institutions'. He continues, 'An international society in this sense presupposes an international system, but an international system may exist that is not an international society'. This means that states may interact without common interests and values, forming a system but not a society (Bull 2002, 13). The English School conception of international society resonates with the idea of a society of state-persons, which means that one can, to some extent, apply the 'domestic analogy' (states as a society of individuals) to understand international relations. States want to construct a society in which they are able to peacefully manage relations among themselves; as part of the process, they promote common values and abide by common rules. More and more states are also willing to agree on principles such as human rights, protection of which requires them to relinquish some sovereign rights and accord human justice a place alongside interstate justice. Vincent (1990, 39) describes Bull's international society as a 'Grotian world' between the Hobbesian rejection of a society of states and the Kantian idea of a cosmopolitan society of individuals.[3] Where the Hobbesian view of international relations is a state of war against all, the Kantian is based on transnational social bonds between individual human beings (Bull 2002, 23–4). The Grotian tradition stands between the realist and universalist traditions and emphasises that common rules and institutions limit conflicts among states. In other words, states are bound by the rules and institutions of the society that they are members of; in addition, they are bound by rules of not only prudence and expedience but also law and morality (25). The Grotian conception of international society is also called solidarist, in contrast to a pluralist view, in which states are able to agree only on certain minimum purposes (Bull 1966b, 52). Although Bull argues in *Diplomatic Investigations* that the members in Grotius' system of are not states but individuals (68), he writes in *The Anarchical Society* that the immediate members of international society are states rather than individual human beings (Bull 2002, 25). Bull's international society takes the state as the principal member but infuses it with solidarism, which makes the system into a society.

Thus, for Bull, international society is characterised by states that are bound by 1) common rules and 2) institutions. Bull (2002, 64) explains that 'rules may have the status of international law, of moral rules, of customs or of established practice, or they may be merely operational rules or "rules of the game" worked out without formal agreement or even verbal communication'. For Bull, there is, first of all, a constitutional principle determining who the members of international

---

3   However, Bull (2002; 39, 49) writes that the international system [in his time] included traits of all the three traditions: 1) war and struggle, 2) elements of transnational solidarity and conflict and 3) cooperation and regulated intercourse among states. For Bull one of these three elements can predominate over the others in different times and places.

society are; second, among these members (which are states for Bull) sovereignty and non-intervention constitute the rules of coexistence (66). Institutions for Bull are an expression of and means for collaboration among states. He continues, '[b]y an institution we do not necessarily imply an organisation or administrative machinery, but rather a set of habits and practises shaped towards the realisation of common goals' (71). Thus, rules are agreed among states, even if only tacitly, whereas institutions emerge as practices or habits. Like rules, institutions enable collaboration among states; that is, they produce enough solidarity to make the system function as a society.

The international institutions, according to Bull (2002, 71), include *balance of power, international law, the diplomatic mechanism, the managerial system of great powers, and war*. Bull (2002, 68) writes that states themselves are the principal institutions of international society in that they make the rules of coexistence (sovereignty and intervention) effective. This makes institutions mechanisms for the enforcement of rules. Wight (1995, 111) and Jackson (2000, 58) have slightly different versions of the institutions and Buzan (2004a) identifies primary and secondary institutions in different interstate societies. For the purposes of this study, it is not of great importance to debate the differences among sets of rules and institutions and make lists of them but to recognise that the principles which determine relations among states also govern spheres of influence, and influence the possible justifications for them.

As I have argued already, a sphere of influence is not listed as an institution or a rule within the English School theory. The concept appears occasionally, but it is never explicitly situated within the international society of the English School, not even by Buzan. I find it very curious that the English School ignores the phenomenon in this way. For example, a sphere of influence could very well be a derivate institution of the managerial system of great powers. If spheres of influence were listed this way among the institutions of international society, it would help to establish their significance and provide impetus for conceptualising the phenomenon further. Luckily for us, Keal did not ignore the concept and its role within the web of rules and institutions. When it comes to spheres of influence, Keal (1983, 2) writes about tacit understandings between great powers and 'rules of the game' instead of laws or written agreements (see also Chapter 2.4). Formally, great powers deny having spheres of influence, but agreements are made that are unspoken or tacit (207). In Keal's estimation, the tacit understandings that underpin spheres of influence provide unwritten rules or guidelines for promoting common interests. These understandings may violate international law but they nevertheless contribute to international order (3).

What we have here is the argument by Bull that international society is built on certain rules and institutions and by Keal that spheres of influence are founded upon 'unwritten rules or guidelines for promoting common interests'. The rules and institutions of international society also offer a relevant framework for conceptualising spheres of influence as representing a special relationship between states. It would be difficult to imagine spheres of influence without the notion of sovereignty, great and small powers, intervention and the balancing game. It should be noted, however, that Bull's rules and institutions are contested concepts in themselves and I will discuss and analyse these concepts as they are defined by the English School. I have left out diplomacy and war, and focused on those institutions which seem most compelling for the project of contesting the concept of sphere of influence. Moreover, because the purpose of this study is not to analyse all possible aspects of the focal rules and institutions, I will confine myself to trying to establish the normative relationship between those rules and institutions and spheres of influence. I believe that by focusing on the normative – the subjugated knowledge which is lacking in the present – I will avoid the pitfall of making spheres of influence dependent on some specific definition of, for example, sovereignty. Exposing spheres of influence to a normative dialogue with the rules and institutions of international society avoids fixing concepts to a particular definition. We can and should still contest the concepts of balance of power and sovereignty even if we argue that they are the framework for understanding spheres of influence.

3.2　Classes of Power and the Balance of Power

Spheres of influence in both the past and the present are viewed as the privileges of great powers. A sphere of influence is an extension of the ideas of hierarchy and inequality in the international system. For the normative reading of *sphere of influence*, this means taking into consideration possible justifications for great power management and the silent acceptance of inequality as the nature of the states-system. If the emergence of the system of states was the beginning of the present international order, then the emergence of the 'great power order' was the beginning of spheres of influence.

In *Power Politics* (1995) *and Systems of States* (1977), Wight discusses the emerging 'great power system' and inequality in international relations.[4] In Wight's view, the grading of powers can be traced back to the beginning of the international system. However, it was in the Congress of Vienna after the Napoleonic Wars, in 1815, that great-power status became regularly established in international politics. On the one hand, the Congress abandoned the old order of precedence among sovereigns, which was based on antiquity of title, and made empires, kingdoms and republics all equal in diplomatic rank. A doctrine of the equality of states became accepted among international lawyers (Wight 1995, 41–2). On the other hand, Wight points out, '[i]n terms of politics, as contrasted with those of diplomatic theory and international law, the Congress of Vienna replaced the old system based on tradition by a system based on power'. Wight (1977, 42) goes

---

4　*Power Politics* was originally published in 1946, and in an extended version, which Wight worked on but did not finish before his death, in 1978. *Systems of States*, a book on Wight's work within the Committee, was compiled by Bull after Wight's death.

on to note in *Systems of States* that '[t]he modern European states-system, while formulating the principle of the equality of states, has modified it by establishing the class of great powers. Since 1907, if not since 1815, their responsibilities and privileges have been recognized in international law'.

Thus, great power management is the context within which spheres of influence can exist and thrive. This makes a hierarchy of different classes of power the prerequisite for spheres of influence. That which Keal calls 'the influencing state' is the great power. 'The influenced state' belongs to the class of small or lesser powers. Kaufman (1976, 27–8) writes on great power influence: 'Furthermore, it was always a condition of acceptance as a world power, that one maintained a position of supremacy in one's own region of the world, and this is a further inducement to the superpowers to subjugate their nearest subsystems'. For Kaufman, becoming a world power requires influence beyond state borders and, specifically, influence in the nearest territories. For Kaufman, a sphere of influence is thus what makes a power great, making the status of great power important for theorising spheres of influence.

There is plenty of discussion on the differences between great powers, regional powers and superpowers (for example Bull 2002, 194–5; Buzan 2004b, 69–72, 76) but my concern here is the lack of interest in defining the class of small or minor powers. All three categories of greater powers can have spheres of influence, rendering the differences between such states less meaningful than looking into what states fall into the lowest category, that of influenced states. States in all three of Buzan's (2004b) classes of power (super, great and regional) are 'great' in relation to small powers and have the capacity to extend influence over smaller states. Perhaps the category of small powers could then be defined as comprising those states which are under the influence of other, greater, powers. Small states are then the objects of power politics – 'satellites' to use the metaphor of influence. On the other hand, small powers can influence the balance of power by shifting allegiances. When Wight (1995, 160) writes about buffer zones he mentions 'trimmers', states which play the great powers against each other A small power can have a stronger economy than a greater power as measured by indicators other than size. Small powers can gain from their close relationship with a greater power, adding to their military strength, economic strength or prestige. Thus, small states are not necessarily insignificant actors. Indeed, a sphere of influence does not necessarily involve total subjugation of the small influenced powers. On balance, the class of small powers is every bit as ambiguous as any other. More importantly, this ambiguity means that the relationship between the great and the small, as well as the direction of influence between them, is not that clear-cut either.

The strict division into great influencing powers and small influenced powers creates an image of one-way influence and the guilt of the great versus the innocence of the small. A great deal of great power management is accepted among states, such as occasional military interventions or the institutionalised hierarchy of the United Nations Security Council. But when it comes to a sphere of influence, a small power is perceived as the victim and the influencing power takes on a negative status. This is one way in which the concept of sphere of influence is used in a pejorative sense: it is seen as predicated on a dichotomy consisting of a bad influencing power and a suffering influenced power. Breaking down this dichotomy would mean discussing the role of great powers as system-level players, with potential positive functions, and the role of small states as influenced powers, both as victims of great power management and as players of power games on their own account. In the end, it would entail looking at the interests of the focal actors but at the same time situating spheres of influence within the international system, that is, as an aspect of great power management and a means of a balance of power.

If the roles given to the influencing and the influenced power in contemporary uses of the concept of sphere of influence are ascribed a pejorative meaning, the same semantic burden is laid upon the concept of balance of power. The pejorative associations of the concept of sphere of influence in the context of the balance of power emphasise the role of small states as objects of great power games. But by connecting spheres of influence and the balance of power with the same objective of preventing a single hegemon from emerging, the normative horizon widens and a sphere-of-influence policy denotes not only hunger for power and subjugation of a weaker party but also a defence of the plurality of international society. Discussing how much influence we can accept for the sake of the system, at the expense of the influenced, sets the stage for a normative debate between spheres of influence and the balance of power.

For Wight (1966a, 153), the concept of balance of power is used in a normative way to denote the principle that such a balance *ought to* be evenly distributed. The balance of power is endowed with a normative element in that it is often seen as a power game which does not treat small states fairly – just like a sphere of influence. This makes it unjust. On the other hand, the balance of power is associated with the positive function of maintaining international order and, more specifically, maintaining a plurality of states and thus preventing world domination by a single power. To repeat Butterfield's (1966, 132) definition of the balance of power: '[a]ll the various bodies, the greater and the lesser powers, were poised against one another, each exercising a kind of gravitational pull on all the rest – and the pull of each would be proportionate to its mass, though its effect would be greatly reduced as it acted at a greater distance'(see Chapter 1.3). If we think about the pendulum idea, it is as if the balance of power is situated within hegemony and dominance: It requires a certain amount of hegemony, which makes international society drift away from independence, but it also prevents a system of empire taking over.

I have already introduced Little's (2007, 34) depiction of the balance of power as a set of scales, but for spheres of influence the question is, What is the relationship between spheres of influence and the balance of power? For Keal, spheres of influence contribute, at least in the influencing powers' view, to the maintenance of a balance of power. Keal (1983, 209) writes, 'So far the argument has been that spheres of influence contribute to order between influencing powers, and hence to order in general, through tacit understanding which serves the goals of social coexistence, and by contributing to what influencing powers perceive as necessary to a balance of power'. In both world wars and the Cold War period, the idea of international influence was always more or less connected with the idea of balance of power. When the term 'sphere of influence' was used to denote colonial relationships, the concern was not so much with international order, which is why Lindley (1926) and Lord Curzon (1907) did not discuss balances of power. The concept of sphere of influence is also rather lacking in the literature on balance of power. The likely reason for this is that balance of power, as a concept, is primarily concerned with the effects of an increase in a state's power through war and conquest, and less with influence. Herbert Butterfield (1966), for example, discusses balance of power at length without mentioning spheres of influence. Nevertheless, the relationship between the two concepts lies in the fact that both are constructed as methods to maintain the system of states and that spheres of influence can help to establish or maintain a balance of power.

We can also compare the justice dimension of the two concepts in order to reflect on their relationship. The idea of a balance of power, unlike a sphere of influence, recognises small states as both victims and actors in the balancing game. Bull (2002, 103–4) writes, '[f]rom the point of view of a weak state sacrificed to it, the balance of power must appear as a brutal principle. But its function in the preservation of international order is not for this reason less central'. For Bull the general balance of power is what matters and if small states must be sacrificed for international order, then so be it. In a contrasting perspective, Butterfield (1966, 142) explains how writers in the eighteenth century thought that a balance of power guaranteed the existence of small powers and actually gave them more room to manoeuvre in terms of foreign policy, as they were not mere 'satellites'. A balance of power vindicated small states (145). For Wight (1966a, 161), in a system that rests on a balance of power small states can sometimes hold the decisive power with regard to the balance, which implies vindication rather than victimisation. In a sphere-of-influence system, small states are not empowered in this way. Neither Keal nor Bull discusses the possibility of small powers being empowered in any way within a sphere of influence, or even having the power to play great powers against each other by choosing the sphere they want to belong to. Thus, with this logic, when a sphere of influence is used as a means to achieve a balance of power, it is always under the full control of the great power and small states are kept on a tight leash. Small states are not able to shift their affinities but rather are at the mercy of the influencing states, meaning that small states have no power where a balance of power is concerned.

Connecting spheres of influence and a balance of power reveals how, for Keal and Bull, a sphere of influence is not a source of vindication of small states – unlike a balance of power may be. What is interesting is the question of whether vindication of small states is how things *ought* to be, because following the logic of 'spheres of influence contributing to order with stability of possessions', it would not seem like a good idea to give small states too much room to manoeuvre.

Butterfield (1966, 145) explains that within the European balance of power, freedom has been promoted before peace precisely because considerations of the balance of power vindicated small states. In a way, this provides the answer to the question posed above: Even if vindication of small states means conflict and war, a choice will be made in favour of a balance of power over a universal empire. There *ought* to be freedom, which means the vindication of small powers, because freedom means freedom from a universal empire. Thus, if the world seems to be sliding into the hands of a single great power, constituting a global sphere of influence, then small states *ought* to be empowered as to prevent this from taking place. This reasoning prompts the conclusion that if spheres of influence are meant to contribute to international order, they need to relate to the logic of a balance of power and, when need be, small states ought to be empowered to engage in the power games. Spheres of influence cannot be stable; they need to exist and change in rhythm with a balance of power.

If we believe Keal (1983, 209–10), who argues that spheres of influence contribute to international order through their contribution to the balance of power, Bull's reasoning about the means to sustain the balancing game offer some normative insights on the matter. Bull (2002, 102–4) argues that international order is maintained through the balance of power, and its main function is to maintain the system of states against conquest and incorporation into a universal empire. Bull continues that the balance of power tends to operate in favour of great powers at the expanse of small ones (103). He explains how the balance of power is necessary for the preservation of the system: 'From a point of view of a weak state sacrificed to it, the balance of power must appear as brutal principle. But its function in the preservation of international order is not for this reason less central' (103–4). The balance of power as a means to maintain the preferred order necessarily violates the rights of individual members of the society of states – just like spheres of influence do – all for the sake of the order. The normative web around spheres of influence is woven out of these elements: the justification of the primacy of the system of states, the justification of violations of sovereignty in the name of the balance of power, and other great power management tools. The historical development, as I have presented earlier, has been one from *de jure* sovereignty to *de facto* great power management.

A balance of power takes precedence not only over the rights of small powers but also over international law. According to Bull, the relationship between balance of power and international law is paradoxical. He writes that the existence of a balance of power is essential for the operation of international law, but maintaining a balance often involves violating that body of law. For Bull, the reason why international law requires the functioning of a balance of power is that the basic rules of international law depend on reciprocity. In the case of a single preponderant power, that power would not need to obey the rules of the society of states and could act as it pleased instead (Bull 2002, 104). Bull writes, 'The requirements of order are treated as prior to those of law, as they are treated also as prior to the interests of small powers and the keeping of peace' (105). This principle applies to the idea of a sphere of influence, if, like a balance of power, establishing a sphere of influence is viewed as a preventive measure against the danger of a universal empire. In such a case, a sphere of influence also necessarily overrides peace, the rights of the small, and law. Order, when maintained by a balance of power and spheres of influence, works to justify the breaking of even the basic rule of the system itself: sovereignty. I will discuss the relationship between international law and spheres of influence later. The section to follow presents the principles of sovereignty and non-intervention.

3.3 Sovereignty and Non-intervention

I have argued that the history of spheres of influence is the history of the system of states. This makes sovereignty of utmost importance for a discussion of spheres of influence. In his *Genealogy of Sovereignty*, Bartelson (1995, 22–4) argues that the idea of sovereignty is the essence of international political theory. Sovereignty explains the international system and defines 'state'. Bartelson asserts that '[…] sovereignty is constituted as a primitive presence from which all theorizing necessarily must depart, if it is to remain international political theorizing' (24). Sovereignty is so powerful a presupposition to a student of international relations that it must belong to the very heart of the idea of sphere of influence. To quote Walker (1994, 62), 'Spatially, the principle of state sovereignty fixes a clear demarcation between life inside and outside a centred political community'. Spheres of influence break the holiness of this demarcation by intruding upon the territory of another sovereign. Spheres of influence essentially involve violation or non-violation of sovereignty; yet this core consideration has prompted surprisingly little theoretical interest.

I treat sovereignty as the principal organising idea of the system of states and as an idea which determines much of the meaning of the concept of sphere of influence. Bull (2002, 8) defines 'internal sovereignty' as supremacy over all other authorities within a given territory and population, and 'external sovereignty' as independence from outside authorities. International theory is interested specifically in external sovereignty and the nature of the system as anarchical. For Wight (1977, 130), external sovereignty is a claim to be politically and juridically independent of any superior. Legal equality of states means a claim of independence of any political superior while at the same time recognising the same claim by all others (23).

The relevance of sovereignty for spheres of influence can be illustrated through the principle of non-intervention, and specifically the difficulty of defining sovereignty and what constitutes a violation of sovereignty. Kenneth Waltz (1979, 95–6) makes an interesting claim in arguing that sovereignty does not mean that states are able to do as they wish. Sovereignty does not mean freedom from the influence of other states: 'Sovereign states may be hardpressed all around, constrained to act in ways they would like to avoid, and able to do hardly anything just as they would like to'. Waltz continues, 'To say that a state is sovereign means that it decides for itself how it will cope with its internal and external problems, including whether or not to seek assistance form others and in doing so to limit its freedom by making commitments to them' (Waltz 1979, 96). Because of the difficulties in defining sovereignty it is not easy to come to terms with the relationship between spheres of influence and sovereignty. Following Waltz's logic, we could enquire whether, in the final analysis, the establishment of a sphere of influence even violates sovereignty. Is it just a relationship of dependency which does not clash with sovereignty? At the same time, the concept of sphere of influence appears to entail a claim that the influencing state violates the sovereignty of the influenced. The problem becomes one of choosing between the idea of a sphere of influence which does not conflict with sovereignty and a sphere of influence which clearly violates sovereign rights. This is where the concept of intervention becomes useful in trying to determine when or if a particular sphere of influence involves a violation of sovereignty. Intervention can constrain the internal and/or external choices of a state to such an extent that it constitutes a violation of sovereignty in Waltz's terms.

Keal (1983, 182) and Wight (1995, 194) both refer to intervention as a means to assert a sphere of influence. Thus, we could conclude that at least interventionist approaches to establishing or maintaining a sphere of influence are in violation of sovereignty. The nature of intervention is still a matter of debate, but at least the concept provides a topical and easily accessible means to discuss whether spheres of influence necessarily involve violations of sovereignty. As an example, when analysing Russia's adherence to some sphere-of-influence thinking, we can estimate how forceful or violent Russia's foreign policy is towards its (imagined) sphere of influence. In other words, by looking at how interventionist Russia's foreign policy is we can possibly say something about the country's approach to spheres of influence. A more interventionist sphere-of-influence policy would then indicate less respect for the sovereignty of the influenced. Yet, in order to pass judgement on the intervention in question, the means and purposes of the intervention would have to be evaluated. Just as an intervention could indicate a sphere-of-influence policy, it could reflect the ideas of 'responsibility to protect' and humanitarian intervention. Thus, as long as respect for sovereignty and the non-intervention principle are negotiated rather than absolute, spheres of influence remain ambiguous too.

According to Vincent (1974, 330–31), respect for the rule of non-intervention means that states recognise the existence and legitimacy of others. The rule of non-intervention is fundamental to the international order of states, because it establishes respect for sovereignty and it determines whether the nature of the system is Hobbesian-Grotian-Kantian or pluralist-solidarist. Intervention belongs to the same category as spheres of influence, balance of power and great power management in that while interventions represent inequality, they are also often accepted and seem to be integral parts of the functioning of the international society. For Wight (1966b, 111), intervention even rises above all other forms of conduct with the controversy it generates:

Intervention perhaps gives rise to more controversy than any other international conduct. Violating the assumption of the equal independence of all members of the society of states, it is *prima facie* a hostile act. Yet it is so habitual and regular that it is impossible to imagine international relations without it; and international law can only make a system out of it by losing touch with diplomatic facts.

Intervention is controversial not only as an act, but also as an idea. As Wight (1966b, 111) puts it, intervention as a concept is fluid and imprecise. Bull describes intervention as interference in another state's jurisdiction over its territory, citizens, and right to determine its internal affairs and external relations. Intervention can be forcible or non-forcible, direct or non-direct, open or clandestine (Bull 1984b, 1). For Stanley Hoffman (1984, 9), intervention can be explicitly coercive, such as economic coercion, and implicit, such as bribery and propaganda bombardment.[5] According to Vincent (1974, 8), intervention is coercive interference accompanied by the use or threat of force. Intervention, just like a sphere of influence, entails inequality in power. To quote Bull (1984b, 1):

> A basic condition of any policy that can be called interventionary in this sense is that the intervener should be superior in power to the object of the intervention: it is only because the former is relatively strong and the latter relatively weak that the question arises of a form of interference that is dictatorial or coercive.

Bull (1984a, 184) asserts that great inequalities of power make interventions possible. Nevertheless, the simple fact of inequality of power between states is not tantamount to interference; inequality is actually inherent in the system of states (187–8). For Bull involvement in a state's sphere of jurisdiction needs to be dictatorial or coercive in nature to be called illegal interference (188). Bull's distinction between dictatorial and coercive intervention and 'the mutual involvement of peoples in one another's affairs' is of course a matter of interpretation and causes disagreements over which actions are to be counted as intervention and which cannot be. But the idea of coercive intervention versus non-coercive involvement offers a perspective from which one can reflect on spheres of influence. As the concept is currently pejorative in tone, references to a sphere of influence imply coercive involvement, but any consideration of the concept in normative perspective would prompt a debate on whether the influence involved is coercive influence or non-coercive, or 'non-forceful involvement'.

What makes the topic of intervention even more complex is the blurring of the distinction between acts of intervention and non-intervention. Wight (1995, 199) writes that non-intervention can be just as positive a policy as intervention: 'Hence the truth of Talleyrand's sardonic remark that "non-intervention is a term of political

---

5   In the same volume, Philip Windsor (1984, 50) argues that economic coercion and propaganda do not constitute intervention since they are a state's normal foreign policy tools; he counts only military force as intervention.

metaphysics signifying almost the same thing as intervention'". Non-intervention can mean support for some cause (other than that achieved by intervention) or its purpose could be to prevent intervention. Hoffmann (1984, 8) puts forward the same claim, pointing out that even non-acts can constitute intervention, also referring to Talleyrand. As regards spheres of influence, non-intervention could signify the acceptance of another power's sphere of influence. It could mean a failure to come to the rescue of a small power about to fall into the hands of the influencing power. In such a case, by analysing policies of intervention and non-intervention, we could determine how spheres of influence emerge as great powers refrain from intervening in territories under the others' influence. Russia's ability to intervene in the territory of Georgia in 2008 and the reluctance of other states to take any counter-actions could be interpreted as Russia consolidating and other powers acknowledging a Russian sphere of influence. Non-intervention could also mean resistance to acknowledging a sphere of influence, for example, in the case of Russia abstaining from participation in the intervention in Yugoslavia and thus abstaining from taking part in causing Kosovo to fall under Western control.

The moral element of intervention is evident. Whereas the concept of sphere of influence does not appear in international law, this is not the case with intervention. In terms of international law non-intervention is the rule, whereas intervention is an exception to that rule (see Bull 1984b, 2). The principle of non-intervention is necessary to the principle of sovereignty. As Vincent (1974, 14) puts it, 'The principle of non-intervention identifies the right of states to sovereignty as a standard in international society and makes explicit the respect required for it in abstention from intervention'. The principle of sovereignty requires that intervention must always be somehow justified. In *The Anarchical Society*, Bull (2002, 138–9) observes that although international law forbids states to intervene in one another's internal affairs, it is argued that considerations of the balance of power sometimes require intervention in order to establish a great power's influence or to resist the influence of a great power. Also Wight (1995, 196) notes how international lawyers have given their blessing to intervention when it is meant to maintain a balance of power. There is also an exception to the rule of non-intervention inscribed in the United Nations Charter. Keal (1983, 183) explains that Article 51 permits an exception to the non-intervention rule whereby intervention can be accepted if it is for self-defence in the event of an armed attack.

According to Vincent (1974, 11), many international lawyers view the motive for intervention as determining the legality of the act. But this causes further confusion as to whether an instance of interference that is considered lawful can be called intervention anymore (11–12). What is unlawful intervention and what is tolerable interference? Although intervention involves the threat or use of force, Wight (1995, 192) explains, even an offer of friendly assistance may be suspect as to its motives and be denounced as intervention. This was the case when the Soviet Union denounced the United States' offer of Marshall Aid to Europe in 1947. Watson (2002, 151) points to the fact that there is a large grey area of pressure and interference where interveners can operate while appealing to international peace and security. Great powers have the leverage to balance between intervention and non-intervention and there is constant dispute regarding the justifiability and illegality of interventions. The idea of a sphere of influence actually offers a solution to the uncertainty of intervention. The advantage Keal (1983, 197–203) sees in spheres of influence is that they contribute to stable possessions and thereby limit the possibility of conflicts. Thus, spheres of influence, under this logic, would serve to limit conflicts over interventions between great powers, for they could freely intervene within their own sphere of influence and would refrain from intervening in those of others. It would not, however, resolve the issue of spheres of influence as potentially subjugating smaller states and violating the principle of sovereignty. For Vincent it is important that intervention is defined as something that is not a permanent state of affairs. Intervention occurs but it also must cease at some point in order to qualify as intervention (Vincent 1974, 8). Interpreting Vincent, a sphere of influence would be considered a permanent state of intervention. This idea is not articulated within the English School, but it could very well be further developed, particularly in the case of Cold War spheres of influence.

Acknowledging the idea of a sphere of influence would then render intervention what might be called *structural intervention*. Bull (1984b, 5) refers to this term, but Philip Windsor (1984, 45) explains it in more detail:

> But at the same time a general assumption persists of a world so dominated, indeed permeated, by sheer power that it becomes almost futile to discuss the question of intervention by the superpowers because it is like asking what contribution oxygen makes to our ability to breathe in the atmosphere.

What Windsor (1984, 46) is talking about is 'a fundamental and permanent form of intervention, even a kind of structural intervention affecting the activities of all kinds of other states in the world'. Windsor (1984, 54–5) explains how the Brezhnev Doctrine was the Soviet version of structural intervention: 'The Brezhnev Doctrine is similarly an appeal to an overriding moral or historical principle, claiming a higher legitimacy than that of international law. [...] The Soviet Union, in other words, has created a higher order of legitimacy for intervention'. Windsor does not consider this to have been unique to the Soviet Union, as the United States also claimed a higher legitimacy than international law by its mission of defending other countries against a universalising foe (57–8). Windsor concludes that whereas the Soviet Union was practicing structural intervention in Eastern Europe, the United States was doing the same in Latin America (64).

Bull (1984a) also comes close to acknowledging that spheres of influence involve acceptance of intervention. He elaborates on intervention within different world orders: In a world with central international authority, the rights of the authority to intervene might be unlimited. In a world of regional international organisations, there might be unlimited power to interfere within particular regions. Similarly, in an order ruled by a small number of great powers, intervention would be accepted within the dominated regions. For Bull any one of the three options would mean a drastic alteration of the current system of sovereign states (Bull 1984a, 185). The two last options – regional international organisations and great powers – could be called spheres of influence, but Bull does not mention the concept in this connection.

Reading from Bull (1984a, 184), abandoning the rule of non-intervention would mean abandoning the right to sovereignty and independence. For Bull not even the European integration or proletarian internationalism could do away with sovereignty and its corollary principle of non-intervention (186). This is so because abandoning the rule of non-intervention, that is, accepting intervention in principle and in practice, would mean the end of the system of states as we know it. Bull is broaching here the question of the nature of international society, which stands to play out as the pluralist-solidarist and pluralist-universalist divide. I pose the questions: Where do spheres of influence fall along the spectrum of international society? How do spheres of influence, when they violate state sovereignty, affect the nature of the international system? Moreover, can spheres of influence replace the system of states and become a world of suzerain systems? And what happens to sovereignty then?

3.4   A Regional Solidarist Order

Discussing the nature of international society makes it possible to situate the concept of sphere of influence more securely at the equilibrium point of the pendulum of international society (see Chapter 2.3). It is not only through the English School that spheres of influence can be theorised in terms of the pluralist-solidarist divide of international society. The tragedies of the two world wars inspired thinkers such as Carl Schmitt to question the viability of the system of states, and resulted in visions of spheres of influence between pluralism and solidarism or universalism (Chapter 4). I argue that the pluralist-solidarist divide helps to contest the concept of sphere of influence and shed light on its meaning beyond the pejorative pall that now obscures it.

In explaining the pluralist-solidarist divide, I begin with Buzan's (2004a) insights. Pluralist international society is state-centric and assumes that international law is made by states (positive law). Pluralism is concerned with the preservation of political and cultural difference and distinctness (46). According to Buzan, solidarists are more concerned with the rights of individuals (natural law), cosmopolitan values and shared moral norms (47).[6] Buzan ponders whether the two are necessarily opposite ideas of state primacy versus a cosmopolitan position or, rather, two ends of a spectrum. Buzan argues that the spectrum option is possible if sovereignty is more of a social contract – something open to negotiation – than

---

6   See Buzan's (2004a, 159) figure depicting the pluralist-solidarist spectrum of interstate society.

an essential condition. At the pluralist end of the spectrum, international society is thinner and collective enforcement of rules is difficult but, at the solidarist end, collective enforcement might be accepted in some areas (49). For some, solidarism means stepping from an international (state-based) into a world (non-state-based) society, but Buzan does not consider it useful to assume that solidarism is tantamount to embracing a world society (57–8). Keeping solidarism as a feature of international society allows one to reason that

> [i]n substantive terms, pluralism describes 'thin' international societies where the shared values are few, and the prime focus is on devising rules for coexistence within the frameworks of sovereignty and non-intervention. Solidarism is about 'thick' international societies in which a wider range of values is shared, and where the rules will be not only about coexistence, but also about the pursuit of joint gains and the management of collective problems of in a range of issue-areas. (Bull 2004a, 59)

The pluralist-solidarist divide is essentially concerned with sovereignty, with intervention as its challenger. In focusing on shared moral norms, solidarism is to Buzan (2004a, 46–7) a more interventionist view of international society. But the spectrum metaphor relieves intervention from turning solidarism and pluralism against each other. Buzan explains, 'In this view, so long as one does not insist that individuals have rights apart from, and above, the state, there is no contradiction between development of human rights and sovereignty. If they wish, states can agree among themselves on extensive guarantees for human rights, and doing so is an exercise of their sovereignty, not a questioning of it' (48–9). Buzan writes that 'sovereignty means different things at the pluralist and solidarist ends of interstate society' (219). He continues:

> In a pure Westphalian interstate society, virtually all intervention is both illegal and illegitimate (except against forces aiming to disrupt or overthrow interstate order). In a thick, solidarist international society such as that represented by the EU, the agreed unpacking of sovereignty, and the establishment of agreements about elements of justice, and the rights of individuals and non-state actors makes many more kinds of intervention both legal and legitimate. (Buzan 2004a, 219)

In Buzan's opinion, sovereignty and intervention can be reconciled within the same international society. Hoffmann understands the role of intervention in international society in a way which fits in with Buzan's vision of a spectrum. Hoffman (1984, 11–12) explains that the question has never been one of international society choosing between intervention and non-intervention but rather of the forms and likelihood of intervention given the nature of the international system as decentralised units without a common superior. Even though for Hoffman intervention is a reality not necessarily because of solidarist tendencies in international society but because of anarchy, he nevertheless implies that sovereignty and intervention can coexist if sovereignty as a principle is understood as something flexible and leaves room for exceptions. Influence, like intervention, has always been a part of the states-system. The same applies to the relationship between spheres of influence and sovereignty: influence does not automatically mean violation of the principle of sovereignty. Spheres of influence and sovereignty can then potentially coexist, for example, when the influenced power accepts its position and when the influencing power offers something in return.

Depending on the interpretation of sovereignty, which is looser at the solidarist than at the pluralist end of the spectrum, intervention is more or less acceptable. In addition, the consideration of justice, such as protection of human rights, loosens up the concept of sovereignty to include the legitimacy of intervention. Is a solidarist international society then also more tolerant of spheres of influence if it is more tolerant of intervention? A sphere of influence could incorporate regional solidarism as a voluntary 'unpacking of sovereignty' and great powers could agree on a certain acceptable level of regional hegemony. Solidarism could make interventions within a sphere of influence a matter of agreement. Solidarism could not, however, explain away the potential for injustice in the case of spheres of influence nor could it likely tolerate the divisions that spheres of influence would create and maintain. If the world is moving in a solidarist direction, it is necessary to look at spheres of influence in a context where sovereignty is not as rigid as it is in a pluralist international society. This opens a way to discuss the normative aspects of justice in the case of spheres of influence in a world where no state can thrive on its own.

Jackson's *The Global Covenant* (2000) deals with the normative order of the system of states and provides some very interesting remarks on sovereignty and intervention. For Jackson (2000; 19, 23), the global covenant signifies 'the underlying moral and legal standards by reference to which relations between independent states can be conducted and judged', and its fundamental underlying ethos is pluralism. International society is a *societas* rather than a *universitas* (105). Jackson's *societas* and *universitas* are other names for a pluralist and solidarist international order, respectively: 'The great political transformation symbolized by Westphalia can be captured conceptually as a reconstruction of European politics from that of *universitas*, based on the solidarist norms of Latin Christendom, to that of *societas*, based on the pluralist norms of state sovereignty, on political independence' (165). Jackson argues that only in Europe or 'the West' are there indications of an emergent *universitas* (127). The European *universitas* is regional and not universal and elsewhere *societas* prevails (127–8). The Peace of Westphalia was the symbol of the political transformation from the Christian order to the system of states (164). In a very Schmittian tone, Jackson appears to prefer *societas* over *universitas*, that is, freedom over hierarchy[7]:

---

7   Schmitt was a proponent of *pluriverse* against *universe*, the latter of which would destroy political plurality in the international system. See more in Chapter 4.3.

The *societas* of sovereign states is the idea and institution that expresses the morality of difference, recognition, respect, regard, dialogue, interaction, exchange, and similar norms that postulate coexistence and reciprocity between independent political communities. The language of *societas* is the language of political freedom as opposed to that of *universitas*, which is the language of political hierarchy and religious or ideological orthodoxy based on a political community of some sort. (Jackson 2000, 168)

It is clear that Jackson's *universitas* has relevance for spheres of influence when he begins discussing the Cold War. According to Jackson, during the Cold War, Eastern Europe, in its subordinate position to Moscow, formed a *universitas* where only the Soviet Union enjoyed the rights of sovereignty and non-intervention. Jackson writes, 'The USSR operated in a fashion that could only be justified, if justified at all, by a concept of legitimate spheres of influence' (Jackson 2000, 255). By contrast, Jackson argues, Gorbachev's speech to the Council of Europe in 1989, an articulation of what was also known as the Sinatra Doctrine, was a declaration of a *societas* ending the Soviet hierarchy in Eastern Europe. It was an acknowledgement of the pluralist norm of international society and a repudiation of the Brezhnev Doctrine. Russia and Eastern Europe thus returned to the *societas* of sovereign states (168, 256).

Jackson's own normative conclusion is that *societas* is the superior order: The pluralist doctrine of non-intervention is the core doctrine of the global covenant and 'to date the modern *societas* of sovereign states has proved to be the only generally acceptable and workable basis of world politics'. To Jackson both the medieval ideological orthodoxy and political hierarchy, and later colonialism represent the type of universitas which the sovereign states have wanted to escape from for the sake of local political freedom (Jackson 2000, 168–9). To that end, for Jackson (2000, 251), the sovereign state has constitutional immunity and a fundamental right to non-intervention, making the ethics of intervention a negative ethics. Jackson writes that 'intervention is prima-facie wrong and must therefore be justified or else it must be condemned' (252). He introduces humanitarianism as one of the current justifications for intervention, but one which goes beyond the rules of the UN Charter (253). In his view, humanitarian intervention has the potential to challenge the *societas*. In an *universitas*, humanitarian considerations would override sovereignty and the question would become whether there is a transformation under way to a global *universitas* where the rule of non-intervention would no longer be the guarantor of sovereignty (251).

The relationship between humanitarian intervention and spheres of influence is interesting, because the concept of humanitarian intervention is so recent that no references to it can be found in the history of spheres of influence. If we look at international society from Jackson's perspective (instead of in terms of Buzan's spectrum), humanitarian intervention represents a discourse against pluralist international society, whereas spheres of influence, even with the potential and likely violations of sovereignty they entail, represent a defence of plurality.[8] In Buzan's spectrum, humanitarian intervention does not automatically signal the emergence of an *universitas* and thus is easier to accommodate with spheres of influence in the middle of the pluralist-solidarist spectrum. The main difference between humanitarian intervention and intervention within a sphere of influence is found in the legitimacy of the two actions in discourses. A humanitarian cause can be accepted as a motive for intervention, while ambitions of creating a sphere of influence cannot. Yet, establishing a sphere of influence and humanitarian intervention are not opposite or separate forms of conduct. A humanitarian cause could be invoked in order to avoid an intervention being associated with a sphere-of-influence policy – as if purifying the motives of the influencing state. Today, humanitarian reasons are the only possible justification for intervention, and if spheres of influence exist, intervention within one can only be defended on humanitarian grounds. If intervention is a central tool of sphere-of-influence policy, and a humanitarian cause can be used as an excuse, then any interventionist state – not only Russia – can be accused of trying to establish a sphere of influence. For many Russian analysts, humanitarian intervention is sphere-of-influence policy in disguise. Humanitarian intervention is a matter of interpretation, hence the disagreement between Russia and Western states on the intervention in Yugoslavia in 1999 and the disagreement on the nature of Russian intervention in South Ossetia in 2008. In fact, Russian analysts often avoid claiming that Russian actions constitute a humanitarian intervention because of the supposedly political uses of the term. For many Russians, Western 'humanitarian interventions' represent a sphere-of-influence policy and for many Western commentators Russian intervention in the territory of Georgia was an expression of a sphere-of-influence policy. Thus, the relationship between humanitarian intervention and a sphere-of-influence policy is not only in how these actions represent solidarism but, and primarily, in how they are justified.

I would say that the establishment of spheres of influence and humanitarian intervention are more interconnected than separated by the discourse on their legitimacy. Likewise, the separation of spheres of influence and humanitarian intervention at the level of the pluralist-solidarist debate is artificial if we challenge the core meaning of solidarism. The problem with Jackson's *universitas* is that we do not know who gets to decide on humanitarian intervention. Who holds the decisive power over the normative? In the case of Watson's pendulum, it is the Empire, but the more vague concepts of cosmopolitan, solidarist and world society leave the questions of agency unresolved. Is solidarism simply a thick international society or is it a cosmopolitan word society? Solidarism needs to be articulated

---

8   For example, humanitarian intervention as *the responsibility to protect* principle, embraced by the UN World Summit in 2005, transfers the responsibility to protect people from states which fail to do so to the international community (see Evans 2008). Responsibility to protect is more closely associated with the idea of *universitas* as a collective and solidarist means to govern international affairs.

also in a concrete political setting, because otherwise we do not know how to situate spheres of influence and humanitarian intervention.

Buzan (2004a, 47–8) writes that the pluralist side is easily identifiable as a system consisting of states but the solidarist side blurs the difference between international and world society because it ties together state and non-state actors. For Buzan, the problem is the impreciseness of the idea of world society. Even though world society occupies a central position in English School thinking, the concept is not systematically elaborated (44). Since Buzan discusses solidarism within the society of states, endowed with sovereignty and the right to intervention, he keeps solidarism within the limits of international society. It makes me wonder at what point pluralism really turns into solidarism.

I argue that humanitarian intervention fits into the cosmopolitan ethos of a solidarist society – an international society of individuals in a single moral community – less than the English School conceptualisations would suggest. To my mind, humanitarian intervention does not jeopardise pluralism as such, but rather – and specifically – the plurality of sovereign *states*. An international society where humanitarian intervention is legitimate is a 'concert of great powers' and/or multiple 'regional *societates*' maintaining a certain level of pluralism. In this order, great powers decide on humanitarian intervention. Even within the EU, which represents a solidarist order for both Buzan and Jackson, greater powers have the final say. In terms of this logic, humanitarian intervention, like any intervention, sits well in a type of solidarist international society, which does not abandon the system of states. Put it another way, humanitarian intervention sits well in a pluralist international society which consists of a plurality of regional units. If we seriously consider regionalism as an alternative to state sovereignty, we have a type of actor that stretches to both the pluralist and solidarist ends of the spectrum. This regionalism challenges the pluralist-solidarist divide by requiring a clarification of agency at the solidarist end and by incorporating solidarism within and pluralism without.

In an argument close to my reasoning regarding the conceptual confusion about solidarism, John Williams (2005, 19–38) asserts that, contrary to the general English School view, a world society does not have to be cosmopolitan. Williams wants to challenge the idea that pluralism belongs to international society and solidarism to world society. He writes that a world society where political activity is principally focused on individuals (and where states are not the predominant actors) can maintain plurality in some form. In other words, diversity can be accommodated in such a society. Williams continues, 'Thus a partly de-territorialised pluralist *modus vivendi* offers a normative agenda for world society' (33). The argument that a world society of pluralism indicates 'non-territorial forms of politics' (Williams 2005, 35) still prompts the question of what exactly happens to territorially bound communities in a solidarist international society or in a solidarist or pluralist world society. The usefulness of the pluralist-solidarist debate is undermined if there is no clarity as to what kind of political organisation is envisioned. Emphasising the importance of regions, Buzan's and Waever's regional security complex – and even more so Hurrell's regional solidarism – offers answers to the contemporary need to make sense of the pluralist-solidarist divide (see Chapter 1.4). But there is no attempt to situate spheres of influence in this debate, because the concept has not been situated at all in international theory. Perhaps the pluralist-solidarist debate does not need spheres of influence, but a sphere of influence can be theorised by situating it within this debate. If we take into account Keal's and, to some extent, Bull's interest in discussing spheres of influence as contributing to international order, it is reasonable to assume that this international order has something to do with pluralism and solidarism.

At the end of the day, by reading the English School we do not find out who it is that would be in charge of a solidarist order or world society. Would it still be states, or a mix of state and non-state actors? Would it be a world organisation – or even a universal empire? The reason why this question is compelling is that the answer to it would make it possible to situate spheres of influence more firmly in the middle of Watson's pendulum or Buzan's spectrum of international society, provided both ends were clearly defined. Sphere of influence emerges out of the English School literature as a pluralist concept, as part and parcel of the system of states, but it also expresses ideas of breaking state borders to form bigger units than states. What makes a sphere of influence diverge from the pluralist ethos of the state is the idea of a regional unit, the *Großraum* for Schmitt (2003) and Carr (2001), Mid-Europe for Naumann (1917) and the 'Good Neighbor Policy' for Lippmann (1945). These regional units are constructed not only out of influence but also out of unity and necessity. This necessity is the prevention of major wars by unifying states to form bigger entities. Jackson, by discussing spheres of influence as an aspect of *universitas,* does make the move towards seeing spheres of influence as part of a solidarist order. Spheres of influence are then regional solidarist orders which allow the pluralist order to survive on the global level. This solidarism is not restricted to 'one humanity' but can include several regional international societies within the international order. The idea of a regional solidarist order also takes the pejorative ring out of sphere of influence. However, given the inadequate definition of solidarism, it remains difficult to imagine what the relationship between spheres of influence and solidarism would be on a global scale: Would solidarism mean the end of great powers and their spheres of influence, or would great powers maintain their dominant position even in a solidarist international society?

3.5   International Law and Justice

This section focuses on English School theory on international law and justice in relation to spheres of influence. It is nothing new to say that influence in international relations is not distributed equally. Some members of the society of states can better proclaim and defend their interests than others (Bull 2002, 53). When one undertakes to examine the justice or injustice of spheres of influence, the first task is to ascertain what international law has to say on the subject. References to international law are also the source of arguments for and against spheres of influence. The relationship between spheres of influence and international law, in the present, rests on the assumption that international law does not recognise a right to a sphere of influence. Rather, it sets limits on pursuing international influence; it does this through the principles of sovereignty and non-intervention, but also through rules on the use of violence. For Keal (1983, 90), it is clear that spheres of influence are inconsistent with the UN Charter's principles of sovereign equality and territorial integrity.

Conformity to or enforcement of law in interstate relations is an entirely different matter than in intrastate affairs. The anarchical nature of the system of states creates an environment in which spheres of influence can exist even if they appear to violate international law. Bull (2002, 126) states that since self-help is a part of enforcing international law, the distribution of power dictates conformity to this law. But it would be too simplistic to claim that the international order is one where great powers take matters of law to their own hands, disregarding the rights of the lesser nations. Bull (2002, 131) argues that conformity to international law[9] and violation of it are not separate forms of conduct. Even when laws are violated, the violation might still embody some elements of conformity, blurring the line between conformity and violation (132). I argue that the same applies to justice. A great power could argue for establishing a sphere of influence (violation) against foreign aggression (conformity or upholding the right of another state to sovereignty). Is not a sphere of influence actually a perfect example of violation and conformity taking place at the same time? If the existence of a sphere of influence implies a relationship between two or more great powers, the sphere of influence has been established not only to influence another state but to prevent another great power from influencing that same state. During the Cuban Missile Crisis (described in more detail in Chapter 5), both parties – the United States and the Soviet Union – expressed their wish to protect the Cuban people from the other superpower's tyranny. What a sphere of influence can be, reflecting on what Bull writes about international law, is a mixture of a violation of the principle of sovereignty and an attempt (even if a self-serving one) to protect the sovereignty of the influenced or to maintain the system of states as the preferred international order.

---

9   Bull defines international law as 'a body of rules which binds states and other agents in world politics in their relations with one another and is considered to have the status of law'. Bull explains that there are rules which states and other agents see as binding them and which constitute an international *society*. It is nevertheless a matter of controversy whether these rules have the status of law due to the lack of an enforcing and sanctioning world government (Bull 2002, 124–5). International law rests much upon self-help, including the use and threat of force. Members of international society often take the enforcement of international law into their own hands, which makes international law function as a part of the balance of power (126). The other members of international society might disagree on which party to a conflict is breaking the law and which is complying with it (127).

Another more or less accepted argument for a sphere of influence is the maintenance of the balance of power. Bull (2002) explains how an interest in the balance of power might clash with international law. Balance of power is a principle that maintains international order but the means of achieving the balance might involve acts of violating international law (138). In this case, we are not talking about justice and the rights of individual states, but of the overriding interest in maintaining a balance of power for the sake of the system of states. Bull in fact comments on this dilemma with regard to international law: 'It is often argued, however, that considerations of the balance of power require intervention in the internal affairs of a state in order to establish a great power's influence in it, or resist the influence of another great power, because of wider considerations of the distribution of power in international society at large' (Bull 2002, 138).

Regardless of systemic considerations and the reasons promoted by the influencing power, the perspective of the influenced state is what matters most when judging the extension of influence. If the influenced state feels its rights are being violated then the argument about protection can hardly justify a sphere-of-influence policy. However, the fact that a state claims that its rights are being violated by a sphere-of-influence policy does not automatically mean that injustice has occurred, or even that any sphere-of-influence policy is being pursued. States can abuse the idea of spheres of influence to get support from other states in a dispute with a greater power. When post-Soviet states voice their anger against what they see as Russia trying to include them in its sphere of influence, they are seeking support from Western states. Because of its pejorative ring, evoking the term *sphere of influence* can be an efficient rhetorical means to draw attention to a cause. The relationship between influencing and influenced states becomes more complex when we do not automatically view small states as victims of a sphere-of-influence policy. It becomes more a question of enmities, alliances and identities than of international law whether influence is accepted or not.

The contemporary discourse has taken a firm stand against spheres of influence expressly due to considerations of justice, even more so than considerations of law. Keal's (1983, 204) stance on the justice of spheres of influence is straightforward: 'The freedom and independence of influenced states is always impaired and no matter how much they contribute to order, spheres of influence are necessarily unjust'. For Keal, even though spheres of influence contribute to international order, this comes at the price of justice (209–10). He explains, 'The injustices inherent in spheres of influence such as inequalities in the distribution of wealth, violation of the doctrine of sovereign equality of states, and the denial of equality of individuals might simply nourish seeds of disorder' (212). Thus the unjust nature of spheres of influence is at the same time a source of disorder. To summarise Keal's argument, spheres of influence might contribute as much to international order as to disorder, but in the end they are based on injustice.

Bull (2002, 75) discusses the meaning of justice as actions considered right in themselves and thus belonging to the class of moral ideas, which are separate from considerations of law, prudence, interest or necessity. Bull explains that there is substantive justice, or recognition of rules about rights and duties, as well as formal justice, 'the like application of these rules to like persons' (76). Bull further writes:

> Demands for 'justice' in world politics are frequently demands for formal justice in this sense: that some legal rule, such as that requiring states not to interfere in one another's domestic affairs, or some moral rule, such as that which confers on all nations the right of self-determination, or some operational rule or rule of the game, such as that which requires great powers to respect one another's spheres of influence, should be applied fairly or equally as between one state and another. (Bull 2002, 76)

Thus, there are two aspects to justice: 1) the contents or the rules stating what course of action is considered right and what is wrong and 2) the equal application of these rules. Curiously, Bull presents spheres of influence as manifestations of formal justice, according to which great powers have equal rights to spheres of influence. Then how about spheres of influence in terms of substantive justice?

Bull argues that the current institutions of international society do not support justice in world politics, but rather international society is at odds with *cosmopolitan justice, human justice* and often with *interstate* or *international justice*. Interstate justice is best served in international society as states may add moral imperatives to the rules of their coexistence, whereas justice for humankind (cosmopolitan) or individuals (human) does not fit in with the workings of international society as it is managed by the states (Bull 2002, 87). Insead of a just international order, Bull sees a hegemony of great powers which leads to systematic injustice:

> Great powers contribute to international order by maintaining local systems of hegemony within which order is imposed from above, and by collaborating to manage the global balance of power and, from time to time, to impose their joint will on others. But the great powers, when they perform these services to international order, do so at the price of *systematic injustice* to the rights of smaller states and nations, the injustice which has been felt by states which fall within the Soviet hegemony in Eastern Europe or the American hegemony in the Caribbean, injustice which is written in the terms of the United Nations Charter which prescribe a system of collective security that cannot be operated against great powers, the injustice from which small powers always suffer when great ones meet in concert to strike bargains at their expense. (Bull 2002, 89; emphasis added)

Systematic injustice is like systemic intervention: it takes place so frequently as to effectuate a status quo and something that is tacitly accepted. In Bull's (2002, 220) worldview the great power order does not provide justice for all, and he doubts whether equal justice within the international society is even possible and desirable. For him it appears that any international order must have its custodians and guardians. In fact, Bull proclaims that the great power order enjoys wide support (221). This means, for Bull, that inequality is a fact of international political life. Bull writes that 'the great powers cannot formalise or make explicit the full extent of their special position' since it would engender more antagonism than the international order could support. For Bull this explains why the society of states is based on equality, rejecting hierarchical ordering (221). Nevertheless, if great powers seem to be both undermining order and denying justice altogether, the legitimacy of their position is eroded (221–2).

Bull (2002, 83) maintains that justice is realisable only in a context of order. If we understand the world as an international society with certain 'rules of the game' – such as spheres of influence being a part of great power management – what are the possibilities for justice? For both Bull and Keal, balances of power and spheres of influence violate justice in relation to small states yet maintain international order. This order also prevents the world from turning into a cosmopolitan society, thus leaving us to settle for interstate justice. An order supporting spheres of influence fits in well with the idea of interstate justice, for it deals with relations among states and not among individuals. It is much harder to evaluate what spheres of influence would mean to human justice than to justice among states. Reading Bull more carefully, spheres of influence do not, in the final analysis, leave much consideration for justice. Instead, Bull refers to 'systematic injustice' in the case of spheres of influence. This translates into formal justice among great powers and systematic injustice against the small.

Based on the English School literature we can discuss spheres of influence as a manifestation of an international order in which sovereignty is not the same for all states and a certain amount of inequality prevails. Thus, the question whether spheres of influence represent injustice is not adequately addressed only by looking at the inequality that they presumptively entail but also by considering the inequality inherent in international society. The reason why inequality seems inherent in a sphere of influence is that we do not have a theory, concept, idea or practice relating to the phenomenon which does not embody this inequality. Even Keal, who recognises some advantages of spheres of influence, cannot argue that they do not violate equality in some way or the other. But what can be investigated is whether this inequality is always necessarily bad, and especially whether it is bad from the perspective of the society of states at large and not only from the perspective of its individual members. It can also be debated whether the relationship of inequality within a sphere of influence has only negative consequences for the influenced states or if those states can still benefit somehow from being within the sphere of influence. We cannot ignore so easily, however, that there is a certain power relation at work even when influence is accepted by the influenced states. Some form of hierarchy and inequality always arises when a sphere of influence is created.

3.6   Influence or Responsibility?

In Chapter 2.4, which deals with agreements on spheres of influence, I explored different concepts that come close to the idea of a sphere of influence. When it comes to justifying spheres of influence, terminology takes on importance. Although Trenin (2009) attempts to differentiate Russia's sphere of influence and interests (see Chapter 1.5.1), I argue that distinguishing between a sphere of influence and a sphere of responsibility is even more pressing. When Lindley writes of protectorates, he means 'protection' given by the influencing power to the influenced at the price of the loss of some, but not all, elements of the protected state's sovereignty. As he explains:

> The assumption by a comparatively powerful State of the duty of protecting a weaker State is an institution of considerable antiquity. In the earlier instances the weaker State might gain the advantage of protection without losing its sovereignty. In the later examples of the older type of protectorate, however, an essential feature of the arrangement has been that the protected State has handed over the conduct of its external affairs to the protecting Power, or accepted its dictation in regard to those affairs, and has thus parted with part of its sovereignty without, however, losing the whole of its independence. (Lindley 1926, 181)

Protection implies something 'good' that can come out of spheres of influence – as opposed to the totally negative view of spheres of influence as forms of domination. This raises the question whether spheres of influence are necessarily always manifestations of systematic injustice based on power politics. Should not those with greater power in fact have more *responsibility* for peace and stability?

Bull offers one answer by distinguishing positive and negative sphere-of-influence agreements. The European expansion was a negative sphere-of-influence agreement, while the agreement on the occupation of Germany by the Soviet Union, United States, Britain and France was a positive one. In the case of Germany, there was a common task – a common *responsibility* – of occupying the territory of the defeated enemy and preventing the resurgence of the Nazis, among other things (Bull 2002, 215).[10] Thus, it is possible to conceptually differentiate positive spheres of influence, ones based on responsibility, from negative spheres of influence. Keal also mentions spheres of responsibility. As an example, he points to France claiming a sphere of influence in Morocco but with the idea that France would preserve order and assist with various reforms there (Keal 1983, 23–4). Likewise, Wight refers to the idea of great power responsibility, claiming that great powers have great responsibilities. They need to protect smaller nations; they must seek to serve, not to rule. Great powers have a managerial role due to their preponderance (Wight 1977, 139). Wight (1995, 43–4) notes, 'For since great powers have wider interests and greater resources than small powers, the main duty of settling international affairs must fall upon them; and it was hoped that they would develop, as it has been said, from great powers into Great Responsibles'.

---

10   Bull (2002, 215) also makes reference to Walter Lippmann's idea of good neighbours and spheres of responsibility, which will be dealt with in more detail in Chapter 4.5.

For Jackson, in general the great powers have a special role in the society of states. He argues in *The Global Covenant* that great powers have a special responsibility for maintaining peace and security in the world, because they can do both the greatest harm and greatest good in world politics (Jackson 2000; 139, 173). Minor powers are not able to contribute to peace and security in the way the great powers can; thus, world peace rests on the shoulders of the great (140–41). Bull (2002, 194–5) calls the special rights and responsibilities of great powers their managerial responsibility. For Jackson, this sort of inequality is quite natural and also desirable. But global security needs supporting institutions other than the class of great powers only: it requires a balance among the great powers against the emergence of a world empire and a concert of great powers which cooperates in the management of world affairs. The concrete manifestation of this order is the Security Council of the UN with its special responsibility for peace and order (Jackson 2000, 201–2).

The responsibility of great powers that Jackson, Wight, Bull and Keal discuss can be refuted, as Jackson (2000, 376) indicates, by saying that it is only a façade masking selfish interests and hegemonial ambitions and an excuse for exploitation and oppression. But if great powers had no responsibility for their actions and if they did not see the need for a normative discourse (justification) they would, as Jackson puts it, only have desires and power:

> The strong would be free to exploit their power to the full. The weak would be obliged to surrender in silence to the hegemon or else face the consequences. Is that how members of international society, great and small, conduct themselves in their relations? I believe the evidence indicates otherwise. (Jackson 2000, 377)

Holbraad (1979, 13) sums up the dual role of great powers within the system of states as follows: 'Thus, they may be seen as both as the potential wreckers and as the "great responsibles" of the world'. Even if the great powers could produce positive influence they would also represent systematic injustice in their managerial role. Acting in concert, great powers might be able to maintain order by a balance of power, but it does not mean that they would rule the world justly. Even if the great powers were called 'the great responsibles', we would be left with the dilemma of injustice versus order.

3.7 Conclusions on the English School

I have tapped the undiscovered pool of English School theory on the relationship between international society, its rules and institutions, and spheres of influence. What the English School account of international society has contributed here is 1) the location of spheres of influence between pluralist and solidarist orders and 2) the relationship between interstate justice and spheres of influence. Spheres of influence belong at the equilibrium point of the pendulum or the middle of the spectrum of international society, as do hegemony or dominance. Similarly, the idea of a balance of power represents a compromise between pluralist and solidarist functions of the international society: a balance of power violates sovereignty within a strict pluralist society and yet it also supports the pluralist system by preventing one single hegemon from prevailing. If sovereignty can be understood as a social contract, intervention does not belong solely to the solidarist end of the spectrum; rather, states can agree on the use of intervention. Not even humanitarian intervention need be a fatal blow to pluralism. Thus, intervention also swings on the pendulum towards the centre. In the spectrum metaphor, sovereignty and intervention can coexist, and so can sovereignty and spheres of influence. The usefulness of applying Buzan's idea of a spectrum lies in its freeing sovereignty from its Westphalian chains, thus liberating the concept of sphere of influence from its pejorative pall. Even though the English School does not locate sphere of influences within solidarism (any more than within pluralism), Jackson's regional *societas* indicates that unity and spheres of influence belong together. I will elaborate on the solidarist idea of spheres of influence in greater substance in the following chapter.

When it comes to the normative question, the problem is between maintaining international order at the expense of the small versus justice for all. According to the English School literature, small states can be vindicated in a struggle for a balance of power but not in a struggle for spheres of influence. In fact, the core question of justice is the right of small states to their independence. Great power influence as such is viewed as acceptable – or indeed even necessary – but a sphere of influence always comes down to the rights of the influenced. I have argued that the matter of justice where spheres of influence are concerned needs further elaboration than is possible with the pejorative use of the term. For example, conformity to international law, which is the source of the notions of international justice, as well as violations of international law, are relevant for contesting the concept of sphere of influence. When there is a struggle over influence, one great power can be accused of violating the sovereignty of the influenced while another can claim to be defending sovereignty against the aggression of the first. In acknowledging intervention as a means to establish spheres of influence, the need arises to discuss what kind of intervention is coercive and what is 'the mutual involvement of peoples in one another's affairs' if one wants to start making lists of what acts make up a sphere-of influence policy. For example, one might ask whether development aid can be the pursuit of a sphere of influence. Conceptually spheres of influence also place limitations on intervention (great powers do not intervene in each other's spheres of influence), giving room for a discussion of normative considerations. Finally, the idea of spheres of responsibility takes the normative question to an entirely new level by giving the practice of establishing spheres of influence legitimacy as such. The next chapter takes the normative issues in this direction.

Chapter 4
Between Nation and Humanity

During the aftermaths of the First and Second World War, many theorists put forward ideas, on the organisation of the international system with a view to saving their own country from peril and securing peace in the future.[1] The significance of these 'grand designs' are explained by William Fox (1944, 159):

> Grand designs are important. They furnish analytical models for public discussion of important problems. They provide criteria by which to test the long-run consequences of various short-run alternatives. Most grand designs are, however, presented by their author as one best hope of avoiding a fresh descent into the maelstrom of global war.

It is the purpose of this chapter to connect these grand designs to the history of spheres of influence. In theoretical terms, the grand designs place spheres of influence in the middle of the pluralist-solidarist spectrum, contributing to a connection between the notions of spheres of influence and international order. Normatively, the designs represent the subjugated knowledge of spheres of influence without their pejorative associations.

The German writers Schmitt and Naumann are well known for envisioning a new world order from a German perspective, Schmitt (2003 [1950]) writing on *Großräume* and Naumann (1917) on Mid-Europe. Schmitt advocated political pluralism in the form of three *Großräume* – Germany being one of them – which would save the world from a universalist conquest. In the United States, the concern was the same: to ensure that the country had the role of a great power and to avoid major war at the same time. To this end Walter Lippmann proposed the United States should rely on the Good Neighbor Policy, which would represent the right kind of influence for a new regionalism. In the United Kingdom, E.H. Carr used the concept of *Großraum* in order to discuss the middle ground between nationalism and internationalism, yet one more affirmation of the usefulness of the pluralist-solidarist debate and the relevance of system-level and normative considerations when contesting the concept of sphere of influence. George Orwell, another Englishman with a perspective on the nature of the society of states, followed James Burnham's idea of a world with super-states, envisioning the dangers of regional universes. Orwell's account casts a dark shadow on the usefulness and legitimacy of spheres of influence.

---

1   For Naumann, the context was World War I and for others World War II and its aftermath.

Naumann, Schmitt; Carr, Lippmann and Orwell were all concerned with the fate of the system of states. Bull (1966a, 36) notes that '[t]he feeling of unease about the system of states is a deep-rooted one in Western thinking about international relations'. This unease was common to these theorists and prompted them to speculate about spheres of influence. Bull expresses the apprehension:

> Whether by a social contract among the nations or by conquest, whether gradually or at once, whether by a frontal assault on national sovereignty or a silent undermining of its foundations, the problem of international relations, if it is soluble at all, is taken to be in the last analysis the problem of bringing international relations to an end. (Bull 1966a, 36)

The dominant storyline of the period of the world wars is that of the struggle between pluriversalism and universalism, the system of states and 'word empire'. What the idea of a sphere of influence represented, with all the different names given to the phenomenon, was a solution to the threat of universalism. It was a compromise in which super-states replaced the deteriorating nation-states and the nationalism that had led to war. This compromise would affect state sovereignty and would strengthen the system of great power management that had been created in the Congress of Vienna. Moreover, a system of super-states, if it were to function on the basis of a balance of power, would prevent not only the destruction of political plurality, but also major wars. The dilemma of the pluriverse versus the universe is still as topical as it was a hundred years ago. There is even more pressure to come to terms with the tension between international society (that of states) and world society (that of individuals). Will territorially bounded communities continue to exist, and if they do, within states or some other units? Will globalisation and the increasing focus on human justice lead to a cosmopolitan world society of individuals, or to a world society which can still uphold plurality? The subjugated knowledge on spheres of influence of the English School, and the theorists concerned with the world wars bring the nature of international society into the limelight in connection with the concept of sphere of influence.

4.1 The Geopolitics of Spheres of Influence

The concept of sphere of influence is generally associated with the tradition of geopolitics[2], which studies the relationship between territory and politics (see Ó Tuathail 1998, 1; 1996, 7). Geopoliticians have been seen as motivated by political ambitions and the use of geopolitics as a tool for power (see Ò Tuathail 1996; 7, 68–9). Classical geopolitics has had a rather bad reputation reinforcing the pejorative associations of the concept of sphere of influence. A typical way of

---

2   Rudolf Kjellén (1864–1922), a Swedish political scientist, was the first to use the term 'geopolitics' and is known for describing the state as a living organism.

understanding geopolitics is found in the following words of Charles Clover (1999, 9): 'Few modern ideologies are as whimsically all-encompassing, as romantically obscure, as intellectually sloppy, and as likely to start a third world war as the theory of "geopolitics"'. Colin S. Gray (2005, 18) explains how many of the critics of geopolitics, like Clover, have viewed geopolitics not so much as an analysis of the problem of international society but as part of the problem itself. Gray continues:

> Geopolitics, like strategy, is an equal opportunity tool of analysis. Each suffers from guilt by association: with conflict, war, and suffering; with some dangerous sounding, even crazy, ideas; and in general with an approach to the world that focuses upon competition rather than co-operation. Some scholars would shoot the geopolitical messenger and condemn the geopolitical message that explains the dynamic spatial dimension to some persisting patterns of conflict in international relations. One might as well condemn medical research for its obsession with disease. (Gray 2005, 27–8)

Spheres of influence are easily associated with such classical geopolitical scholars as Halford Mackinder (Heartland), Nicholas Spykman (Rimland), A.T. Mahan (Seapower), Friedrich Ratzel and Karl Haushofer (organic state theory and *Lebensraum*). Ó Tuathail (1998, 5) calls the work of this group 'imperialist geopolitics'. Haushofer's *Lebensraum* (living space) in particular offers an idea of expansion in the most pejorative terms. Brian W. Blouet (2005, 3) explains how Haushofer wanted the expansion of Germany to include all German-speaking peoples and the creation of a greater Germany. However, Gray (2005, 27) argues that Haushofer cannot be accused of being the evil genius behind Nazi expansion to achieve world domination. Spheres of influence are by definition – those definitions we have available – related to power, and ultimately to conflicts and the exercise of power using violence, that is, exactly what geopolitics is 'obsessed with'. The vision of the evilness of geopolitics, represented in particular by German geopolitics, and its association with the concept of sphere of influence has contributed to the concept's pejorative meaning.

Spheres of influence as circles on a map owe much to Halford Mackinder's (1861–1947) concept of the Heartland.[3] Mackinder has influenced, for example, Schmitt (2003, 37) and Nicholas Spykman (1944), who used Mackinder's Heartland concept in order to develop his own: Rimland. Paul Coones (2005; 65, 80) argues that during the last decade there has been a growing interest in the concept of the Heartland in certain political and intellectual circles in Russia ('Eurasianism'). Mackinder was a geographer and a political geographer, rather than a theorist. His Heartland is not really a sphere of influence, but the notion does reflect Mackinder's fear of the emergence of a single world power and his defence

---

3   See The Geographical Pivot of History (2004 [1904]) and Democratic Ideals and Reality (1996 [1919]) from Mackinder.

of the system of states. What Mackinder (1996, 106) produces are terms which describe territories and their power relations, as the well-known dictum states:

> Who rules East Europe commands the Heartland;
> Who rules the Heartland commands the World-Island;
> Who rules the World-Island commands the World.

For Mackinder (1996; 198, 65, 67, 50), the Soviet Union comprised much of the Heartland, and World-Island meant the joint continent of Europe, Asia and Africa. North and South America, Britain, Malaya, Japan and Australia are smaller islands, or satellites, on Mackinder's map. In the idea of the Heartland, a sphere of influence is reduced to a territorial metaphor, which urges us to content ourselves with a map of influences and power struggles instead of thinking about what spheres of influence mean for international society.

Spheres of influence are present as circles on a map in geopolitical literature, where they represent a balancing game and a facet of geostrategy. The geopolitical intention is to discover who will rule the world and how, not to discuss matters of sovereignty, intervention, justice and other themes which relate to the pejorative associations of the present idea of sphere of influence. Imperialist geopolitics represents spheres of influence as aspects of geostrategy, the association of geography and military elements with politics. Moreover, there is no comprehensive engagement with the idea or the concept of sphere of influence, because the imperialist dimension does not capture the originality of the phenomenon. Those geopolitical visions which have ended up in this book not only reinvent spheres of influence as a new form of territorial organisation but also explain their *raison d'être* in terms of international order. I do not want to eliminate the territorial element from spheres of influence, and the writings I have chosen do articulate the spatiality of spheres of influence. But they also add something more: the idea of a society of states, and even the pluralist-solidarist debate. This means that even though the visions presented in my sources come with rather nationalist aims, they are combined with considerations of the institutions and rules of international society and normative questions.

If geopolitics does not offer enough tools for theorising spheres of influence, neither does the realist school of IR. My selection of sources in this chapter represents realist voices, like that of E.H. Carr, but the realist school as such is not the source for this study of spheres of influence. The reason is again the same: the pejorative uses of the term *sphere of influence* call for an investigation of the order/justice axis, which is not covered by the realist accounts. Moreover, there is not even much interest in spheres of influence to be found. For John Mearsheimer (2001, 14), the three most influential realists of the twentieth century are Carr, Hans Morgenthau and Kenneth Walz. If we look at the latter two, which are not studied in this book, Morgenthau's *Politics Among Nations* (1993) deals with imperialism but not at all with spheres of influence. Waltz's *Theory of International Politics* (1979) is even less concerned with spheres of influence.

Waltz comes closest to the topic by discussing the advantages of a bipolar great power order over a multipolar order. According to Waltz, contrary to the general view, interdependence does not necessarily enhance possibilities for peace, because conflicts take place specifically among those actors which are in contact with each other (138). For Waltz, interdependence in a multipolar system means vulnerability and instability, whereas a bipolar system is more stable and less conflict-prone (138–45). Even though Waltz admits that wars of lesser scale have been fought within the bipolar system that prevailed during the Cold War (182), he does not explore the relationship between conflicts, bipolarity and spheres of influence. If we look at Mearsheimer's *Tragedy of Great Power Politics* (2001; 40–42, 140–42, 247–9), it mentions the idea of 'regional hegemons' and their balancing game, but does not discuss the relationship between the hegemon and its subordinates.

After the Cold War, geostrategising in the spirit of reducing spheres of influence to a territorial notion was continued by Zbigniew Brzezinski[4] (1998, 2004) and Saul B. Cohen (1964, 2003, 2005). The world-view of Brzezinski is a very 'Mackinderian' one with its emphasis on the leadership of Eurasia in the grand battle for influence. Brzezinski has promoted the United States' world leadership as the alternative to both anarchy and the rise of a rival power, that is, a new rise of Russia. Cohen (2003, 3–5) wrote about 'world realms' in a book published in 1964 and continued to make the same statements even 30 years later. Cohen divides the word into different realms dominated by a central power. In explaining what a realm means, Cohen writes, 'A national state (the meso-level) may dominate the geopolitical region within which it is located, and forge the framework of a geopolitical realm' (3). But just like Brzezinski, Cohen does not engage in conceptualising influence in terms of political theory. Samuel Huntington, even though he mentions spheres of influence only four times in his *Clash of Civilizations* (2007), elaborates a similar view. Huntington's famous thesis is that future conflicts will evolve between civilisations instead of states. What Huntington proposes – in a claim relevant to the study of spheres of influence – is that civilisational blocs develop around 'core states'. Core states attract culturally similar countries to 'bandwagon' with them (3118). Huntington writes:

> A world in which core states play a leading or dominating role is a spheres-of-influence world. But it is also a world in which the exercise of influence by the core state is tempered and moderated by the common culture it shares with member states of its civilization. Cultural commonality legitimates the leadership and order-imposing role of the core state for both member states and for the external powers and institutions. (Huntington 2007, 3131)

---

4   Brzezinski is a Polish-American political scientist who also had a career the as United States National Security Advisor to President Jimmy Carter from 1977 to 1981. He has a very critical view of Russia, and Russian scholars and politicians often quote these criticisms.

Huntington emphasises cultural affinity, which we can see in Naumann's work discussed in the following chapter, but this does not make Huntington's sphere of influence acceptable in any way for the majority of people who view spheres of influence pejoratively. This negative view is based on the 'clash' – the inevitability of conflict – and, in addition, the injustice that are seen as part and parcel of spheres of influence. The clash of civilizations is an idea which has gained wide acknowledgement, but it does not offer tools for a theoretical conceptualisation of spheres of influence concerned with discussing justice and international order.

The present understanding of spheres of influence leans towards the Mackinderian tradition of pointing out territorial struggles for power, making *sphere of influence* a catchword or a metaphor rather than a contested concept. The following conceptualisations of a sphere of influence, which bind international order to a normative agenda, promote the aim of contesting the concept and exploring the subjugated knowledge of the present.

4.2   Friedrich Naumann and Mid-Europe

If geopolitical tradition in general is often associated with the concept of sphere of influence, so is, in particular, the German tradition. But less frequently does the name of Friedrich Naumann (1860–1919) come up in this context. Naumann's work *Central Europe* (1917) (German original *Mitteleuropa* 1915) is not only a contextualisation of the idea of sphere of influence in terms of the fate of the German state, but also a theoretical piece leading the way for a wider discussion on international order and the disintegration of the system of states. Naumann's vision of a Mid-Europe[5] (*Mitteleuropa* in German) is interesting in the sense that it comes close to advocating regional integration yet it maintains the power relation of the influencing and the influenced states which is integral to the concept of sphere of influence. Mid-Europe is not a project which brings states together on an equal basis – which is why Naumann can also be seen as broaching the relevant normative questions – but the way that Naumann defends his vision of regional solidarism makes Mid-Europe a rather different entity from a sphere of influence as understood today.

In *Central Europe* (1917), Naumann elaborates his wish to create a Central European Union, or Mid-Europe.[6] For Naumann (1917, 179), 'the United States of the World' was far distant, but he took the view that groups of humanity were

---

5   The title of the book is *Central Europe* in the 1917 translation, but *Mitteleuropa* within the text is translated as 'Mid-Europe'. It seems in the translation Mid-Europe (also Central European Union) denotes the union of states Naumann promotes, while Central Europe refers to a geographic region.

6   Naumann was not the only German promoting the idea of Mid-Europe. See Heffernan (2000) for the broader German discussion on Mid-Europe, and also on Ratzel's Lebensraum, the idea of living space for Germany and the theory of the organic state.

emerging and that Mid-Europe would be one of them. These 'central points' (the Great States) were on the rise, counteracting the power of the state (179–80). Naumann proclaimed that there was a growing unity of nations which belong to neither the Anglo-French Western alliance nor the Russian Empire but to the Central Powers of the German Empire and the Austro-Hungarian Dual Monarchy (1). This Mid-Europe would be the new German-led Great State. The context for Naumann's vision of Mid-Europe, just like the visions of other like-minded theorists, was the end of the old international order:

> All the allies in the Great War feel without argument that neither now nor in the future can small or even moderate-sized Powers play any large part in the world. Our conceptions of size have entirely changed. Only very big States have any significance on their own account, all the smaller ones must live by utilising the quarrels of the great, or must obtain leave if they wish to do anything unusual. Sovereignty, that is freedom to make decisions of wide historical importance, is now concentrated at a very few places on the globe. (Naumann 1917, 4)

Small states had become dependent on great powers; large-scale industry and super-national organisation had seized politics (Naumann 1917, 4). For Naumann Germany was too small, as were Austria and Hungary, to survive a world war. He concluded, 'Hence to-day the Central European Union is no chance but a necessity' (5). It was not with Russia that Germany should unite; rather, if it were to maintain an individual course Germany would require a union with Austria-Hungary (60–61). Mid-Europe was to be the fourth power among the other three great organisms; that is, Great Britain, America and Russia (182).

For Naumann (1917; 15, 23, 25) unification was a political necessity; not unifying would mean political suicide. The economic Mid-Europe would battle for success amidst other unions, and states which could not keep up in the race would fall into third- or fourth-rank sovereignty (189). While the leaders of economic world-groups would be the greater states, small states could no longer choose isolation, and instead needed to decide which union they would or could join (194). Naumann was concerned that the German people did not understand the greatness of the older world-group economic areas (211). Germany could no longer keep up with them alone. He claimed that unless Mid-Europe emerged as a separate centre of power it would fall into being a satellite nation (180).

Naumann explains that a proper mixture of enforced unity and freedom draws the satellites in closer to the centre of power (182). He identified different strategies to insert influence: Russia rules with fear but also with the magnetic power of the Russian spirit (183). The English, instead, request as long as possible, and only after that do they command whereas the American Great State represents the third way – 'the most non-military great human organism that has ever existed' (184). Naumann observed that these Great States were not mere administrative districts but entities intermediate between nation and humanity with a specific essence that held the union together (185).

Naumann thus establishes an idea of spheres of influence expressed very much in Cold War terms: satellites around the sun. But he also discusses differences between forms of influence, approaching Bull's (2002) three forms of preponderance: *dominance, hegemony* and *primacy* (see Chapter 2.3). For Naumann the special essence of the union held it together but at the same time the rulers exercised differing means of control: the Russian Great State was built on coercion while the American on free will, with England standing between the two (Naumann 1917, 182). Thus, again, instead of separating good and bad, or just and unjust influence, it is possible to take the coercive element of unification into consideration and start building the language of influence on that basis.

Naumann's ideas were written for the political elite of Germany and for those states which Naumann dreamed would become the new Mid-Europe. He knew that there was strong opposition to his vision in Germany, not least in Austria and Hungary (Naumann 1917; 15, 19). Naumann tried to explain that Austria-Hungary without allies would be even more lost than Germany without allies (23). He also wanted Germans to let go of nationalism for the sake of Mid-Europe (11–12). Mid-Europe would be built upon the German language, but Germans would have to display tolerance and flexibility with regard to neighbouring languages (108). Naumann envisioned that Germany would be the leader, the nucleus, of the new Union. Mid-Europe was to become a historical and political entity, not only an economical union (35). He exclaimed, 'You must think of these stretches of country as a unity, as a brotherhood of many members, as a defensive alliance, as a single economic district!' (3–4). Naumann thought that it was not enough to build the Union on economic considerations alone, which is why he speaks of a common soul and common historical consciousness of the peoples (44). Here Naumann's Mid-Europe reminds one of an entity governed by a suzerain as the beloved and revered father (in Chapter 2.2).

Sovereignty would be an obvious concern in the new Mid-Europe. For Naumann, the creation of Mid-Europe would mean centralisation of certain political activities, but without sacrificing sovereignty. Mid-Europe was not an entity that would destroy sovereignty: 'No State becoming a partner in the new super-State will consent to sacrifice thereby its political dignity, its own sovereignty which it has won with difficulty and defended with its blood' (Naumann 1917, 254). The dignity of the state must not be touched, Naumann proclaimed. For Naumann, even though the word 'super-State' is used, Mid-Europe was not a new state, but a union of existing states, with sovereignty remaining the organising principle (255). According to Naumann's vision no state could be forced to join the union. He emphasised the traits and rights of the satellites even though Germany was the central power. Although Naumann proposed the harmonisation of many laws in the political and economic union, he wanted the joining states to retain their political independence (272). At the same time, the union had to have its military dimension, which naturally created political limitations but also offered a safeguard through the joint army (281).

Naumann's Mid-Europe was also an ambitious imperialist project, as he reveals when examining the economic considerations in resisting the power of the other great states. First, Mid-Europe would need further regional accessions to become greater than the existing dimensions of Germany and Austria-Hungary (Naumann 1917, 272). He added that Mid-Europe would need its share of overseas colonial possessions (198), going on to predict, 'Our Central European home population would be the centre of the life of an economic body which stretched out its grasp into other quarters of the globe' (203). This was thus not simply a regional union of states, but a union that leaned on the idea of overseas possessions as a necessity for economic success.

Naumann's German-led Mid-Europe clearly has something to do with a sphere of influence. Both are 'between nation and humanity'; they may be seen as a solution to the demise of the nation state. If we look at Naumann's vision, excluding its imperialist ambitions, it is quite far from the pejoratively tinged concept of sphere of influence that we embrace today. Mid-Europe sounds much more acceptable because it is justified, not by power political games but by the survival of cultural uniqueness, freedom in plurality and independence over Eastern domination. In addition to embodying a survival story, Mid-Europe is not an empire which will strip its constituent parts of their identity and sovereignty.

Naumann took pains to justify the Central European sphere of influence and maintained the use of cultural affinity in organising the 'Central European Union'. Membership needed to be voluntary, based on the brotherhood of nations, bearing in mind the absolute necessity of this development. Naumann did not scare his readers with the threat of a world hegemon, but rather warned about the demise of Mid-Europe as an independent centre of power. He wanted at least an illusion of sovereignty to prevail over the idea of total merger into one unit. He was nevertheless in favour of colonial expansion in order to keep up with the other great unions. But, most importantly, Naumann reflected Mid-Europe against the emerging international order at the time, where small states were becoming satellites of the great ones. This approach of his has important theoretical value for the present discourses on spheres of influence, which take no interest in the broader questions of international order. In their connecting spheres of influence with international order, and considering the possibility of the end of the Westphalian system of states and the emergence of a system of unions of states, thinkers such as Naumann and Schmitt are necessary literature for understanding spheres of influence. The world today is caught in the crossfire of regional integration projects and still-strong nationalistic sentiments. Somehow, the world is between nationalism and humanism, just as Naumann felt it was almost a hundred years ago. This is also where Carl Schmitt situates his articulation of a sphere of influence.

4.3 Carl Schmitt, Nomos and *Großraum*

When writing about spheres of influence, one cannot avoid discussing the work of Carl Schmitt (1888–1985). According to Mika Luoma-aho, Schmitt's Weimar writings are overemphasised in relation to his later works on international law and geopolitics. The reason for undervaluing the post 1936 writings was Schmitt's association with the Nazi regime (1933–1936). As Luoma-aho (2000, 703) writes, later Schmitt avoided topics related to domestic politics and concentrated on international relations. Schmitt's interest in international relations led him to discuss the *Großraum* (literally, 'large space'; figuratively, large spatial sphere). Schmitt's theory on international order was born in a specific context with a concern for the future of Germany after the war, but it has relevance even today, not least when theorising *sphere of influence*. Schmitt's association with the Nazi regime can be seen to have influenced his geopolitical ideas, but we should also ask how much his Nazi sympathy has affected our reading of his work; that is, our reading of *Großraum* as the pejorative sphere of influence.

Schmitt's *The Nomos of the Earth in the International Law of the Jus publicum Europaeum* (2003) was first published in German in 1950 (*Der Nomos der Erde im Völkerrecht des Jus Publicum Europaeum*).[7] The translator's introduction to *The Nomos of the Earth* describes Schmitt's idea of *nomos* as 'a community of political entities united by common rules'. It continues, 'It is the spatial, political, and juridical system considered to be mutually binding in the conduct of international affairs – a system that has obtained over time and has become a matter of tradition and custom' (Ulmen 2003, 10). At the core, Schmitt is talking about the same international order, the same basic idea of a society of states, as the English School; with the state as the 'decisive entity' of the political. This is why Alessandro Colombo (2007, 22–5) calls Schmitt's theory 'realist institutionalism', where the realist game of power politics is understood as an institution, and international anarchy is placed in a societal and juridical web. But what is important for the history of spheres of influence is the point when Schmitt begins theorising on the collapse of the institutions of the society of states. It was in describing the danger of modern states being at the verge of extinction from the political map of the world that Schmitt developed his vision of spheres of influence. Without exploring Schmitt's concept of *nomos* in detail we are unable to grasp the meaning of *Großraum*.

Schmitt's concept of *nomos* is the background for understanding his vision of how states should have been organised in post-War Europe. For Schmitt (2003, 70) *nomos* means 'the immediate form in which the political and social order of a people becomes spatially visible – the initial measure and division of pastureland, i.e., land-appropriation as well as the concrete order contained in it and following from it'. Schmitt further explains that *nomos* is not only the measure of dividing and situating a land but includes the political, social and religious order that follows from it (70). *Nomos* is not something fixed, for new manifestations of world-historical events will always give rise to a new *nomos* (78–9.) However, Schmitt argues, not every land-appropriation constitutes a new *nomos* even though

---

7   Louiza Odysseos and Fabio Petito (2007, 1–2) call it the masterpiece of his intellectual production, a work that should be acknowledged as a classic of International Relations.

a *nomos* always includes a land-based order and orientation (80). A change needs to occur in international law in order for seizure of land to create a 'new *nomos*', that is, 'a new spatial order of international law' (82).

The reason why *sphere of influence* as a concept is situated specifically in classical geopolitics can be found in Schmitt's definition of *nomos*: it is a social order that is made spatially visible. *Nomos* is a social order, as it is for the English School, but at the same time it is a spatial order of dividing land and constructing borders. Perhaps this is also the reason why spatiality, the geopolitical dimension of spheres of influence, is emphasised over other dimensions. It is emphasised quite rightfully: the spatial element is at the core of spheres of influence as long as international relations is concerned with states and their borders. 'Sphere' is the spatial element and when states begin to arrange themselves into unions, blocs, super-states, centres of power – whatever one wishes to call them – we witness a spatial order based on spheres of influence.

A sphere of influence also tends to imply territorial proximity of the influenced states to the core, which is why influence in distant territories is not viewed as a sphere-of-influence policy as readily as relations between the core and its surrounding states. Kaufman's (1976, 11) 'direct sphere of influence' not only means that the influence is *de facto* instead of *de jure* but also that the states have a geographical proximity. Spatiality makes sphere of influence a physical entity, and as such it is easier to imagine the orbit as circles on a map. This leads to assuming that if Russia has a sphere of influence somewhere, it is within the post-Soviet space. Likewise, it is more difficult to imagine a United States sphere of influence because of the blurring of the spatial element into varying military, economic and ideological influences around the globe. Nevertheless, Schmitt's *nomos* is more than just spatial; it is also political and juridical, and this is where it becomes a conceptualisation of spheres of influence based on visions of international order and the society of states.

Nomos becomes important for Schmitt (2003, 56–66) when he compares the pre-global order – medieval Europe's unity of international law, *respublica Christiana,* supported by an empire and the papacy – to state-centred international law, the first global order of international law. This new age was founded on a spatial order of balance and it meant secularisation with the elimination of the holy empire and the imperial house of the Middle Ages (127). This was the epoch of *jus publicum Europaeum*, international law among sovereign territorial states, which prevailed from the sixteenth century to the end of the nineteenth century (126–7). It was an order determined by Europe for the rest of the earth. Schmitt called the new *nomos* a marvellous product of human reason because it ended the religious wars of the Middle Ages and rationalised and humanised war (141–2, 151). This function of 'bracketing war' is what makes states so important to Schmitt. For him it is the system of states that has made it possible to limit wars. By contrast, the end of sovereign states, and the emergence of a world hegemon, would mean that once *the political* (the ability to separate friend from enemy) was gone, a door would be opened to global interventionism.

Schmitt describes the territorial changes within a spatial order of the *jus publicum Europaeum* and illustrates the role of great powers. First, 'the procedures for territorial changes in European international law were developed by the Great Powers at the major peace conferences in the 18th and 19th centuries' (Schmitt 2003, 185). Schmitt claims there are different principles at work whose purpose it is to maintain the present order and its established members, one of which is 'delimitation of spheres of influence' and 'affirmation and recognition of great spheres of special interest' (185–6). Great powers are the strongest members of the spatial order, and thus they march at the forefront of development (190). This primary status also requires recognition from others, which makes it in fact the highest form of recognition in international law (191). The practice of recognition, according to Schmitt, had an important effect on the spatial structure of the order of international law. Great powers could participate in European conferences and negotiations and could acquire colonies. Schmitt elaborates this point, saying, 'Recognition as a Great Power became and remained a legal institution of international law, as important as recognition of a new state or government' (191). In his view, since great powers were the leaders of the spatial order, they were in a position to recognise major territorial changes (190–92). Schmitt took the institution of great power management as an institution of international society, in English School terms, but also as to denote a legal institution. Here Schmitt was pushing the limits of the system of states with sovereignty as its core principle, making way to discuss the role of the great and the small within a *Großraum*.

The spatial order of Europe was based on political balance; it was the foundation of international law. Schmitt (2003, 189) writes, 'The pervasive commonality of the spatial order is more important than everything usually associated with sovereignty and non-intervention'. Just like Bull then, Schmitt took the view that order took precedence over sovereignty. He was also openly in favour of the balance of power as the ordering principle, noting 'the great practical superiority of the concept of balance, because therein lies its capacity to achieve a bracketing of war' (198). Moreover, just as Keal saw the order spheres of influence could produce, Schmitt saw the war-limiting effect of balancing. The English School vision of order and great powers, and Schmitt's vision of *nomos* and its leaders are very much alike, and testify to the importance of taking this shared view of the system of states seriously when reflecting on the present images of international order and spheres of influence.

Finally, after his extensive explanation of the previous *nomos* of the earth, Schmitt addresses the topic of the future *nomos*, which in his view began with the collapse of the Eurocentric spatial order. What worried Schmitt was the growing power of the United States. Moreover he (2003, 227) was concerned by what he saw as the decline of *jus publicum Europaeum* into a universal international law lacking distinctions. European order was becoming part of the spacelessness of general universalism (230). Schmitt notes that at the same time as a new spatial order of universalism from the United States was challenging the traditional European order, there was also a new process of 'several different spheres (*Großräume*) of international law' that appeared on the scene (231). More specifically, Schmitt identified what he saw as the threat of universalism as coming from the West and hoped that a new regional organisation of the global political map would be the solution. Schmitt was concerned about the fact that Europe had lost its central position and did not even seem to have noticed it (233). What the Europeans had overlooked was that the recognition of new (non-European) states in international law had destroyed the *system* of states and was replaced by a *collection* of states randomly joined together by factual relations rather than by any spiritual or spatial consciousness (234). As Schmitt states, 'With this rejection of international law, Europe stumbled into a world war that dethroned the old world from the center of the earth and destroyed the bracketing of war it had created' (239). Put into English School terms, Schmitt thought that international *society* was turning into an international *system*. What is more, the weakening of society at the expense of the system would lead to a world war.

Schmitt was not fond of the idea of a World Government, or a solidarist international society with common morals. It was not only that Schmitt disliked the idea of a single sovereign; he had an aversion to any system of international society where spatial distinctions would disappear, whether dictated by the United States or a World Government. Schmitt (2003; 241, 244) was critical of the League of Nations' choice of universalism over pluriversalism, which he termed the 'Geneva dogma'. As Schmitt saw it,

> The development of the planet finally had reached a clear dilemma between universalism and pluriversalism, monopoly and polypoly. The question was whether the planet was mature enough for a global monopoly of a single power or whether pluralism of coexisting *Großräume*, spheres of interest, and cultural spheres would determine the new international law of the earth. (Schmitt 2003, 243–4)

The League advocated universalism instead of pluriversalism, a position which Schmitt was not happy about. At the same time, the League failed to create a universal world order, since the Soviet Union and the United States were absent (Schmitt 2003, 245.) Schmitt thought that the alternative of a plurality of *Großräume* was not discussed at the time of the League of Nations. What was at stake was a balanced spatial order against a centrally ruled world – pluralism against universalism, polypoly against monopoly (247). A World Government was not what Schmitt wanted. He envisioned something else to counter the threat that universalism posed to *the political*, the society, and even the system, of states. That something was a sphere of influence: '*Großräume,* spheres of interest, and cultural spheres' (243–4).

It was not only the Europeans themselves who were to blame for their plight at the time. Schmitt put much of the blame on the United States for destroying political plurality. The United States was making its own rules of the game. As early as December 2, 1823, the Monroe Doctrine had shielded the Western

Hemisphere from further land appropriation by the European powers (Schmitt 2003, 238). Yet, the United States controlled the foreign policies of states within the Western Hemisphere even though they were considered 'sovereign'. They were in fact within the spatial and political sphere of influence of the Monroe Doctrine. Schmitt explains the relationship as follows:

> [...] the controlled state's territory is absorbed into the spatial sphere of the controlling state and its special interests, i.e., into its spatial sovereignty. The external, emptied space of the controlled state's territorial sovereignty remains inviolate, but the material content of this sovereignty is changed by the guarantees of the controlling power's economic *Großraum*. (Schmitt 2003, 252)

The United States' *Großraum* was something where the shell, or outer layer, of sovereignty is maintained but the content of it is sacrificed. This sacrifice meant that:

> The controlling state had the right to protect independence or private property, the maintenance of order and security, and the preservation of the legitimacy or legality of a government. Simultaneously, on other grounds, it was free, at its own discretion, to interfere in the affairs of the controlled state. Its right of intervention was secured by footholds, naval bases, refuelling stations, military and administrative outposts, and other forms of cooperation, both internal and external. (Schmitt 2003, 252)

The controlling state, thus, has the right to maintain order as it pleases and the capacity to interfere and intervene. The spatial sovereignty of the controlling state is extended to include other states within its sphere of influence, but formally sovereignty still remains in the hands of the controlled state. This was the case with the Monroe Doctrine; this is the case with a *Großraum*; and this is also the basis for depicting spheres of influence in the present. The states within the spatial order of the Western Hemisphere – the Caribbean and Central American states – thus belonged to the United States' sphere of spatial sovereignty (253).

According to Schmitt (2003, 296) the United States was faced with a choice between isolation and intervention – a choice between a transition to the plurality of coexisting *Großräume* or a global claim to world power, and with it, global civil war. The threat of this interventionist policy was that it transformed the concept of war from one of interstate conflict to one of intrastate struggle; that is, into a civil war (299). What the Monroe Doctrine ultimately came to represent was a new spatial order – global universalism lacking any spatial sense – replacing the old one. Political control and domination were based on intervention, which destroyed the *nomos* of sovereign territory (252). The Western Hemisphere was not the only target; eventually the United States made the claim for global interventionism and refused to recognise territorial changes that it considered illegal anywhere (307).

Thus, the true challenge to the old *nomos* came from the United States and its proclamation of the Monroe Doctrine in interventionist terms. The wording 'Western Hemisphere' was now intimately connected with the Doctrine, as it became a *Großraum* in the sense of international law (Schmitt 2003, 281–3). In the beginning, the Doctrine meant a defensive line of isolation directed against the powers of the Old Europe, but drawing such a line also gave the United States the freedom to undertake its own land appropriations in the hemisphere (286). This isolation created a new spatial order by separating, politically and morally, a sphere of guaranteed peace and freedom (New World) from a sphere of despotism and corruption (Old World) (289). In the next chapter, where I discuss Cold War practices, this aspect of spheres of influence will become even more evident. If we step beyond seeing spheres of influence as a structural matter of hierarchy, inequality and a struggle for a balance of power, we find a discourse of justification, of 'us and them', of freedom and tyranny. Moreover, for Schmitt, if there was a moral line between the Old and the New World, it was also territorial and historical: the Western Hemisphere was a territory with its own historical tradition (286). I argued before that the idea of sphere of influence subsumes a spatial or territorial dimension. I would now assert that it also includes the idea of some moral, historical or cultural closeness. This makes a sphere of influence look like a regional arrangement something that encompasses a delimited territory of states that are somehow related – or at least related in the opinion of the central power.

According to Schmitt (2003, 353), the Eurocentric *nomos* met its destruction in World War One and a division of the world into East and West became reality. Schmitt listed three alternatives for the future order. The first was that one of the great powers would emerge victorious and the dualism of East and West would be replaced by a complete unity of the world under a sole sovereign (354). For Schmitt this was the most undesirable alternative – this was universalism. The second option was an attempt to restore the balance of power of the previous *nomos*. The third was a balance maintained by several independent *Großräume* which needed to be homogenous internally but differentiated externally (355). Schmitt already saw the Western Hemisphere as one, and Eastern Europe as the second new territorial *Großraum* (305). Ulmen (2003, 19) writes that Schmitt saw Germany as being too small to be a world power but too big to disappear from history. Thus Germany could not survive the destruction of the state-system on its own. According to Luoma-aho (2007, 36), the Soviet Union, as well as the British and Japanese empires, also had their respective *Großräume* in Schmitt's eyes. A German-led *Großraum* in Central and Eastern Europe would balance the two universalistic powers of the United States and the Soviet Union maintaining the political pluriverse as the prevailing international order (Freund 1995; Luoma-aho 2000; 2007, 41).

Schmitt explained the dissolution of *jus publicum Europaeum* through international law (see Schmitt 2003, chapter 2). The international law that Schmitt idealised was the spatial international law developed in Europe, not least because its great achievement was the bracketing of war. Even though Schmitt declared that the challenger of *jus publicum Europaeum* was the United States, which had its own spatial international law that allowed universalist-humanitarian interventions; Schmitt also blamed the Europeans for mistaking the universalising of international law for a victory of European international law (233). In fact, Europe itself made *jus publicum Europaeum* global through land appropriations (231–9). Schmitt could not stand universal international law. He considered it the end of European international law, because it was universal law that lacked all distinctions; it embodied a general universality and meant the destruction of the traditional global order. Thus, Schmitt began to see the development of an international law specific to *Großräume* as desirable. He was afraid of the United States' *Großraum* not because it created this kind of spatial international law – after all spatial differentiation was what Schmitt sought – but because it could turn into a universalist monster. As I understand it, for Schmitt, the globalisation of European international law was not the focal problem until Europe's domination over that law was jeopardised.

The question remains, what is the form of international law, if any, that lies between the separate spatial international laws? Will anarchy still prevail between *Großräume,* and will there be international societies instead of a single international society? Does Schmitt's system of *Großräume* mean suzerain-state systems? Schmitt leaves these questions quite open when he focuses on exploring the universalist threat. We can, nevertheless, detect a certain formality of influence within Schmitt's schema. For Schmitt (2003, 252) the right to intervention was based on agreements and treaties, making it possible to claim that the action taken was no longer intervention. When Schmitt writes about *Großräume* as separate spheres of international law, he cannot be talking about informality and tacitness. In this respect, one could argue that Schmitt's idea is a legal system more resembling colonialism and suzerain-systems, and less the spheres of influence which Keal wrote about. Looking at history from the perspective of the present, the tacitness of influence is not necessarily a distinctive feature of a sphere of influence. The present understanding embodies the pejorative associations, but it also embodies a sphere of influence which is imperialist. Even the Cold War sphere of influence, though tacit, was well established and included treaties, such as the Warsaw Pact. The ideological divide was also concrete and evident. If we think about Russia, it is often accused of trying to establish its sphere of influence by formal means – integration. Yet, because of the pejorative associations of *sphere of influence*, the integration project of the European Union in all its legality is not described as a sphere of influence.

Whereas Naumann's vision of Great States seems to be situated more in the spatial order of states, with his defence of sovereignty and national sentiments, Schmitt's *Großraum* takes the idea of spheres of influence a step further by legitimising them and creating a new spatial order of international law. This new spatial order of *Großräume* means a loosening of the Westphalian notion of sovereignty but does not mean the creation of a solidarist international society. Instead of solidarism, Schmitt clings to the pluralist system in the new form it takes. Schmitts Großräume are spatial solidarist entities within a pluralist system, blurring the line between the two ends of the spectrum, yet not specifying how much "society" would be incorporated in the relations between the new political entities. Schmitt did not explain the idea of *Großraum* nearly as thoroughly as he did the idea of a *nomos* of the earth. It is Schmitt's conceptualisation of international order and the moral stance that particular is good while universal is evil that accounts for his succeeding in giving the concept of sphere of influence a place in the history of international theory.

4.4 E.H. Carr: Nationalism versus Internationalism

E.H Carr (1892–1982) is a well-known British historian, journalist, diplomat and theorist on International Relations. He is less known, however, when it comes to the topic of spheres of influence; which is surprising considering his use of the term *Großraum*. Carr's *The Twenty Years Crisis* was published in 1939, reflecting on the results of the First World War, and *Nationalism and After* in 1945, outlining visions for international order after the Second World War.[8] Luoma-aho (2007, 44) suggests that Carr's conception of the political is adopted from Schmitt, even though Carr does not refer to Schmitt directly: both insisted that politics took place in a pluriverse of states in the context of violence. As Carr (1965, 49) saw it, within a national community the concentration of authority in a single organ would result in totalitarianism and the same applies to the international system, which is why a multiplicity of authority is required. In essence, Carr relied on the same idea of the duality of pluriverse and universe as Schmitt did – or, as Carr termed them, nationalism and internationalism – and the need to find a middle ground between them.

Just like Schmitt and the English School, Carr (1965) recalls the history of international order: a state-system emerging from medieval Christendom. The period Carr admires is one which began with the Napoleonic Wars and ended in 1914 (6). For Carr, this was a period which was successful in balancing between internationalism and nationalism: the asserting of claims to statehood by nations existed side by side with the creation of a single world economy (6–7). Carr's own nationalism caused him to admire the English supremacy in the world economy, which explains his enthusiasm for the post-Vienna order. But British supremacy ended in the First World War and the nineteenth-century economic system was ruined. What followed the war was a 'catastrophic growth of nationalism and the bankruptcy of internationalism' due to the increase in the number of nations (17–18). Carr writes, 'Down to that time the influence of nationalism had been to diminish the number of sovereign and independent political units in Europe'. The conditions of the period, the military and economic developments, favoured the concentration of power, but instead dispersal of authority was taking

---

8 I use the 2001 edition for *The Twenty Years Crisis* and the 1965 edition for *Nationalism and After*.

place all over the globe (24). The change compared to the previous order was that independence and statehood were assigned no more by might (by virtue of power) but by right (40–41). Carr did not view the equality of nations as proclaimed in the Charter of United Nations as being possible in the way that equality of individuals is (42). He thought states are simply too disparate in size (43). Like Schmitt, Carr did not advocate a 'supreme world directorate' that would follow the bankruptcy of nationalism or requests for the emancipation of the individual to equal a 'sentimental empty universalism'. The world was not united enough for a universal authority (44).

These are the observations Carr made about the history of the system of states. What is noteworthy when discussing spheres of influence is the dualism of nationalism and internationalism, and Carr's interest in the location of power in international relations. What Carr would have liked to have seen was a power structure that is called great power management in English School terms. Carr (1965, 34–7) made a prediction concerning the possible fourth period after the Second World War. Even though nationalism was still strong, the main forces of the world – the United Kingdom, the United States and the Soviet Union – were not built on nationalism in the old sense. According to Carr the world might well have been facing the end of 'the ideology of the small nation as the ultimate political and economic unit' (36). What Carr (2001, 211) thought that he saw was the concentration of sovereignty, a 'clearly marked trend towards integration and the formation of even larger political and economic units', which started in the latter part of the nineteenth century (212). For Carr it was a dangerous fiasco when nationalism and disintegration were resumed in 1918; instead of political and economic disintegration, the post-war order would have required larger units (211–12). Making a reference to Naumann's Mid-Europe Carr (2001, 212) notes that the process of concentration continued:

> The United States strengthened their hold over the American continents. Great Britain created a 'sterling *bloc*' and laid the foundations of a closed economic system. Germany reconstituted *Mittel-Europa* and pressed forward into the Balkans. Soviet Russia developed its vast territories into a compact unit of industrial and agricultural production. Japan attempted the creation of a new unit of 'Eastern Asia' under Japanese domination. Such was the trend towards the concentration of political and economic power in the hands of six or seven highly organised units, round which lesser satellite units revolved without any appreciable independent motion of their own. (Carr 2001, 212)

Thus Carr saw a change in the post-war order. There was no return to the pre-1914 world, nor would sovereignty remain static. Territorial power had not always been centred on sovereign states and it was uncertain whether it would be in the future either (Carr 2001, 210–11). Carr's focal question was, 'Will the nation survive as the unit of power?' (209). Carr went on to predict that in the future sovereignty will be more blurred and indistinct than at present. Sovereignty had marked the distinctiveness of the authority claimed by the state after the medieval system. But 'when distinctions began to be made between political, legal and economic sovereignty or between internal and external sovereignty, it was clear that the label had ceased to perform its proper function as a distinguishing mark for a single category of phenomena' (Carr 2001, 212). Thus, Carr questions the whole idea of state sovereignty as the organising principle of international order, since its original meaning did not fit the conditions at the time. For Carr we had already lost sovereignty as a principle, and in the reality of international affairs sovereignty was also becoming obsolete. Based on Carr's observation, basing the idea of sphere of influence on assumptions about sovereignty is problematic if sovereignty no longer adequately describes the 'present conditions'– if it ever did. With this logic, if there never was sovereignty other than in principle, then 'violations of sovereignty' poorly describe what spheres of influence are about.

Carr states that in the future units of power will likely not take much account of formal sovereignty. He does not see why there should not be units consisting of formally sovereign states as long as the effective authority is exercised from a single centre. Nevertheless, these units would not be recognised by international law (Carr 2001, 213). What Carr means is the *informal* concentration of power, not a system of *Großräume* that would replace the system of states in the eyes of international law. Moreover, Carr suggests that international order cannot be based on naked power alone; there needs to be consent, whether it be forced or not, on the order (216). To sum up, for Carr the concentration of power is informal and does not require a change of international law, but does necessitate consent among the great powers.

Even though for Carr the future order would not be built on international law, he uses Schmitt's terminology:

> If these predictions are realized, the world will have to accommodate itself to the emergence of a few great multinational units in which power will be mainly concentrated. Culturally, these units may best be called civilizations: there are distinctively British, American, Russian and Chinese civilizations, none of which stops short at national boundaries in the old sense. Economically the term *Großraum* invented by German geo-politicians seems the most appropriate. The Soviet Union is pre-eminently a *Großraum*; the American continents are the potential *Großraum* of the United States, though the term is less convenient as applied to the British Commonwealth of Nations or the sterling area which are oceanic rather than continental agglomerations. (Carr 1965, 52)

Compared to Schmitt's analysis, there had to be a British and not a German *Großraum* between the two other great powers (Carr 1965, 53). Carr did not want Britain to end up as subordinate to the United States or the Soviet Union, but to lead a Western European *Großraum* (71, 73). Moreover, Carr makes it clear he does not promote 'a division of the world into a small number of multinational units exercising effective control over vast territories and practising in competition and conflict with one another new imperialism which would be simply the old nationalism writ large and would almost certainly pave the way for more titanic and devastating wars'. Carr admires the nineteenth-century order of only a few great powers which could decide on matters of war and peace, with small states agreeing to this practice, and wishes that would be the model for the future (53). It is the old great power order that Carr is referring to rather than a system comprised of suzerain rulers.

Carr (1965, 54–5) doubted the viability of small nations as independent entities in a world where neutrality was no longer possible, and where small states could no longer contribute to collective security. In Carr's view, the only way for a small nation to maintain independence and contribute to international security was 'by willingly merging some of its attributes into the common pool'. This would also solve the problem caused by the principle of national self-determination, a product of the nineteenth century that has caused impracticably small units of power (56). Carr considers it natural for human beings to form groups of varying size and purpose. The multi-national units of power would not have to kill national feeling and culture; instead they could offer overlapping and interlocking loyalties (59). The new political units should not be based on national exclusiveness but on shared ideals and aspirations, just as Naumann envisioned. Carr wanted to avoid the multi-national units manifesting nationalism at a larger scale. The concentration of power should advance tolerance of the national and not the opposite (66). Carr is constructing an image of two different ways to concentrate power: One represents a nationalistic-imperialistic project ending up in more wars and the other advances tolerance and shared values. Carr does not explain the difference between the two types of influence well enough, but conclusions can nevertheless be drawn. First, nationalism is the core issue. It has the potential to ruin the beautiful idea of *Großräume*, just like it ruined the system of states. Second, Carr expresses the idea that there is a tolerant *Großraum* and a imperialist *Großraum*, meaning that a sphere of influence has the potential also to benefit all the members of international society, not least because of the order it produces, in the form of the tolerant *Großraum*.

Carr had a vision of a union of the great and the small which would not mean the formation of empires but a union of states with at least some level of independence. Interestingly, at the same time Carr (1965, 58–60) proposed a world security organisation, supported by the three great powers for the management of some collective forces and strategic bases. Even if Carr was not very consistent or clear in his vision of this organisation and its relation to the system of *Großräume*, the idea of a world security organisation in a world of *Großräume* is an aspect lessening the pejorative burden of the concept of sphere of influence when reflected against George Orwell's vision of isolated regional units (Chapter 4.6) or the Iron Wall which separated the Western and Eastern blocks not too long ago. Moreover, the idea of a world security organisation adds the global solidarist agenda into the framework. If Schmitt's vision lacked an explanation of the relations among Großräaume, then Carr's security organisation provides an idea of how to manage relations between the great entities as a society. This means that the relations between *Großräume* are important in the sense that they take us back to Bull and Keal's argument of great power management contributing to international order (Chapter 2.6). If this element of great power management is lacking in a vision of spheres of influence or *Großräume,* the justification for endangering sovereignty all but disappears.

The logic of trying to solve the dilemma of war and nationalism by organising the system of states into a system of *Großräume* is noteworthy for contesting the concept of sphere of influence with its present pejorative connotations. Even though Carr's solution sounds like a triumph of the inequality of states, he is not as much of a 'realist' as he may at first seem. Matters of justice are not alien to Carr. He (1965, 61) declared, quite radically, that the primary function of international order is not to maintain the status quo or rights of nations, but to improve the life conditions of ordinary people. Carr does not seem to take the state at face value, but rather places individuals before it. Even if a sphere of influence on a theoretical level is mainly concerned with relations among states, the pejorative associations of the concept, especially the images of the Cold War, nevertheless encompass the human factor. Then the question becomes, how does a sphere of influence affect the people inhabiting the territories influenced? I believe that this is the one question that should be focused on more squarely when discussing spheres of influence.

Carr can make us consider whether his emphasis on social justice over nationalism could be applied to the logic of spheres of influence. Is a sphere of influence in fact a progressive idea (like it is for Carr) instead of a regressive one? Could it not be seen as progressive and at times justified if we place human beings front and centre instead of clinging to the principle of state sovereignty and the nation-state? After all, protecting people is the cause that promoters of humanitarian intervention appeal to in order to justify violations of sovereignty, the use of force and violence in general. Carr (1965, 69) insists that small or medium-sized nation states lack the resources to provide well-being for their people. He puts forward proposals on common action, conventions, a General Staff and trade agreements as the measures needed to create the British *Großraum* (72) – proposals which bring to mind the present practice of integration and not forceful domination. Are the peoples of the small states better off if they can let go of their state's sovereignty and accept a merger into bigger entities? Or is Carr just as utopian as those he accuses of being so, when he is dreaming of prosperous and humanistic spheres of influence?

Carr's concern was war and peaceful change as he tried to make sense of a world free of the problems caused by nationalism and internationalism alike. He offers the solution of larger units to war-causing nationalism and its counterpart, utopian internationalism. The solution cannot be a fantasy for Carr; it needs to be based on the realities of life. And in reality regionalism was more practical than universalism: 'The history of League of Nations, beginning with the insertion in the Covenant of the original Monroe Doctrine reservation, bears witness to the persistence of attempts to escape from a theoretical and ineffective universalism into a practical and workable regionalism' (Carr 1965, 45). Internationalism for Carr meant universal dominion. He (2001, 78–81) thought that world peace, based on the 'harmony of interests' that internationalism proclaimed, was certainly desirable but its problem was that it could be used to mask hegemonic political interests. Carr notes, '[…] pleas for international solidarity and world union come from those dominant nations which may hope to exercise control over a unified world'. Moreover, those states which desire a position in the dominant group usually invoke nationalism against the internationalism of the dominant powers (79). The core problem of utopianism was that in the end, in a concrete political situation, selfish national interest would win out over any sense of common good (80). This is why, in his view, the emerging order that was challenging the system of nation-states had to be based on pluralism. This meant a compromise 'between the past confusion of a vast number of nations, great and small, jostling one another on a footing of formal independence and equality, and the well-knit world authority which may or may not be attainable in the future' (Carr 1965, 52).

Carr insists that power is and will be the determining factor in world affairs. Thus,

> [t]he new international order can be built only on a unit of power sufficiently coherent and sufficiently strong to maintain its ascendancy without being itself compelled to take sides in the rivalries of lesser units. Whatever moral issues may be involved, there is an issue of power which cannot be expressed in terms of morality. (Carr 2001, 216)

Carr is a realist, sceptical about utopian dreams, which is why his stand is so strong. The realist paradigm has obviously left its mark also on the present understanding of spheres of influence. This is why the possibilities of the concept have not been explored outside the realist worldview of power politics. Carr is important to the concept of sphere of influence for situating it in the framework of problems with nationalism and internationalism, and especially by expounding on how spheres of influence could solve the problems of nationalism. Carr's sphere of influence cannot be built on nationalism and he argues that larger political units can improve the living conditions of citizens. What is more, Carr pointed out the blurring of sovereignty and the difficulty of discussing sovereignty which was never truly realised. Again, if we relax the idea of sovereignty, spheres of influence are not always and necessarily a violation of sovereign rights; that is, a sphere of influence does not inevitably deserve a pejorative interpretation.

4.5   Walter Lippmann and the Good Neighbor Policy

Schmitt and Naumann proposed a new global political order for rescuing Germany from being absorbed by other great states and for the sake of pluralism. Schmitt and Naumann had their American counterparts who were interested in regional arrangements and developing a scheme for great power relations and relations among the big and the small. One of these visionaries is Walter Lippmann who, along with President Franklin Roosevelt, envisioned international order in terms of the 'Good Neighbor Policy'. Lippmann's and Roosevelt's basic concern was the question of what kind of influence would be the right one for the new regionalism.

According to Warren F. Kimball, in a meeting with Winston Churchill in 1941, Franklin Roosevelt put forward a proposal whereby the United States and Great Britain would together police world affairs until an international organisation could be formed. This police force was later expanded to include Russia and China. Roosevelt's post-war plan included proposals that great powers would act as guarantors of peace, that colonial empires would be disbanded and that other states would be disarmed (Kimball 1991, 85). Aleksandr Fursenko and Timothy Naftali (1998, 9) write that Franklin Roosevelt rejected the policy of Theodore Roosevelt from 1904 which asserted that the United States could intervene in the domestic affairs of the countries of Western Hemisphere. The new policy from 1933 onward would be that of non-intervention with the name 'Good Neighbor Policy'. Lippmann took the concept of Good Neighbor Policy and formulated the idea of the United States having a sphere of responsibility within the Western Hemisphere.

Ronald Steel (1999, xviii) calls Lippmann (1889–1974) America's greatest journalist. Lippmann received the Pulitzer Prize in 1958 and 1962 for his newspaper column 'Today and Tomorrow'. His journalism had a great impact on politics, along with his personal contacts with prominent politicians. For example, Steel argues, Lippmann's editorials for the New York *World* helped to prevent an American invasion of Mexico (xivv). In addition, Lippmann was advisor to Woodrow Wilson, contributing to the Fourteen Points. Yet he stayed away from both politics and academia, influencing politics through his writings and personal relations. Lippmann's writings did not go unnoticed within the English School either. Lippmann's revulsion of imperial ambitions, and his support for upholding American ideals – in the form of the Good Neighbor Policy – were acknowledged by both Bull (2002) and Keal (1983).

For Lippmann, like his contemporaries, the world wars formed the context for thinking about international order. Lippmann (1945, 131) felt that a new world order could emerge from the ruins of the war, and with it a long peace. Lippmann pondered the war events in Europe in *Some Notes on War and Peace* (1940). He lamented the balance-of-power system in Europe and the lack of an authority to bind together the European nations (38–44). Lippmann saw Europe as an entity in itself, which would not flourish as a diversity of nation-states; but instead as a union, which required a centre of order:

> If this is correct, then the great question of the war is whether there will be established a new and durable center of civilized union and authority, capable of repulsing attack, large enough and strong enough to exhaust the aggressors,

and able in the end to admit and absorb into its unity the civilized peoples of the western world (Lippmann 1940, 45–6).

In Europe, small states had put their independence in the hands of the system of the balance of power, whereas in the New World relations among the great and the small were founded upon the Good Neighbour Policy (Lippmann 1945, 81). Relying on a balance of power was the mistake Europe had made. Instead, in the New World, a more successful policy had been developed. Lippmann thought that this model, successfully implemented in the Western Hemisphere, could form the basis of a new international order. A clearly spelled-out policy was needed that would tie nations together into unions of 'good neighbors'. Bull called the idea of good neighbours represented by Roosevelt and Lippmann 'spheres of responsibility'. Bull (2002, 215–16) writes that what Lippmann spelled out in *U.S. War Aims* (1945) was an idea that the post-war international order should be based on a division of three or four spheres of responsibility where each great power or combination of them would secure peace. Lippmann in fact proposed that the world order would be 'composed of the great regional constellations of states which are the homelands, not of one nation alone but of the historic civilized communities' (87–8). Lippmann argued that international order could no longer be established on the basis of collective agreements among individual national states; rather these had to be concluded among groups of national states (64–5).

For Lippmann (1945, 65), this organisation of the world meant the strategical systems of the Atlantic Community (the United States, Western Europe and Latin America), the Russian Orbit, China and later some constellation(s) in the Hindu and Moslem worlds. Lippmann was also prepared to counter voices against United States' dominance over Europe from people who would rather have seen a European federation. But Lippmann did not see Europe as a single geographic and strategic entity that could form a political union (125). The main reason for this was that Germany would inevitably be its nucleus (126). Lippmann argued that war as it was known at the time was being fought precisely to prevent this from taking place (127). For Lippmann, European unification could be implemented only by preventing German domination, and this could be done within the framework of the Atlantic Community (128).

Fundamentally, Lippmann was as nationalistic in his visions for international order as any other theorist presented here (see Lippmann 1945; 49, 53–7, 208–10). The purpose of introducing the Good Neighbor Policy was primarily to secure the Western Hemisphere as a distinct region free from interference from the outside. In order to resist outside conquerors in the spirit of the Monroe Doctrine Lippmann (1945, 73) called out for a common foreign policy since '[a] house divided against itself cannot stand'. For Lippmann, the Good Neighbor Policy was a substitute for an empire (85). The common foreign policy Lippmann called for did not mean political federation or a formal treaty of alliance, but rather a network of agreements and understandings. Lippmann explained, 'The Atlantic nations remain separate sovereign states but they form a living community'

(77). The regional systems should be based on the Good Neighbor Policy of non-aggression, co-operation and good will and not on a policy of neutrality that depended on balancing between great powers (82–3). Lippmann made sure his proposal would be appreciated also by the small states, portraying the Good Neighbour Policy as a two-way game:

> The Good Neighbor relationship is one in which small states and a great one in the same area of strategic security become allies in peace and in war. The great state provides *protection* – which the technology of modern war being what it is – no small state can provide itself. The small state reciprocates: it provides strategic facilities needed for the common defence, and it uses its own sovereign powers to protect its great neighbor against infiltration, intrigue, and espionage. Insofar as the small state makes this critical contribution to the security of the neighbourhood, *its independence is of vital interest to its great neighbor.* (Lippmann 1945, 83–4; emphasis added)

According to Lippmann, a great power provides protection for its small neighbours as compensation for the contribution they make to ensuring the security of the region. The independence of the neighbour is 'of vital interest' to the great power and that will guarantee the protection of the neighbour states. As this protection comes with a price, Lippmann emphasised that small states can only assure their rights by general acceptance of the duties of the Good Neighbor Policy. Lippmann writes, 'We must not, as many do, identify the rights of small nations with their right to have an "independent" foreign policy, that is to say one which manipulates the balance of power among great states'. For him small states were too small compared to big states to pursue anything other than the Good Neighbor Policy (Lippmann 1945, 84). There was simply an ever-growing disparity between the greatest states and others (137–8).

For Lippmann the relationship between the great and the small did not involve injustice; rather, it was a win-win relationship in which the great offered protection for the price of commitment by the small to certain duties. Moreover, the small states were not innocent actors, but like any other states can play the games of power politics if given the chance. This was the most just system Lippmann could envision for the smooth working of the international order and the prevention of war. Justification of influence through arguments on reciprocity, common to Naumann and Lippmann alike, is the second foundation of justifications for spheres of influence, the first being their contribution to international order. With the idea of reciprocity, sphere of influence takes the influenced state itself to possess meaningful agency and interests, instead of only being an object of great power politics. In a way, to place small states in this kind of sphere of influence is to rescue the small state as much as possible in the face of concentration of sovereignty. In other words, it means the vindication of the small state, not its subjugation. My point is, when we look at spheres of influence through the lens of international theory, namely theory on order, we can turn that which seems evident around into an idea that normally does not cross our minds. It is not a unique thought to picture small states benefiting from cooperation or integration with greater powers, but it is definitely a forgotten thought when it comes to spheres of influence.

Like Schmitt, Naumann and Carr, Lippmann dismisses the idea of a universal society in the form of a world government charged with policing humankind. As Americans had successfully implemented regional policies through the Monroe Doctrine, the Pan-American Union and the Good Neighbor Policy, Lippmann (1945, 190) asked why they should promote a universalist doctrine. First of all, no state would give away its legislative and executive power to such a world government (183). Moreover, any comprehensive world organisation can only reinforce national measures of security, not replace them (160). According to Lippmann, diplomatic relations dealing with security and prevention of war should be left to 'national states', acting within regional groups (167). Here, he holds on to plurality in world politics as much as Schmitt does.

Lippmann did not believe that separate states could form a world organisation but he did think that if single sovereign states combined in their neighbourhoods, and neighbourhoods combined into larger communities, then these constellations could participate in a universal society. Lippmann's thinking here is along the lines of Carr's, arguing for the incapability of the nation-state to guarantee peace. If we compare this thinking to Schmitt's and Naumann's, we see that the German scholars did not call the capabilities of the state itself into question, as Lippmann (and Carr) did; quite the contrary, they felt that the international order had taken a turn in an irreversible direction. For Naumann and Schmitt this new world order was one where no small states, or any states at all, could survive. If we look into the present, which is still a conflict-ridden age, the same challenges of nationalism and disparity of power remain in international relations. Europe has indeed found a way to unite (although it has not eliminated nationalistic sentiments), but for most parts of the world, Lippmann's dream of 'Good Neighbors' remains unattained. I believe Lippmann's ideas are still valid in the present day, and they offer an interesting perspective on spheres of influence, not least because of his emphasis on peace.

In Lippmann's (1945, 138) view, the world order that was forming around regional actors was crucial for world peace. He notes, 'The regional grouping of states in combined strategical systems is, therefore, indispensable to the general security of great and small nations alike, and to the stabilization of the relations among states'. Peace would be determined on the basis of great powers' willingness to rest within their orbits:

> Under the regional principle I am advocating, it would be held to be an overt act of aggression for any state to reach out beyond its own strategical orbit for an alliance with a state in another orbit. Within the same strategical neighbourhood alliances are good: neighbours must and should combine for their common security. But alliances are bad if they disrupt the solidarity of a neighbourhood; they are entangling and interventionist if they bring an alien power into the midst of a neighborhood. (Lippmann 1945, 136–7)

The problem remains, as Keal (1983, 211) notes, that spheres of influence are not stable. If they are not stable, there is not much prospect for peace. Lippmann would allow spheres of influence for all the great powers, which would then act in a concert. Lippmann was nevertheless concerned about whether Russia was willing to keep within its orbit and whether any concert with Russia would guarantee peace. Lippmann still believed that a concert would be the foundation of a new order (Lippmann 1945, 91). And 'concert' meant first and foremost the relationship between the United States and the Soviet Union (132). For Lippmann, a direct war between the two was as impossible as a war between an elephant and a whale – if only the two countries refrained from reaching out for allies within the orbit of the other (134–5). Furthermore, Lippmann considered it possible to solve the emerging ideological disparity between Western democracy and Russian totalitarianism by meeting the Russians as allies and proposing to them that they commit themselves to democratic freedom (150–51). To put the matter in Cold War terms, both superpowers would have their own spheres of influence which would lead to stability and avoid major war. For Lippmann this meant stabilisation of relations among states, both great and small (138). Coming at a time and place such as the United States in the midst of the Cold War, Lippmann's call for partnership was powerful. Reading at the current time and place, a post- Cold War Europe where genuine partnership with Russia is still a dream yet to come true, Lippmann's call sounds topical. In Europe, Germany is perhaps the only country with pragmatic relations based on economic partnership with Russia without the shaming and blaming practice. The United States has failed in the resetting and rebuilding of relations time and again. This is the legacy of the ideological drift between the two worlds.

It was not only Lippmann's concern for peace in general and the rights of small nations in particular that makes him an advocate of the idea of sphere of responsibility. For Bull (2002, 215), the difference between a negative sphere of influence and a positive sphere of influence (or responsibility) is that the negative influence takes the form of expansion while the positive is agreed upon and somehow accepted by the small states. Lippmann tries to make the case that his Good Neighbor Policy is something more acceptable, responsible and based on collaboration than what is traditionally understood in the case of spheres of influence. Lippmann (1945, 87) writes,

> Objections present themselves at once to the views expounded in this book: they are that the world will be divided up into spheres of influence each dominated by a great power, that within these spheres the smaller and the weaker states will come under the influence of the great power, and that the huge constellations of states may become rivals and enemies.

Lippmann explained that the regional groupings had already been formed and that that development should not be prevented. Any hope for stabilising international relations rested on the perfection of these regional groupings

(Lippmann 1945, 188). Disputes, when they emerge, should be settled within the neighbourhood in question without the interference of any outside actors. Lippmann feared a purely regional dispute could escalate into a global dispute if several great powers became involved. For Lippmann, attempts at a global settlement would not guarantee justice any more than success. Failed attempts at global settlement of regional disputes could even result in global war. Licence given to universal intervention means it would be used (189). The Good Neighbor Policy was the remedy to shifting alliances caused by power politics. Lippmann's regionalism tried to prevent these shifting alliances so that each state would recognise that it belonged to only one larger strategic zone of security (190). This would not guarantee that no wars would emerge between the regions, but stabilising the alliances would remove the most provoking forms of interference and intervention, which are a cause of great wars (191). Here one sees Lippmann the pluralist talking: 'In this view of things the horrid antithesis of nationalism and internationalism subsides' (193).

Going back to Roosevelt's original idea of good neighbours, Kimball (1991) explains how there was confusion within the United States about the two approaches to coercion (a sphere of influence) and leadership (Good Neighbor Policy). Kimball writes that '[i]n the immediate, practical sense, the Monroe Doctrine in the era of World War II was a sphere of influence conception that gave the United States self-assigned special "responsibilities" in the Western Hemisphere'. Kimball sees the Good Neighbor Policy, in the end, as having been a reformulation of the Monroe Doctrine based on hegemony and not an equal partnership (123). In the Good Neighbor Policy there remained a dilemma of how to exert influence without the use of power (125). Kimball asks, 'But how are the regional "policemen" to avoid the Orwellian temptation, even necessity of creating a sphere of influence in their region? How is such a region different from a Pax Britannica, a Russian Empire, or a Monroe Doctrine?' (96). For Carr (2001, 215), the Good Neighbor Policy was by no means separated from power: 'The "good neighbour" policy of the United States in Latin America is not the antithesis, but the continuation of "Yankee imperialism"; for it is only the strongest who can both maintain their supremacy and remain "good neighbours"'. Keal (1983, 24) also identified the problem of who would 'police the policemen' in a proposal put forward by President Roosevelt after World War Two for an international order of four policemen. Wight as well warned of the double standards of great powers, which would justify their actions as enforcing peace and security; at the same time, they wish to monopolise while simultaneously monopolising the right to create international conflict (Wight 1995, 42–3). For James Burnham, Lippmann's contemporary, the Good Neighbor Policy was simply a propagandist name and by no means a policy that would guarantee the sovereignty of a great power's neighbours. Burnham (1941, 263) strongly argued that the Good Neighbor Policy meant 'the *de facto* elimination of independent sovereignty in all nations and colonies of the area except the United States, and thus the creation of a single interrelated territory so far as *de facto* political sovereignty goes'.

A critical look at Lippmann's vision of the great regional constellations shows that it attempts to come to terms with the aspect of power politics in constructing regional constellations but it cannot be seen as a serious alternative to the proposals put forward by Naumann, Schmitt or Carr. There is an emphasis on protecting the small states and maintaining world peace, but that is not unique to Lippmann's proposal. Rather, the Good Neighbor Policy is an attempt to justify, in more acceptable words than sphere of influence, *Großraum* or super-state, the emerging order of great power management. Yet, Lippmann was more optimistic and specific in describing the relationship between the great powers as one which would be based on collaboration and acceptance of the limits of influence. He even believed that democracy, which Russia should also be persuaded to embrace, could be the prevailing ideology in international relations.

4.6   George Orwell and the Totalitarian Super-states

George Orwell[9] (1903–1950), was a well-known English novelist and journalist.[10] In addition to novels such as *Animal Farm* and *Nineteen Eighty-Four*, he left behind a body of diary entries, essays and newspaper journalism. Orwell died at the age of 46 of tuberculosis, leaving us to wonder at what he might have written during the years of the Cold War if he had not passed away. Even though Orwell did not live to witness the emergence of the international system that he himself foresaw, his input into the history of spheres of influence is significant.

It comes as no surprise to anyone who has read Orwell's works that his novels were politically motivated. Orwell himself was passionate about political developments to such an extent that he volunteered to fight in the Spanish Civil War in 1937. Paul Anderson (2006, 28) describes Orwell's political orientation as an engagement with the 'dissident anti-Stalinist revolutionary socialist left that was obsessed with the degeneration of the Bolshevik revolution'. Furthermore, Anderson (2006, 32) writes that Orwell wanted to see democratic socialism as the prevailing form of political organisation and saw this threatened by Stalin's carving out a sphere of influence. It was the future of the state, post-war Europe, democracy and the common people that Orwell passionately debated. He could not avoid the topic of spheres of influence, for they loomed on both sides of his home country.

Orwell wrote from his sense of justice, mixing propaganda with prose style. Orwell fused political purpose with artistic purpose, making his voice far more widely heard among people than any political scientist or commentator. Even though Orwell's work is not focused on spheres of influence, the powerful images of the super-states in *Nineteen Eighty-Four* must have made an impression on readers, thus contributing to our understanding of spheres of influence. In *Nineteen Eighty-Four,* which Orwell finished in 1948, we find the antithesis to the spheres

---

9   Orwell's real name was Eric Arthur Blair.

10   See Newsinger (1999) on Orwell's life and political thought.

of influence which would save political plurality, prevent war and create a new functioning international order. This was *a totalitarian sphere of influence*. It is Orwell who describes a world based on spheres of influence in its most oppressing and cruel form.[11] Orwell focuses on the totalitarian system that Winston Smith witnessed in London. In the novel, one can also see and, perhaps even more, sense the international system that is the context for Mr Smith's experiences. Orwell's fictional world consists of three super-states – Oceania, Eurasia and Eastasia – which are constantly at war with each other. One is always allied with the other, with the third party being the enemy. Russia, which has absorbed Europe, forms Eurasia, and the United States, which has absorbed the British Empire, forms Oceania. Eastasia consist of China, Japan and fluctuating parts of Manchuria, Mongolia and Tibet. Orwell (2000, 859) calls these super-states separate universes where 'almost any perversion of thought can safely be practised'. The borders are not stable but 'the balance of power always remains roughly even, and the territory which forms the heartland of each super-state always remains inviolate' (854). Fighting occurs in some distant disputed areas but there is never any attempt to invade enemy territory (855). It sounds like the super-state system promotes stability and, in fact, some sort of peace for the masses.

For Naumann the acceptance of citizens and their loyalty to the great state was crucial, likewise Lippmann envisioned international influence as responsible foreign policy, not something that would lead to totalitarianism. What makes Orwell's fiction the antithesis of, say, Lippmann's sphere of responsibility is the crucial difference of motive. Where Lippmann's sphere of influence is designed to prevent war, Orwell's fictional world-system is in place to maintain war. In *Nineteen Eighty-Four*, war is the means to control people by fear and hatred, and thus it is needed for the sake of the order. Peace is not desired in a system which is based on total control of the people. Particularly illustrative of this mindset is the motto of 'the Party' of Oceania: 'War is Peace'. Wars are not meant to be won but instead they maintain a balance of power and prevent conquest by any world empire. In fact, in some ways war between the super-states is peace in much the same sense as the peace which the non-prosaic visionaries hoped super-states would create:

> War, however, is no longer the desperate, annihilating struggle it was in the early decades of the twentieth century. It is a warfare of limited aims between combatants who are unable to destroy one another, have no material cause for fighting and are not divided by any genuine ideological difference. (Orwell 2000, 854)

This world is actually not so different from Schmitt's and the others' international order, except for the emphasis on the perverse effects of

---

11   See 'Chapter III: War is Peace' in *Nineteen Eighty-Four* (2000), where Orwell explores the system of super-states.

totalitarianism. The existence of super-states, even in a constant state of war, limits conflicts and maintains international order. Yet, the relevance of Orwell's novel lies in the gloomy image of spheres of influence it conveys. I have argued that we need to transform this pejorative orientation into a normative debate and for this reason I have sought to bring forth arguments *for* spheres of influence. But we also need to acknowledge arguments *against* spheres of influence and Orwell provides one: spheres of influence which create and perpetuate injustice, repression and violence. Orwell's construction of a system of super-states works as a warning story of great power order gone badly awry.

Less well-known than *Nineteen Eighty-Four* are Orwell's columns. During the period 1943–1947, Orwell wrote a weekly column to the *Tribune* (with a gap of 21 months while he worked as a war correspondent to the *Observer*) (Anderson 2006, 2). These columns included Orwell's insights into the logic of spheres of influence. Orwell's inspiration for portraying the world of super-states came from Burnham's *The Managerial Revolution* published in 1941 (see Newsinger 1999, 106–7). Orwell (1946) summarises in an essay on Burnham's thinking the essence of *The Managerial Revolution*:

> The new 'managerial' societies will not consist of a patchwork of small, independent states, but of great super-states grouped round the main industrial centres in Europe, Asia, and America. These super-states will fight among themselves for possession of the remaining unclaimed portions of the earth, but will probably be unable to conquer one another completely.[12]

Even though Orwell in many ways refutes Burnham's predictions on the new world order, he endorsed the prediction of the weakening of the small and the increasing power of the great. The threat of 'the totalitarian super-states world order' was not fictional, but very concrete for Orwell. He (2006b, 2006c) wrote in *The Tribune* on 2 February and 19 October 1945 that the world was indeed splitting up into two or three super-states, or great empires, just as Burnham predicted. In 'As I Please 7', written in 1944, Orwell (2006a) argued, again referring to Burnham that Britain was decadent and bound to be rapidly conquered by Germany. After the conquest of Britain would come the attack on the USSR and Russia's 'military weakness' would cause her to 'fall apart to east and west'. Orwell writes, 'You are then left with three great super-states, Germany, Japan and the USA, which divide the world between them, make ceaseless war upon one another, and keep the working class in permanent subjection' (85).

In his columns Orwell describes international order in the same manner as in his novel, saying that states will be at permanent war with each other but the war will not be very intensive or bloody. He sees these super-states, which are ruled by

---

12   Later Burnham (1947) discarded his visions of super-states and opted for an American world empire, a *democratic world order* as he prophetically coined it, because of the dangers of the atomic weapon and the universalist ambitions of the Soviet Union.

a self-elected oligarchy, as cut off from each other, self-sufficient and in no need of trading with each other (Orwell 2006b, 240; 2006c, 249). Orwell (2006b, 240) writes:

> If these two or three super-states do establish themselves, not only will each of them be too big to be conquered, but they will be under no necessity to trade with one another, and in a position to prevent all contact between their nationals. Already, for a dozen years or so, large areas of the earth have been cut off from one another, although technically at peace.

Orwell foresaw what was to come after the war: the Iron Curtain. Two super-states embraced the world order of preventing interconnectedness as much as possible. This was not the prospect that other visionaries of spheres of influence portrayed. Quite the opposite: at the core of spheres of influence lay the ideal of great powers managing international relations in concert. The super-states were indeed expected to keep away from each other's spheres of influence; but not to isolate themselves economically or culturally. *International society* would prevail in a system of spheres of influence as much as in a system of nation-states. For Carr and Lippmann new regionalism, *Großräume* or the Good Neighbor Policy was to be built on great power management. For Bull and Keal spheres of influence similarly operated as a means to manage relations among the great powers not as a means to divide the world into disconnected entities. Again, Orwell expresses the legitimate concern that the super-states would become hostile towards each other, in which case unification could indeed still promote political plurality but would no longer promote peace in the true sense. According to Orwell's prophecy, something fundamental would happen to international society; it was as if it would split in pieces and lose its global character. Only two suzerain powers would remain. If we think about international order, this kind of development would be an even more drastic new *nomos* than that which Schmitt described. The scary truth which lies within Orwell's fiction is that the world witnessed the emergence of two separate, antagonistic super-states; one of which exhibited totalitarian features after the Second World War, and has not yet fully recovered from it.

Although Orwell sides with Burnham in predicting the division of world into super-states, he criticises 'that school of thought' for its contempt for the common person and ignorance of the strength of democracy – its power of criticism (Orwell 2006a, 85). For Orwell, the sphere of influence of a super-state presupposed a totalitarian system. He does not see super-states as capable of offering respect for the common person, or of upholding truth, and thus upholding democracy. Orwell is explicit about the impossibility of incorporating international influence of the super-state with democratic government. Super-states simply cannot be democratically governed, and thus they cannot pursue any good. This is the view that still persists today. Perhaps this, coupled with our bad memories of the Cold War, is one of the reasons why we are so afraid of spheres of influence in the present. Orwell himself believed in the possibility of the all-mighty super-states and their totalitarian nature. Orwell's account is an image of Cold War spheres of influence as comprised of super-states or great empires which are totalitarian by nature, possess the atom bomb, are self-contained and which maintain 'peace that is not peace' (Orwell 2006c, 249).

4.7 The Shared Concern

According to Luoma-aho (2007, 52):

> Schmitt was quite possibly the first theorist of international law and international relations to articulate what exactly happened when President Monroe gave his seventh annual address to the United States Congress, and what had really begun almost a decade before in the Congress of Vienna: the dismantling of the Peace of Westphalia.

Perhaps Schmitt was the first, but he certainly was not the only one. The common concern for the majority of these thinkers was the need to solve the problem of nationalism as the cause of major wars. If this was not an openly stated goal, the idea of breaking national boundaries – willingly or by force – and connecting peoples, was.

All the theorists presented here were interested in international order, not simply the fate of their own state. Essentially all shared Schmitt's concern for universalism. Orwell was less occupied with political plurality than with political freedom. Lippmann and Carr put more emphasis on the prevention of major wars than their German counterparts, but Schmitt and Naumann both sought a peaceful world. For Lippmann and Naumann alike, non-forceful unification was a necessity, because people needed to accept the new political units. Schmitt was more concerned with the concept of *nomos*, and was not specific regarding the details of the actual unification. Carr's concern was also war and order: he declared the end of small states and dreamt of a British *Großraum*. Some were more concerned with matters of peace than others, but all attempted to paint a picture of some sort of super-states which would be the actors in the future international order. The predictions, or fears, came true in the form of the super-states of United States and the Soviet Union; although not in the way the scholars had perhaps hoped. In fact, Schmitt's and Naumann's fear was actualised: Germany lost the war and its position as a great power. Carr's England did not succeed in becoming a pole of power either.

Naumann, Schmitt, Carr, Lippmann, and Orwell relied on the idea of a balance of power when explicating international order. On the one hand, the balancing system is seen as the core problem and, on the other, as the ultimate solution. Schmitt based his ideal world on the idea of a balance of power: balance meant pluralism and 'no balance', universalism. For Schmitt, the necessity of spheres of influence as the basis of the new system of balance lay in the fact that the system was becoming that of two balancers with universalist ambitions. Either of them could gain too much power, turning the world into a single empire unless a third force was found. Initiated by the Monroe Doctrine, the development was towards *Großräume*, or balance through spheres of influence. There could be no balance of power within the past system of states. Carr found balance in regionalism, which he situated between the bankruptcy of nationalism and empty internationalism.

Roosevelt and Lippmann were concerned that small states could abuse balance-of-power politics. In a sense, they saw a balance of power as working just like Butterfield (1966, 142–5) described when he argued that it gave small states room to manoeuvre. Lippmann set the idea of balance of power against that of a Good Neighbor Policy. The former resulted in war, while the latter in order. For Lippmann, a balance of power, as it allowed the small states 'run around free', was the source of disorder and war; by putting small states on a leash with the Good Neighbour Policy, war could be avoided. Thus for Lippmann the argument goes that the system of 'responsible spheres of influence' was an alternative to a balance of power. In the end, Lippmann is simply proposing a balance-of-power system based on his idea of good neighbours, and not a system that lacks a mechanism for maintaining a balance of power.

In Orwell's fantasy-world of *Nineteen Eighty-Four*, a constant state of war enforced by a totalitarian government was a means to achieve a balance of power among the super-states. Orwell's warning is powerful in all its extremity, because it is based on the perspective of an individual. It lacks the nationalistic perspective of wanting to make one's own state the model super-state. It is a story of how the super-state are all corrupt and rotten. The system is rotten from the inside and the international order is based on the perverse equating of war with peace. Orwell lacks a general perspective on sovereignty, the role of small states and the development of international order. Yet, by the same token, he is not confined to the map metaphor, but focuses instead on the nature of the influencing state. The significance of *Nineteen Eighty-Four* derives from the fact that its popularity is based on something quite different compared to any theory of international politics. *Nineteen Eighty-Four* was made into a movie and references to Orwell's imaginary world in popular culture are frequent (see Wikipedia on George Orwell). Even if extreme totalitarianism is the prominent theme of *Nineteen Eighty-Four*, the super-state system is the context for the emergence of 'doublethink' and 'Big Brother'. Thus, Orwell's writings, and especially his prose, are known to people not educated in International Relations, and have a much wider audience. Clearly, Orwell's sphere of influence represents cruelty and injustice at their utmost, complying with and reinforcing the pejorative associations of the concept today.

Another common line of thought – sometimes overt, sometimes more hidden – is that the *normality* or *necessity* of power is what justifies spheres of influence. It is not an abnormality that an inequality of power emerges, if it is seen as a part of the social life and functioning of international relations. In fact, spheres of influence prevent tyranny and the disappearance of *the political* – pluralism

– from the international arena, by dividing power according to the principle of balance of power in a new form. The nation-states in Europe failed to achieve a balance of power among themselves; war eventually prevailed. Nationalism urged states to take up arms. Thus, something bigger than the nation-state was needed as the seat of power, although such bigger entities also ran the risk of ending up either as world tyrannies or engaged in major wars with each other. But as the nation-state system was in crisis, and the world was already moving in the direction of a world empire or world government, spheres of influence, super-states or *Großräume* offered a solution in between the two other options. Power seemed to be the basis of all the international systems in sight, since humanity was too divided for a solidarist society to emerge on its own. Even Lippmann, who wanted to cut power out of the equation, could not fully escape the fact that even in the Good Neighbor Policy, sovereignty would not be the same for all.

The conceptualisations of super-states and *Großräume* offer important insights as regards the justice and injustice of spheres of influence. In general, for the theorists presented here, justice was not a top priority, and inequality of power was a fact of political life. Justice in the super-state was not a choice as such; it was more a question of convincing the influenced states that they needed to unite under the power of the centre in order to survive. Thus, justice was instrumental, and not a value. Bull and Keal discussed the justice of spheres of influence in the context of the system of states, not challenging the premises of that system; whereas Naumann, Schmitt, Carr, Lippmann and Orwell proceeded from the view that there could be no system of states based on sovereign equality anymore. Even so, the rights of influenced states were a concern, because super-states could not be built by force. Thus, Naumann, Carr and Lippmann expressed sympathy for influenced states and wrote of the importance of small states' acceptance of being dominated.

But, as small states still existed, as the system was only on the verge of destruction, the proponents of a new system needed to justify the systematic injustice that would emerge with it. For Naumann, Schmitt and Carr, unification was a necessity. Schmitt's focus was on the universalist threat, and Carr's was on the problems of both nationalism and internationalism. Naumann, like Schmitt, was worried about the future of the German state, and Carr was concerned about the future of Britain. For Lippmann, it was the good-natured approach that made spheres of influence look like they would benefit all parties involved. Orwell, by contrast, could not find justification for the super-states which came with totalitarianism, and resulted in 'brain death' for the human beings who were subjects of the system. For Lippmann, since the United States was a democracy, its rule was just, and non-democratic states simply needed to be converted. Orwell was concerned for the fate of the common people inhabiting the super-states. Naumann and Carr alike expressed sympathy for the people. Naumann insisted on voluntary unification and saw Mid-Europe as a brotherhood of nations. Carr, with all his realism, thought that the foundation of international order lay in improving people's living conditions. I think that when it comes to the normative dimension of spheres of influence, it is precisely the human perspective that we are lacking. I will return to this topic in the concluding chapter.

Naumann, Schmitt, Carr, Lippmann and Orwell all used different terms to describe their visions of regional solidarism. Even though the actual term *sphere of influence* appears rather infrequently within the literature of the period, knowledge on the term was available already at the time since it was used in the context of describing colonial influence. One possible reason for not using the term *sphere of influence* could, indeed, be its association with colonial practices and the need to find new terminology. Lippmann's case is clear: he wants to defend influence with a term which has no negative overtones, and this could very well be the reason why others avoid the concept as well. Schmitt's reference to spheres of influence also attests to his equalling them somewhat to his conception of *Großräume*. But the lack of use of the term does not mean that the theorists were not writing about spheres of influence. I argue that the grand designs during the period of the world wars, based as they were on the connection between influence, international order and justice, strongly relate to the idea of sphere of influence. Geostrategy does not reach these far corners of the ambit of the concept; and empire lite, regionalism and integration do not have the history and centrality that the concept has within the vocabulary of the discipline. I am opening up the criteria – or the terms of discourse, as Connolly (1993) would put it – for an appraisal which can incorporate the normative dimension and questions of order into what at present remains an uncontested concept. What I envision, based on the history of thought presented above, is a sphere of influence situated between nation and humanity.

For a history of spheres of influence, the period of the world wars offers an untapped pool of ideas. Whereas the Cold War practices such as those seen in the Cuban Missile Crisis, are currently connected with the concept of sphere of influence, the discussion on the concentration of sovereignty and the possible benefits and drawbacks of creating super-states are not. Schmitt's ideas are perhaps the best known, but no serious thought is given to his or to others' visions on spheres of influence. At present, the international system is in a state of confusion about the principle of state sovereignty, unification of states, inequality and balance of power; giving all the more reason to look into the past, where confusion and uncertainty resulted in theories on spheres of influence.

Chapter 5
The Burden of the Cold War

The historical memory of spheres of influence points strongly to the era which started after the Second World War and ended in early 1990s. When we think of spheres of influence we remember the divisions, the superpowers and their blocs, the ideological battle, and the Cuban Missile Crisis; and we remember how Russia lost its sphere of influence and the United States could freely pursue its universalist ambitions. The purpose of this chapter is not to tell the story of Cold War spheres of influence in its entirety or even comprehensively; it is to raise questions on Cold War spheres of influence by discussing them on the conceptual level. Examples from the Cold War have already been illustrated in the chapters on the English School, and the historical setting is clearly visible in the School's work, but this chapter goes into the period in more detail. The purpose of this chapter is twofold:

1. To look at the conceptual insights of Keal, Kaufman and Vincent, as well as Bull, on the consolidation of spheres of influence with means such as interventions. Keal and Kaufman offer perspectives on the formality and legitimacy of influence, which help to problematise the current pejorative associations of the concept.
2. In order to reflect on actual Cold War practices, I present the Cuban Missile Crisis as an example of a collision of spheres of influence. Again Keal and Kaufman provide much of the material because of their theoretical focus, but as discourses of justification, speeches of Kennedy and Khrushchev are explored as well.

In its simplicity, the Cold War understanding of a sphere of influence is that of a foreign policy aimed at controlling smaller states for the sake of position, prestige and the balance of power. It is influence for its own sake: any increase in the quality and quantity of influence is that much influence taken away from the rival power. Spheres of influence were interpreted through 'imperialist geopolitics' and a realist worldview. They implied not only an ideological divide but also military superiority or inferiority and resources for prosperity. Looking more closely at the Cold War reveals that fundamentally, despite the realist power calculations, spheres of influence were an aspect of international order: the threat of universalism if the balance of power should fail, great power management, questions of sovereignty and intervention, tacit understandings, stability of possessions, and even considerations of justice. Yet, we lack theoretical studies on Cold War spheres of influence, just like we lack interest in the relationship between spheres of influence and international institutions after the Cold War.

The Cold War made spheres of influence visible; the world became the battlefield of superpowers' military, political, cultural and economic influence. The result was that the Cold War manifestations of influence ended up overshadowing the earlier history of spheres of influence. Hence, the concept of sphere of influence came to be understood in the meaning ascribed to it during the Cold War. What is wrong then with associating the concept of sphere of influence with the Cold War? First, it is problematic to use the concept without contesting it, as I have argued throughout the study. Second, it is problematic to rely on an understanding of spheres of influence that is based on the history of the Cold War without first contesting the interpretations of that history. Given our lack of knowledge and interest in the conceptualisations of the phenomenon, what do we really know about the Cold War spheres of influence? Third, the problem of transposing Cold War images into the present is that the Soviet Union and the Berlin Wall no longer exists. Even without drama such as that seen at the end of the Cold War, the world is being transformed all the time. States change; their relations change; new states appear; and some old states disappear. Even if the institutions of the society of states stand rather firm, they, too, are under pressure whenever a new order emerges. Thus we should constantly renew our knowledge of what constitutes a sphere of influence, as long as people continue to use the concept and it captures something essential about territorial influence. We are better equipped to do this when we study our history.

5.1   Consolidating Spheres of Influence

According to Keal, after the war, in 1941, the Allies (the United States, Britain and the Soviet Union) approved the Atlantic Charter, which denied a right to aggrandisement or territorial changes against the wishes of the people concerned and gave sovereign rights and self-government to those who had been deprived of them (Keal 1983, 65–6). Against the spirit of the Charter, spheres of influence crept into international practices and became a legacy of the war (66). At first, spheres of influence were determined by the occupation of specific regions. Where the Soviets were present, the Western powers stayed away and vice versa. The Soviet Union stayed out of the affairs of Italy and Greece, and the United States and Britain out of Romania, Bulgaria and Hungary (84–6). This is how spheres of influence worked as the 'exclusion of other powers', to cite Keal's definition.

Keal (1983, 80) continues explaining the consolidation of Cold War spheres of influence which began already in 1939 when the Soviet Union signed the non-aggression pact with Germany, which included a secret protocol dividing Eastern Europe into spheres of influence. For Keal, Stalin's hegemony over Central East Europe was '[…] not compatible with the principles of the Atlantic Charter and was bound to bring the United States and the Soviet Union into conflict' (84). The Soviet Union's consolidation of its sphere of influence is a rather unpleasant memory for Europe, and it is not surprising in this perspective that the pejorative image persists.

Keal writes that the United States opposed a Soviet sphere of influence in Eastern Europe but that through its actions and inactions it in fact allowed it (Keal 1983, 93; also Davis 1974, 170). In fear of its rival's further expansion, the United States did not want to recognise the Soviet sphere of influence but did nothing in practice to oppose it (Keal 1983; 94, 96). As the Soviet influence became more and more overt towards the end of 1945, the United States started to act according to the principle of balance of power (97–8). On 12 March 1947, President Truman asked Congress for aid to Greece and Turkey to resist Soviet pressure. This became known as the Truman Doctrine (see also Vincent 1974, 188–93). Keal writes:

> Most of the states in eastern Europe already had a communist government and 'way of life' and the region had been privately acknowledged by United States officials as a Soviet sphere of influence. In effect the speech drew a line between these states and those where Soviet influence was not established. It was a formal declaration that the United States would resist any extension of the Soviet sphere of influence beyond its existing limits. As such it marked a resignation on America's part that eastern Europe was a Soviet sphere of influence. (Keal 1983, 99)

Other steps taking the United States closer to consolidating its respective sphere of influence were the recommendation for a collective defence in North America and Western Europe, strengthening regional order in Latin America and treating Soviet influence in Eastern Europe as irreversible (Keal 1983, 101). Behind the Marshall Aid Plan (1947) was an idea that economic support to Western Europe would diminish the conditions for Communism to spread (101–2). In other words, it was an attempt to prevent Soviet influence from spreading westwards (102). This was, of course, against Soviet interests. Keal observes, 'The Marshall Plan provoked the Soviet Union to further consolidation and the extent of Soviet influence was made clear by Poland, Czechoslovakia and Finland, all of which would have preferred to have participated in the plan, declining to do so' (107). In addition to preventing Czechoslovakia and Poland from joining the plan, the Soviet Union consolidated its sphere of influence through a pro-communist coup in Czechoslovakia in February 1948 (104–5). Here Keal is explaining the practice of how the superpowers took control of the territories of the globe: dividing them, excluding each other, at times challenging one another while at others accepting one another's influence, and accepting this as the post-war international order. The idea of inaction as an acknowledgement of a sphere of influence is interesting and I have referred to it earlier in the context of intervention (Chapter 3.3). This means that Cold War spheres of influence were established as a mixture of extending influence, finding the territorial limits of that influence, and abstaining from interference, intervention and other involvement.

For Keal and Kaufman, the Cold War represents a consolidation of spheres of influence, making them a *normal* practice of international relations. Kaufman (1976, 195) describes the 'decisive presence' of the Soviet Union in Eastern Europe and the United States in Latin America as a normal state of affairs. He (1976, 28) observes, 'All the countries located in the two spheres of influence have suffered from penetration by the superpowers to varying degrees. In some cases, the intervention has been permanent with annexation being the final solution'. In the same vein, Keal (1983, 104) states, 'Thus, the lines were drawn: what had been going on since before the end of the war was now explicit and open'. The openness and normality of the two spheres of influence is the reason why we associate spheres of influence with the Cold War. To invoke the term 'sphere of influence' in the present is to evoke not the *Großraum*, Mid-Europe, super-state, Good Neighbor Policy or the Great Responsibles, but the ideological hegemonic ambitions of the Soviet Union and, to a much lesser extent, the United States.

5.2   Interventionist Policies

When we look at Keal's, Kaufman's and Vincent's accounts of Cold War superpower relations, we find not only the concept of sphere of influence but also intervention, the Monroe Doctrine, universalism and the Good Neighbor Policy. All the way from Naumann to Keal and the English School, from 1915 towards the end of the Cold War the same themes attend the idea of a sphere of influence. Thus, the clarity that related notions bring to the concept of sphere of influence is not only the legacy of the period of the world wars, but also of the Cold War.

When Keal explains how spheres of influence became the normal state of affairs, in the case of the United States, he refers to the Good Neighbor Policy and the Monroe Doctrine. According to Keal, the United States' vision of the post-war order was that of universalism. World affairs would not be governed by spheres of influence and a balance of power but by international cooperation and organisation. Roosevelt was opposed to colonialism and power politics, and supported the self-determination of peoples (Keal 1983, 67). According to Keal, the United States argued that spheres of influence belonged to power politics, which was not the way to a lasting peace (69).[1] He goes on to note, 'In place of power politics there would be collective security under the control of a universal organization' (70). According to Keal, Roosevelt saw great power 'policemen' acting as good neighbours (rather than as 'influencing powers') in the interests

---

1   Lynn Davis wrote in 1974 that throughout the war the United States was against spheres of influence, the tradition that had caused the outbreak of the war in the first place. For the United States achieving peace required a collective security organisation. Davis notes that American officials never saw the Monroe Doctrine or United States' relations to Latin American states as analogous to Soviet or British influence in Europe, which they so feared (Davis 1974; 141, 143).

of world community with the explicit approval of other great powers (71). Thus, officially, the United States opposed spheres of influence despite some dissident officials who favoured them (71–2). Kaufman (1976, 181), too, examined the Good Neighbor Policy, and remarked how the Monroe Doctrine became more acceptable in Latin America as a result of Roosevelt's approach:

> It is important to note that the greatest progress towards the acceptance of the Monroe Doctrine on a continental basis was made during F.D. Roosevelt's 'good neighbour' policy, committing Washington to refrain from military intervention in the Southern Republics. During the years 1933–65 no direct military intervention took place in the region.

Even though Kaufman writes that the United States refrained from military intervention, Keal's insight is that, in the end, Roosevelt's vision of world order was not too different from one with spheres of influence and great power management. The role of weaker states in this system of collective security was very much like that within a sphere of influence (Keal 1983, 70). What Keal implies is that a sphere of influence can have different names but in the end it involves the same conduct. In other words, if a foreign policy practice falls within the definition of a sphere of influence, then regardless of the name given to it, it is still a sphere-of-influence policy. The terms used to describe a particular form of conduct may then signify a difference between accepted and deprecated policy. Thus, for Roosevelt the term 'policemen' signified an acceptable policy, whereas 'spheres of influence' were disapproved of. What we are broaching here is the question of how to make influence acceptable. The Good Neighbor Policy is not necessarily a policy designed to thwart spheres of influence, but one establishing a sphere of influence by disapproving of intervention, thus 'selling' the position of being influenced more easily.

Cold War spheres of influence are inevitably related to interventions. Vincent (1976, 107–12) discusses the fluctuations in United States' interventionist and non-interventionist interpretations of the Monroe Doctrine, where the element of legitimacy appears again. According to Vincent, the American approach to Latin America until 1918 was interventionist, but at the Inter-American Conference in Buenos Aires in 1936 a protocol of non-intervention was signed (113). He writes:

> What was remarkable was that the United States should bind herself by treaty to the observation of an apparently absolute rule of nonintervention, allowing none of the exceptions with which she had increasingly indulged herself. By signing and ratifying such a protocol, it seemed that the United States had finally succumbed to the Latin American doctrine of nonintervention. (Vincent 1974, 113)

Before 1936 the United States had resisted the call of Latin American countries to adopt the principle of non-intervention in their mutual relations, but here 'Franklin Roosevelt's Good Neighbor policy had extended to the international legal relations of the American States' (Vincent 1974, 115). This was influence without intervention, making influence more acceptable, and in Vincent's estimation transposing non-intervention from a principle to a term in a treaty was quite remarkable. However, this tendency of American foreign policy was short-lived. Vincent explains how already before the Second World War hemispheric solidarity was becoming the foundation of relations between the United States and Latin America. Especially after Communism entered the hemisphere, the Monroe Doctrine became accepted as a guiding principle for the hemisphere (193). Where the original Monroe Doctrine opposed the old European order extending to the Western Hemisphere, the Cold War transformed the Doctrine into one opposing Communism, at the same time broadening the idea of extrahemispheric intervention and counter-intervention against it (208). Vincent also interprets the Truman Doctrine as an extension of the Monroe Doctrine (the exclusion of the old European order) into a worldwide doctrine of counter-intervention (193). This meant the extension of influence from the regional to the global level. Here Vincent is pointing to the transformation of the United States' policy from non-intervention to a sphere-of-influence policy firmly founded upon interventionism. He thus establishes the connection between Cold War spheres of influence and the policy of intervention.

It seems that the capacity for and use of intervention came to define much of the relations between the influencing and the influenced powers during the Cold War, again adding to the present pejorative interpretation of *sphere of influence* and taking us further away from the justifications of influence. Both Keal (1983, 141–3) and Kaufman (1976, 29–30) mention the Johnson Doctrine as the interventionist principle establishing the United States sphere of influence in Latin America. The United States intervened in the Dominican Republic in 1965 after internal power struggles in that country. This the United States saw as a threat to the inter-American system and peace in the hemisphere (Keal 1983, 141). President Johnson claimed there were outside agents, that is, communists, trying to seize control and this prompted the United States to announce its position, which became known as the Johnson Doctrine (142). The United States first argued that the intervention was conducted in order to protect Americans living in the Dominican Republic, but the justification was soon extended to include responsibility for law and order in the country, preventing the spread of international communism and, ultimately, protection of the hemisphere (Keal 1983, 142; Vincent 1974, 202–4). But if intervention became characteristic of the United States' influence, both regionally and globally, how could it be justified? We can try to answer that question from the Soviet perspective by invoking the idea of structural intervention.

The case for justifying intervention is found in Windsor's (1984, 54–5) notion of structural intervention. Reading from Vincent, the Soviet Union's internationalism was a form of structural intervention in which the nation-state was downplayed to an extent where intervention was considered an internal conflict. Vincent (1974, 146–7) observes that after the Russian Revolution there was no room for the norm of non-intervention, because Russia had substituted class for nation and imperialist war for civil war. In Cold War terms, Russia had formed its sphere of influence, a realm where intervention was normal and acceptable. The establishment of the Communist International (Comintern) in March 1919, and its strengthening in 1920 made respect for national self-determination all the more insignificant for Soviet Russia (Vincent 1974, 152–3). Conversely, in Soviet relations with Asia, national freedom was declared as a means to counteract imperialist oppression (153–4). Vincent writes, 'It is possible to establish this dualism as a theme of Soviet foreign policy between the two wars containing a revolutionary motif which led to interference with the affairs of other states and a motif of accommodation which proclaimed noninterference at the formal diplomatic level' (155). Here we see the unease over the principle of non-intervention which Russia had yet to overcome: simultaneous upholding and violating of the principle of non-intervention. A present-day example is found in Russia's fiercely resisting intervention in principle – seen in its opposing the interventionism of the United States – yet resorting to intervention in South Ossetia in 2008.

According to Vincent (1974, 184–5), non-intervention as a legal principle was defended by the Soviet Union but was superseded by interests derived from socialist internationalism. Moreover, adherence to the principle of non-intervention did not prevent the Soviet Union offering support for national liberation movements by invoking the Soviet idea of sovereignty, which recognised the right to self-determination of each nation irrespective of its statehood or lack of it (185). For Vincent, it was the Brezhnev Doctrine justifying Soviet invasion in Czechoslovakia, as outlined by S. Kovalev in a *Pravda* article in 26 September 1968[2], which established the policy of structural intervention (177–8). Vincent describes the Soviet Union's discursive strategy as one turning the matter of sovereignty upside down: by interfering in Czechoslovakia, the Soviet Union in fact claimed it had upheld the country's sovereignty against internal and external counterrevolution, and had by no means violated it (178). Thus, the Soviet Union's actions were only protective and defensive. Hence, intervention which becomes so well established as to lead to certain degree of legitimacy acknowledged by other great powers is justified by a power relation that seems evident, natural and too strong to be challenged from without. When this legitimacy, derived from 'structural intervention' or the establishment of a sphere of influence that no other great power challenges, is coupled with the rhetoric of upholding the sovereignty or the rights of the people of the country intervened in, we have the elements which made Cold War interventions possible and even acceptable. The interconnectedness of spheres of influence and intervention becomes all the more clear.

Thus far we have established the narrative of consolidating spheres of influence. The United States turned its back on non-intervention and the Soviet Union had already established its interventionist sphere of influence policy in the Molotov-Ribbentrop Pact. If adherence to the non-intervention principle of the United

---

2 Brezhnev restated the 'doctrine' in a speech at the Fifth Congress of the Polish United Workers' Party on 13 November 1968.

States made the Monroe Doctrine and spheres of influence more acceptable, what happened when non-intervention was abandoned? The answer on the part of the Soviet Union was to establish intervention as the state of affairs – structural and permanent intervention, which, as the argument goes, is no longer intervention. For the United States in turn, legalising influence through treaties offered a means to consolidate intervention as a part of its sphere-of-influence policy.

5.3   De Facto or de Jure Influence?

Keal devoted pages to explaining how spheres of influence were agreed upon. His conclusion was that the interventions (in Hungary, Czechoslovakia, the Dominican Republic and Cuba) during the Cold War and the conspicuous lack of reaction to these by the rival superpower testify to *the tacit understanding* of spheres of influence (Keal 1983, 154). According to Keal, tacit understanding 'stems from perceived common interests and it is achieved through unilateral acts or the conspicuous absence of certain acts together with the response or lack of response to those acts' (151). Keal further explains that post-war spheres of influence were unilaterally consolidated but at the same time required implicit, by no means open, acquiescence from the other party (114). For Bull (2002, 216) as well, understandings relating to spheres of influence were not formal or drafted in a treaty but based on reciprocal declarations of policy or 'behaviour of the parties which is *as if* in conformity with a rule, even though that rule is not agreed, not enunciated nor even fully understood'. In addition, Bull claims there was no 'free hand' given to the other superpower, but rather the United States and the Soviet Union had an interest in and maintained contact with the other's sphere of influence (217).

Kaufman points out how there is *de facto* recognition of the superiority of one's rival in the respective sphere of influence; condemnation is only verbal. He notes how world peace was more important than the goal of liberating the oppressed countries from their ideological opponent, referring to what Keal deemed the contribution of spheres of influence to international order (see Chapter 2.6). Kaufman also indicates that there was an understanding if not mutual agreement on spheres of influence. He calls this 'legitimacy by omission', 'tacit acceptance' or 'indirect compliance' with the superpowers' right to protect their spheres of influence (Kaufman 1976, 21–4). For Kaufman the 'decisive presence' of the Soviet Union in Eastern Europe and of the United States in Latin America was a normal state of affairs (195). *De facto* influence and tacitness are not, however, the whole story. I have already pointed to the ideas of the normality of spheres of influence, structural intervention, acceptance, and treaties on non-intervention, all of which indicate the prospect of formalising and legitimising spheres of influence.

When writing about colonialism, I introduced Kaufman's idea of *de facto* and *de jure* spheres of influence, and pointed out how Kaufman interprets the former as a sphere of direct influence. Kaufman's (1976, 10–11) sets out to argue that a sphere of influence is a product of the Cold War and is characterised by informality and geographical proximity.[3] He goes on to put forward the idea of separating *de jure* and *de facto* also in the Cold War period. This means that during the Cold War there was also influence which was more formally, not only tacitly, agreed upon. Keal makes the interesting remark that the Soviet Union had *de facto predominance* in Eastern Europe while the United States managed to create predominance by a *juridical framework* in Latin America. Keal (1983, 114) writes, 'The nature of the influence it exerted was not of the same kind as the Soviet Union exerted in eastern Europe, and the United States was able to establish its predominance, to some extent, through a formal institutional framework'.

Kaufman's (1976, 179) argument is that *de jure* influence is more legitimate, more acceptable from the point of view of the influenced states. Keal explores how this influence was established at the Inter-American Conferences (Havana 1940, Rio de Janeiro 1942 and others) by following the Monroe Doctrine's spirit of keeping non-American powers out of the continent. Moreover, Keal refers to regional settlement of disputes being affirmed by Article 52 of the United Nations Charter and the Inter-American Treaty of Reciprocal Assistance. Finally, in 1948 the Organization of American States (henceforth OAS) was formed further legitimising the regional security arrangements, that is, spheres of influence (Keal 1983, 107–9, see also Vincent 1974, 195–6). After 1955, the Soviet Union had its juridical framework, the Warsaw Pact, which was also an organisation for protection against an outside attack. It is possible that Keal does not take the Pact into consideration here, because it came into being at a later period, when spheres of influence were already established.

Kaufman further explores the differences between the United States' and the Soviet Union's influence. According to Kaufman (1976, 34), inequality is manifested in different terms for the two superpowers: The Soviet Union dominates its satellites in the political field and the United States in the economic, social and educational sectors. Moreover, there are fewer limitations on political and ideological freedom in Latin America than in Eastern Europe. Many Latin American countries enjoy freedom of the press, freedom of speech, and political pluralism (36). The Soviet Union allowed diplomatic or other relations with capitalist countries, whereas the United States did not allow diplomatic relations with communist states. The Soviet Union, nevertheless, had tighter political control overall (38–9).

All in all, the *de jure* side of Cold War spheres of influence implied a certain acceptance of the influence, not only by the other influencing power but also by the influenced states. It even implied a legal framework, a treaty or an organisation. Regardless of this acceptance, Keal and Kaufman still speak of spheres of influence, meaning that for them a sphere of influence *de jure* is not by definition different

---

3   Although Kaufman (1976, 181) makes the remark that in the case of the United States the country's sphere of influence has a longer history, he nevertheless writes that spheres of influence developed specifically after the Second World War (11).

from a sphere of influence which is imposed against the will of the influenced states. In present usage, a sphere of influence is always involuntary. The reason is discursive: how could we speak of a sphere of influence in a pejorative manner if it were not a tool of oppressive power politics? Reading Keal and Kaufman, a general image is beginning to emerge of Soviet influence being more oppressive (political), whereas American influence is softer and more legitimate. The importance of Keal's and Kaufman's analysis is that in bringing to the fore *de jure* influence it allows us to relax the exclusively pejorative understanding of spheres of influence to a notion of influence that is not necessarily implemented against the will of the influenced and by force. This discussion of *de facto* and *de jure* influence has not lost its relevance and could contribute to a discussion on the means of influence (of Russia, the United States, European Union, China and other great powers) in the post-Cold War era.

What we can also conclude from the Cold War consolidation of spheres of influence by means of intervention, legal mechanisms and softer approaches is that the attempts to understand spheres of influence during the Cold War relied extensively on foreign policy doctrines. By evoking the different sphere-of-influence doctrines – the Monroe, Truman, Johnson, and Brezhnev Doctrines – Keal, Kaufman and Vincent were able to make sense of spheres of influence by relating them to significant historical signposts and the people behind them. These doctrines are not the truth about spheres of influence, but they are the milestones which have defined *sphere of influence* and continue to do so. Evoking the Brezhnev Doctrine in order to criticise Russian foreign policy becomes a powerful discursive tool because of the associations with Cold War spheres of influence and interventionism it embodies. At the same time, the Doctrine is useful in conceptualising *sphere of influence* because it provides an explanation of historical events, embodies a discourse of justification and exemplifies structural intervention.

5.4   The Legacy of the Cold War

Both Keal and Kaufman acknowledge the good and the bad sides of spheres of influence. Keal (1983, 157) views spheres of influence as potentially contributing to international order (see Chapter 2.6). Tacit understandings between the superpowers are based on the common interest of avoiding a nuclear war (156). Where Keal is concerned about conflicts between the superpowers and a nuclear war, Kaufman concludes that tight control has diminished the number of conflicts among the members of a subsystem. When there have been conflicts, they have arisen as a consequence of an attempted emancipation from a controlling superpower (Kaufman 1976, 196). The Cold War order rested on a balance of power, but Bull (2002, 109) thought that it did not rest on 'general collaboration or concert among the great powers concerned'. The Cold War balance was not the same as the nineteenth-century European balance-of-power system, which was based on rough equality of the five members, a common culture and a common objective of balance (109–11). Keal and Kaufman, the latter less directly, indicated that a tacit understanding of spheres of influence, and thus also of a balance of power, among the two superpowers existed that was based on the avoidance of a nuclear war.

The Cold War international order is not something we can be particularly proud of. Even if we were to agree that some wars were avoided or some stability was maintained by Cold War spheres of influence, we could not justify the practice in the present. The power of the Cold War image is that it is a true example, from a very near past, of how spheres of influence divided people and how an ideological divide, military competition and antagonism almost led to a nuclear war. Accordingly, it is fair to say that we should remember the Cold War spheres of influence. We certainly do not want to repeat those mistakes. If we have forgotten the order-producing mechanisms in spheres of influence, the reason is straightforward: it was not a particularly good order. It was not even a particularly successful pluralist order, because 'the pluralism of two' did not really represent freedom, even though it did prevent the emergence of a world empire.

Clearly, the Cold War spheres of influence represented injustice. This is where I make my own normative statement; Keal and Kaufman were of the same opinion. Keal (1983, 212) recognised that spheres of influence were inherently unjust. Kaufman was perhaps even more concerned for the sufferings of the influenced states. Kaufman (1976, 11) describes a sphere of influence as a 'prison' condition for the countries of the controlled region. Even Cuba, which Kaufman describes as a deviant case, an exception to the inescapable prisoner status, suffered from the limitations imposed by a superpower (197). The Soviet Union could not 'free' Cuba from the United States' sphere of influence (197–8). In Kaufman's view, the aim for a superpower in its sphere of influence is to keep the controlled countries in a position of dependency (31). He writes that superpowers undermine and try to replace governments that have failed to maintain the values of the bloc (82). 'Satellite states' also renounce their interests in their external affairs for the benefit of the superpower (83). Kaufman further declares that the people of the dominated regions feel that their misfortunes are caused by the exploitative relationship to the superpower (83–4). Today, in the discourses on spheres of influence, the prisoners of political and economic influence are the post-Soviet states; thus, the notion of imprisonment is one association that the concept of sphere of influence has carried along with it over the years.

In addition to (the illusion of) stability and order, there is the question of formality and legitimacy of influence – expressed in the distinction between *de facto* and *de jure* influence – as the subjugated knowledge of the Cold War. It is subjugated because presently only *de facto* influence is seen as influence constituting a sphere of influence. This means that, for example, a treaty establishing a union of states is not seen as forming a sphere of influence because it lacks a clearly defined central power, and because it signifies influence *de jure*. Nevertheless, present discourses on Russia's influence constitute an exception to this rule: if Russia's influence is described as *de jure,* it means a sphere of influence of 'the self-serving suzerain' or imperialist power, not a legitimate form of influence – even if an influenced state accepts its position. In the case of Russia, attempts to establish influence via a treaty or an organisation are deemed instances of a sphere-of-influence policy. One example is the Russian proposal for a European Security Treaty put forward by President Medvedev in 2008, which Foreign Minister Lavrov (2010) defended in the following way:

> It is strange to hear people say that our initiative is an attempt to return to the
> 19th-century policies of 'spheres of influence'. On the contrary, the Treaty offers
> a real opportunity to rebuild Euro-Atlantic politics on a collective basis and will
> help redeem the time lost after the end of the Cold War.

In 2011 when then-Prime Minister Putin suggested a 'Eurasian Union' as the future integration project for the post-Soviet space, the idea was greeted with suspicion elsewhere even though Putin (2011) affirmed that '[a] state must only join on its sovereign decision based on its long-term national interests'.

In the present uses of the term *sphere of influence* no legal means of bringing states together appear, except in the case of discussing Russia's influence. In general, there is no room to discuss spheres of influence as being legitimate. Keal and Kaufman argue that both formality and informality are found in the arrangements of spheres of influence. Yet, the present age does not debate spheres of influence as much in terms of their level of formality as it does by classifying the states that exert the influence. This is why it does not make much difference how Russia exerts its influence; the fact that it does so is adequate for the condemnation of that influence. Thus, even when using softer methods of influence, Russia is still viewed as pursuing a sphere of influence. It is not only that *de jure* and *de facto* influence can be distinguished; there is also a question about the legitimacy of influence when it is related to a specific state. Keal and Kaufman suggest that a sphere of influence can be something different for different actors. The United States and the Soviet Union did not have the same type of legitimacy for their influence; yet, Kaufman and Keal used the concept of sphere of influence for both. Because they both had a definition in mind (exclusion of the other power, violation of sovereignty and mostly tacit agreement) they could refer to both the Soviet Union's and the United States' conduct using the same term regardless of the differences. At the same time, the United States' influence appears to be more acceptable, because it is founded upon treaties; it is more *de jure*.

Acceptable or not, for Kaufman and Keal, it is not the name of the state which determines whether its policy may be deemed one of establishing a sphere of influence; it is the policy itself, which is defined in relation to the prevailing international order. Thus, in this case, *sphere of influence* is not a pejorative expression and there is no need for Keal and Kaufman to describe the United States' influence in some other terms (such as the Good Neighbor Policy). My ultimate point here is that Russia, like any other state, is a member of international society and exerts its influence within the context of the world which its decision-makers see around them. We simply cannot ignore the Russian political imagination, which consists of opposition to the United States' interventionism and a fear of being estranged from the great power club. This imagination affects, if not defines, Russia's foreign policy. Even though Russia is the successor of the Soviet Union, and even if we conclude that the Soviet Union engaged in an unjust practice in maintaining a sphere of influence, this is not a case of guilt by association. Indeed, it was Mikhail Gorbachev, the last head of state of the Soviet Union, who ended the 'festival' of spheres of influence by abandoning the Brezhnev Doctrine and who demanded disarmament, the withdrawal of the country's military presence in Eastern Europe and strengthening of global institutions like the United Nations. Gorbachev's approach meant a clear break with previous policies. I believe we need to take a fresh look at Russia's policy of influence, a perspective that does not cling to the country's Cold War image. This means discussing the legitimacy and the nature of spheres of influence in general, and in the case of Russia in particular.

5.5 The Cuban Missile Crisis

We are still missing some elements of the Cold War story: the collision of and competition for spheres of influence, and the nuclear factor. These I would like to discuss by exploring the Cuban Missile Crisis in 1962, although this is not the only collision of the superpowers. We could very well discuss the Vietnam War (1955–1975), the Berlin Blockade (1948–1949), the Soviet war in Afghanistan (1979–1989) or some other battle over spheres of influence. But the Cuban Missile Crisis represents 'crossing the line', embarking on influence in the territory of the other superpower, and thus challenging the stability of international order as established by spheres of influence. More importantly, the missile crisis centres on nuclear weapons and encourages an examination of the meaning of the nuclear factor where spheres of influence are concerned.

In analysing the Cuban Missile Crisis, Paul Keal's work is presently the only available source that makes it possible to take the concept of sphere of influence up a notch theoretically. When it comes to finding out what happened in the missile crisis, I rely on Fursenko's and Naftali's *'One Hell of a Gamble': Khrushchev, Castro and Kennedy, 1958–1964* (1998) and *Khrushchev's Cold War: The Inside Story of an American Adversary* (2006).[4] A few other works are used as supplementary sources. In *'One Hell of a Gamble'*, Fursenko and Naftali share the story of the Cuban Missile Crisis using secret documents from archives that have been opened since the collapse of the Soviet Union. In order to exemplify the political discourse that Keal as well as Fursenko and Naftali refer to, I analyse excerpts from speeches by President J.F. Kennedy and General Secretary Nikita Khrushchev.

---

4   On the Missile Crisis see also Graham Allison's and Philip Zelikov's *Essence of Decision* (1999).

The Cold War was a time of constant threat of nuclear war. This gave a special meaning to the balance of power and great power management. That the United States and the Soviet Union possessed nuclear weapons created a unique concentration of power where maintaining the status quo became a matter of life and death for all of humanity. The threat of nuclear war materialised in the collision of spheres of influence in the territory of Cuba. In terms of theory, we are dealing with the ideas of stability of possessions and limiting conflicts through spheres of influence in the nuclear age. Even though in the present we sometimes forget that the Bomb still exists – not only as a symbol (a material representation) of power, but also as an actual weapon of mass destruction – the fact is that nuclear deterrence makes struggles for spheres of influence extremely dangerous, which is the lesson of the Cuban Missile Crisis. Unfortunately there is as little discussion on the meaning of nuclear weapons for spheres of influence as there is conceptual discussion on spheres of influence to begin with.

In January 1959, Fidel Castro, along with his brother, Raúl, Ernesto 'Che' Guevara and others from the 'July 26 movement', overthrew the Cuban dictator Fulgencio Batista. This was the beginning of a socialist Cuba which would seek the company of the Soviet Union. Castro considered the Americans imperialists and was irritated by the naval base in Guantánamo on Cuban soil, which reminded him of Theodore Roosevelt's 'big stick' diplomacy (Fursenko and Naftali 1998, 5–7). According to Fursenko and Naftali, Fidel Castro was well aware that the time of Franklin Roosevelt's Good Neighbor Policy was over. The United States once again opted for an interventionist foreign policy by participating in the overthrowing of Jacobo Arbenz's regime in Guatemala in 1954. In that same year, the OAS signed the Caracas Resolution, which included a commitment by its members to joint action in case of communist infiltration (9). This was the background to Cuba's resistance to American influence.

According to Fursenko and Naftali, when Castro took over Cuba, neither the United States nor the Soviet Union knew what course he intended to pursue. The Soviet Union was cautious in supporting Cuba, because it was uncertain of the country's ambitions. In Cuba, the communists were not in complete control of the government. Moreover, as Fursenko and Naftali explain, Guevara and Castro's brother Raúl were members of the communist party but Castro was not a Marxist; he was a 'Fidelista'. In the end, Castro made his choice and pledged his allegiance to communist ideology. Finally, the situation in 1960 was that Cuba was sliding into the socialist camp and the United States 'seemed prepared to accept this violation of its sphere of influence' (Fursenko and Naftali 1998, 55).

After January 1961, Cuba and the United States had no diplomatic relations and very little mutual trade (Fursenko and Naftali 1998, 83). The Kennedy administration could not just sit and watch Cuba turn into a communist Soviet outpost, however, and thus developed a plan for a military invasion using Cuban exiles to overthrow Castro; this was launched on 15 April. A curious aspect of the plan and its execution was that, according to Naftali and Fursenko, Kennedy was concerned about the worsening of the United States' international reputation and for this reason wanted to avoid offering air support (93). The United States did not want to be seen by the world as an interventionist aggressor. Due to this cautiousness, the operation, known as 'the Bay of Pigs Invasion', completely failed (97).[5]

What can be concluded here is that international institutions worked to limit states' actions even during the unique bipolarity of the Cold War: sovereignty and the non-intervention principle had not lost all meaning. The United States and the Soviet Union could not act as they pleased, especially because they had to consider each other's reactions. The Soviet Union was cautious in supporting Cuba, for the sake of good relations with its opponent, and the United States feared for its reputation in the case of full-blown military intervention. If we compare the time of the missile crisis and the world today, some things have not changed. The ideological orientation of another state, be it close by or far away, is still a concern, even to the extent that a great power is ready to intervene. Even the argument has not changed: intervention is resorted to for the sake of the people. It is still a means to put an end to dictatorship or tyranny, or to protect human rights. Cuba was a manifestation of this same paradigm – intervention to save a people from an oppressive ideology, albeit in a very different international order.

For the United States, a communist outpost in the Caribbean was not acceptable; the reason was not only the Soviet threat, but also the legacy of the Monroe Doctrine. Keal (1983, 113) explains:

> After Guatemala it was Castro's government in Cuba that became the focus of United States anxiety about the infiltration of international communism into the hemisphere. By the time Kennedy became President, the United States regarded Cuba as a Soviet satellite and as a transgression of the Monroe Doctrine that could not be tolerated.

Keal's insight is that considerations of the peace and security of the United States overrode the independence of Latin American countries to decide on their internal matters. The threat was of course that those states would also fall under Soviet influence. The Cuban association with the Soviet Union was a threat to the balance of power in the region (132). Moreover, Keal (1983, 113–14) writes that the United States had the right to determine what the threats to peace in the hemisphere were and what was considered an acceptable form of government in each state of the hemisphere. If we link this to the more general context of international order, the United States would seem to be following the principles laid down as early as in the 1815 Congress of Vienna about great powers' rights to decide on matters of international security. In this perspective, what we are dealing with is not something peculiar to spheres of influence or to the Cold War superpower rivalry but merely an old tradition of great power management. The idea of a sphere of influence needs to be understood as something that emerged with

---

5   See Fursenko and Naftali (1998, 77–100) under 'Bay of Pigs'.

great powers and lives with great powers. Conceptually, a sphere of influence is situated between the universe and the pluriverse and which is intimately connected with the principles of sovereignty and non-intervention. I would submit that any conceptualisation of a sphere of influence must rely on the notion of international society and that as a practical policy the pursuit of spheres of influence always emerges as a part of international order. A sphere of influence belonged to the framework of international society, both as an idea and a foreign policy tool, even during the Cold War.

For the United States, the dilemma was to justify intervention and make it look like something other than a sphere-of-influence policy, which had such a negative ring to it. On 20 April 1961, President Kennedy gave an address before the American Society of Newspaper Editors explaining the Bay of Pigs invasion. He (1961) explained how intervention was against the American tradition and international obligations, but at the same time stated:

> Should it ever appear that the inter-American doctrine of non-interference merely conceals or excuses a policy of nonaction – if the nations of this Hemisphere should fail to meet their commitments against outside Communist penetration — then I want it clearly understood that this Government will not hesitate in meeting its primary obligations which are to the security of our Nation!

Thus, exactly as Keal points out, if it was a question of the country's security, the United States' considered that it had the right to act, even abroad. Moreover, inaction could be even worse than intervention if it led to accepting communist penetration. This is the logic whereby a small state's sovereign rights can be violated for the sake of the greater good. Because of international order – the extreme division of the world into two camps – inequality had become the foundation of international relations. It was the right of a great power to decide what was acceptable in its 'neighbourhood' and what was not — and for the United States communism was not.

Kennedy made it clear that in light of its own actions on the 'bloody streets of Budapest', the Soviet Union had no cause to deplore the United States' actions. He (1961) observed,

> It is not the first time that Communist tanks have rolled over gallant men and women fighting to redeem the independence of their homeland. Nor is it by any means the final episode in the eternal struggle of liberty against tyranny, anywhere on the face of the globe, including Cuba itself.

Kennedy (1961) wrote how the spreading threat of Communism turned support and help for the people into a reign of terror where discontent was repressed and self-determination disappeared. When reading these justifications for taking action, the idea of the inherent injustice of a sphere of influence becomes blurred. It becomes a matter of perspective: justice in whose opinion? In a concrete political situation, justice is not abstract; it is defined by those involved. The Cold War struggles for freedom against tyranny are perfect examples of spheres of influence representing either alleged deprivation or a declared bestowal of freedom.

According to Fursenko and Naftali, the day Khrushchev decided to send Warsaw Pact weapons to Cuba, in late September 1959, was the day when Khrushchev decided to take the risk of a military clash with the United States by pursuing interests in Latin America. Fursenko and Naftali explain, in the logic of spheres of influence, that '[f]or the most part, Stalin had left Latin America to the United States. It was America's backyard, too far away for a man who had never traveled outside his own sphere of influence in Eastern Europe'. Khrushchev, however, did not fear to cross the old barriers of spheres of influence when looking for allies (Fursenko and Naftali 1998, 12). Ultimately, the Soviet support extended beyond conventional weapons. Fearing that the Cubans could side with China, and receiving a report indicating that the CIA was recommending preventive war against the Soviet Union, Khrushchev, for the first time, on 9 July 1960, spoke of extending the nuclear umbrella over Cuba (50–52). Fursenko and Naftali write:

> The Soviet Union had never stationed ballistic missiles outside of its borders. But Khrushchev had broken rules before. Stalin had never seriously considered making inroads to Latin America. The idea of a missile gambit, which began in Khrushchev's mind as a work of inspiration, even whimsy, stayed with him. (Fursenko and Naftali 1998, 171)

Fursenko and Naftali (1998, 180) quote Khrushchev's statement at a meeting of the Defence Council of the Soviet Union where he insisted that nuclear missiles would not only protect Cuba but would equalise the balance of power. The missiles would eliminate the strategic imbalance, the military inferiority (187). Fursenko and Naftali write, 'But a concern for Cuban security alone cannot explain why the Soviets took the risk of sending their most expensive and dangerous weapons seven thousand miles to an island republic'. Other reasons motivated Khrushchev: Kennedy's decision to resume nuclear testing in April 1962, the lack of progress in the negotiations over Berlin and the American activity in Southeast Asia all posed a challenge to the Soviet Union (183). The Soviets wanted to do more than just save Castro; their reasons for crossing the line were the balance of power, the nuclear balance and projecting power into the Western Hemisphere (180–88).[6]

When the Soviet Union finally reached out of its comfort zone and approached the borders of its competitor, the move was not motivated only (if at all) by its interest in Cuba as such. Khrushchev did not involve Castro in the negotiations

---

6   Fursenko and Naftali (2006; 469, 471) write that the missiles were placed in Cuba as a political threat, a restraint on the United States regarding Cuba, with no aim of unleashing a war. Taubman (2005, 535) also asserts that the missiles were meant to frighten and not to be fired.

with Kennedy at any point (Fursenko and Naftali 2006, 490; Holbraad 1979, 69). In the terminology of postcolonial research, this was a case of marginalising Cuba, and later also marginalising the Cuban interpretation of the history of the crisis (see Laffey and Weldes 2008). If the Soviet Union was uncertain about supporting Cuba in the first place, it was even more uncertain about providing military support lest something that was a minor relationship should turn into a conflict between the superpowers (Fursenko and Naftali 1998, 23). The Soviet foreign policy bureaucrats were against fulfilling the request made by Cuba to supply them with Polish weapons, but it was Khrushchev who saw the revolution in Cuba as being too important to deny it assistance (23–4). Khrushchev also believed that for the United States general détente was an important enough reason to ignore Cuba in order to maintain good relations with the Soviet Union (44–5). What comes to light here is the significance of international society for the consolidation of spheres of influence. Institutions and rules were at work, and both the United States and the Soviet Union restricted their actions because of them. With the restrictions created by the desire to act as a member of this society, the act of pursuing spheres of influence reflected not only national interests but also an interest in maintaining peace and order in general.

Keal concludes that the threat to the security and ideology of the hemisphere came not from Cuba's internal developments but from Soviet intrusion. The threat was ultimately about what the Soviet Union could do in and from Cuba; it could use Cuba in order to strengthen its nuclear and strategic balance with the United States or use it as a base for communist infiltration in Latin America (Keal 1983, 153–4). According to Keal, the conflict involved a dispute between two influencing powers over the limits of spheres of influence. The interventions in Czechoslovakia and Hungary, by contrast, were a matter of the influencing power acting against the influenced (134). Two observations follow: 1) we are dealing with a *collision*, exactly that which should challenge Keal's idea about spheres of influence producing order and stability, and an event which was, nevertheless, bound by the existence of international society; 2) if we look at the history of spheres of influence, the great power competition for survival is always there. If sovereignty is fluid, intervention a contested idea, and justice a matter of interpretation, then great power rivalry is the one thing we can establish with reasonable certainty as a defining feature of spheres of influence when we look at the history constructed to date. Noteworthy for the present pejorative understanding of spheres of influence is that if there has to be another great power against which a sphere of influence is constructed, this can hardly be a purely imaginary adversary. If Russia is trying to establish a sphere of influence, against whom is it being created? Where is the other great power with a sphere of influence? And why would Russia see the United States, the EU, China or some other entity as the other influencing power?

What followed the Soviet support for Cuba and the United States' Bay of Pigs invasion was the missile crisis. The Soviet Union delivered 36 R12 missiles to Cuba by the end of September 1962, and the first shipment of nuclear warheads reached the island on 4 October. On 15 October, American U2 flights spotted some of the missiles (Fursenko and Naftali 1998, 216–22). As Fursenko and Naftali argue, President Kennedy was reluctant to answer the Soviet threat with military action; he wanted to try diplomatic means. But the problem was that the more time the diplomatic solution took, the less likely military success became. If the Soviet Union were able to make the missiles operational, the United States would embark on what would be a suicidal mission in trying to destroy them (26). The tension was great and spheres of influence were bringing the world to the brink of war – instead of contributing to peace and stability. Despite the initial constraints by international society, this was 'stability of possessions' failing in the most tragic sense. According to Fursenko and Naftali (1998, 235), avoiding a military solution as the first option; the United States answered with a naval 'quarantine' preventing additional offensive weapons reaching Cuba.

President Kennedy (1962) gave a speech on the crisis on 22 October. In the speech he stated that the purpose of the missile bases had to be to provide a nuclear strike capability against the Western Hemisphere. Kennedy referred to international agreements by stating:

> This urgent transformation of Cuba into an important strategic base – by the presence of these large, long range, and clearly offensive weapons of sudden mass destruction – constitutes an explicit threat to the peace and security of all the Americas, in flagrant and deliberate defiance of the Rio Pact of 1947, the traditions of this Nation and hemisphere, the joint resolution of the 87th Congress, the Charter of the United Nations, and my own public warnings to the Soviets on September 4 and 13. […] The United Nations Charter allows for regional security arrangements – and the nations of this hemisphere decided long ago against the military presence of outside powers. Our other allies around the world have also been alerted. (Kennedy 1962)

For Kennedy, American interests in Cuba were legitimate and the country's sphere of influence could be justified on the basis of international law. In fact, Kennedy's assertion of regional arrangements is like Schmitt's idea of spheres (*Großräume*) of international law. Kennedy was not saying that there were tacit agreements about spheres of influence. He was saying that the Western Hemisphere constituted a legitimate *Großraum* which was under attack. There was also a voice similar to Naumann's in Kennedy's claim for a regional international law. Kennedy insisted that Cuba was well known for its special and historical relationship to the United States and the entire Western Hemisphere. In the light of the legality of the United States' sphere of influence, and the special relationship of the Cuban and American peoples, the Soviet Union had pulled a stunt constituting a 'deliberately provocative and unjustified change in the status quo' (Kennedy 1962). In addition, Kennedy (1962) accused the Soviet Union of attempts at world domination and assured that the United States was ready to take action if the safety and freedom of peoples the United States was committed to were threatened.

In letters to President Kennedy dated 23 and 24 October 1962, Khrushchev, like Kennedy, invoked international agreements:

> I must say frankly, that the measures indicated in your statement constitute a serious threat to peace and to the security of nations. The United States has openly taken the path of grossly violating the United Nations Charter, the path of violating international norms of freedom of navigation on the high seas, the path of aggressive actions both against Cuba and against the Soviet Union. (Khrushchev 1962a)

> You wish to compel us to renounce the rights that every sovereign state enjoys, you are trying to legislate in questions of international law, and you are violating the universally accepted norms of that law. (Khrushchev 1962b)

Both superpowers claimed to be on a mission to protect freedom and peace; that is, they were on the side of the law. Bull (2002, 211) writes that in fact both the Soviet Union and the United States have mainly appealed to peace and security – and not ideology, doctrinal rectitude or human justice – in justifying their interventions. This, for Bull, meant that they valued international order over norms of justice (212). I agree that international order and peace were the main concerns for the two great powers after the conflict unfolded in full, but also the language of justification was strong and even showed a humanitarian dimension. Again, I draw the conclusion that justification mattered because of concerns for international society. Khrushchev (1962c) wrote to Kennedy on the 26th offering to remove the missiles if the United States would promise not to invade Cuba. He also wrote that the Soviet military aid to Cuba was solely for 'reasons of humanitarianism', to support its revolution against outside attack, and not as a means to interfere in Cuba's internal affairs. It is hard to imagine how humanitarian reasons were at the heart of Soviet foreign policy here, but it is easy to understand that positions were defended with appeals to such a noble cause.

Khrushchev proposed to Kennedy on 26 October that if the United States ended the naval blockade and refrained from invasion in Cuba the Soviet Union would destroy its armaments in Cuba (Keal 1983, 137–8). The next day (27 October) Khrushchev wrote again to Kennedy, without waiting for a reply to his previous letter, and presented additional demands for the settlement of the crisis. The letter stated that the United States had surrounded the Soviet Union with missiles located in Britain, Italy and Turkey and claimed that this was an unfair situation. Khrushchev proposed that the Soviet Union would remove its missiles from Cuba if the United States would remove its missiles from Turkey (Khrushchev 1962d). Curiously, Khrushchev was an eager reader of Walter Lippmann's columns. Fursenko and Naftali (2006, 487) write that Khrushchev appreciated Lippmann's realism and his insight into international relations. During the Cuban Missile Crisis, on 26 or 27 October 1962, Khrushchev was given the column Lippmann wrote in *The New York Herald Tribune* on 25 October. In the column, Lippmann proposed that the superpowers dismantle both the Soviet base in Cuba and the US base in Turkey. This idea possibly influenced Khrushchev (1962d) and prompted him to propose, in a letter of 27 October, the removal of missiles in Turkey. Fursenko and Naftali (2006, 488) even put forward the question whether President Kennedy might have delivered his message through Lippmann, since he knew of Khrushchev's enthusiasm for reading Lippmann's columns. In the end, the United States accepted the offer to refrain from invading Cuba but the agreement on the Jupiter missiles in Turkey would be concluded later under a secret protocol (Fursenko and Naftali 1998, 278–87).

Ultimately, the United States got its way, without a military invasion. Khrushchev did not want a war and eventually the Soviet Union returned the missiles to where they came from (see Fursenko and Naftali 1998, 277). To quote Fursenko and Naftali, '[Kennedy] could not go to war in the Caribbean with any hope of prevailing. He had tried to achieve some measure of parity with the United States to defend Soviet interests in that region; but clearly he had failed' (260). Keal (1983, 141) writes that by withdrawing the Soviet Union accepted that Cuba was in the sphere of influence of the United States. The crisis was settled on 28 October with a promise from the Soviet Union to withdraw the missiles, but there were still difficult negotiations ahead on how to implement the agreement (Fursenko and Naftali 2006, 493; Taubman 2005, 577). I will end my account of the incident here and look at the contribution of the missile crisis to our present understanding of spheres of influence.

5.6   A Re-reading of the Cold War

The Cuban Missile Crisis is an excellent example of how the struggle for spheres of influence encompassed ideology, 'contamination', fighting tyranny or imperialism, and defending the freedom of the people. *Sphere of influence* is not an idea which belongs exclusively to the Cold War, but it definitely has features which make Cold War spheres of influence special. At the same time, the concept of sphere of influence relates to ideas on international order, that is, to international theory expounded by the English School, especially because that theory was born in the midst of the Cold War itself. Keal saw the missile crisis not as a matter of Cuba's conversion to communism as such but as the expansion of the Soviet sphere of influence. International order was also at stake, and war between the superpowers was the risk worth taking in a conflict over Cuba.

Even though the spheres of influence in the Cold War were based on tacit agreements, Kennedy argued for the legality of an American *Großraum*. Khrushchev did not spare words in appealing to international law. This, coupled with hesitation about turning a minor matter into a superpower conflict and the need to justify influence, prompts me to state that concerns for international order affected the decisions on questions of influence. It was Bull's international society at work. The missile crisis is also an example of the dangers of spheres of influence;

it almost ended in a nuclear war. Because of the instability of spheres of influence and the balance of power, a struggle between two influencing powers took place and spheres of influence failed to provide for stability of the powers' possessions. Yet, spheres of influence, although almost leading to nuclear war, did not, in the end, fail to provide for international order during the Cold War. World War Three never materialised and spheres of influence maintained the bipolar order. In fact, what I am able to read from the Cuban Missile Crisis is that somehow the nuclear threat overrode the powers' considerations regarding their spheres of influence. Keal, and Fursenko and Naftali, seem to agree that international order – and maintaining it by nuclear parity – was a major motive for both parties. The Soviet Union gave up; it could not achieve nuclear parity and it could not extend its military influence to the Caribbean. The Soviet Union was ready to back off, because, in the end, luckily, peace was more important.

The role of small powers comes into the limelight in the Cuban Missile Crisis. In the case of Cuba, sovereignty was defended and violated at the same time. Intervention was resorted to. Yet the small power was no victim. Although Cuba was ignored in the negotiations, marginalised as an object of superpower rivalry, it was able to choose its side and play 'the big game'. Castro wanted to join the Soviet bloc; he wanted the Bomb. The people were less enthusiastic, but of course it was not for them to decide. Moreover, given that Cuba agreed to the Soviet influence, was the relationship anymore that of being part of the Soviet Union's sphere of influence, or was it an alliance? This is the general question of where we draw the line between a sphere of influence, an alliance, integration, and so on, when it comes to the consent of the influenced state.

The role of small powers includes influencing balances of power. The Cold War balance of power is generally viewed as something Wight called a 'simple balance', that is, 'selective concentration upon the greatest Powers'. But Wight argues there has never actually been, in Western international society, a simple balance. There have always been lesser powers around or between the dominant powers (Wight 1966a, 152). A simple balance is only possible in an international system of established, stable *Großräume*. As long as small states exist as independent powers, no matter how small they are, as the Cuban case testifies, balance is achieved by controlling the moves of the small powers. This destroys the dream of perfectly working great power management and it destroys the idea of perfect hierarchy. The Cuban Missile Crisis proves that not even the Cold War was built upon a simple balance; even tacit agreements on spheres of influence could not create a simple balance. Maybe this is why Lippmann did not trust the balance of power, but believed that there must be a way to divide the world along lines of responsibility, willingly and in good spirit (see Chapter 4.5).

If we re-read the Cold War, one inevitable question is whether spheres of influence provided for international order in the case of the Cuban Missile Crisis. Did the tacit agreement on spheres of influence cause the crisis, prevent its escalation, or both? This is a discussion on the conflict- and war-preventing mechanism of spheres of influence, a discussion completely absent from IR today.

In the present understanding of the concept, *spheres of influence* are a source of conflicts, not checks on violence and war. I have yet to encounter a statement from a non-Russian affirming that Russia's sphere of influence contributes to stability and helps to limit conflicts. In this light, the Cuban missile crisis is an example of how *due to* the struggle for spheres of influence and the balance of power the superpowers came close to starting a nuclear war. Because of spheres of influence, the United States took great pains to plan a military invasion to overthrow Castro. Because of spheres of influence, Khrushchev delivered nuclear armaments outside Soviet soil for the first time. One could even put the blame on spheres of influence for Cuba's turn towards communism and the loss of many lives in Castro's purges. It all makes sense: spheres of influence can lead to this. In any human endeavour, power has the potential to lead to death and destruction. But power has another side too, and the historical discourses on spheres of influence reveal that they may be vehicles for exercising 'responsibility' or using power for the sake of order.

If we turn the matter the other way around, we could say that respect for spheres of influence eventually prevented escalation of the conflict. Keal writes that the role of spheres of influence as means to limit violence became obvious in the case of Cuba. They created a restraint on great powers interfering in territories that they perceived as falling under their rival's influence. In fact, respect for them prevented a nuclear war (Keal 1983, 205). This claim can be refuted, of course, and I would say that it was rather the *fear* of nuclear war that prevented such a war. But what Keal means is that considering the antagonistic system, the existence of the fatal bomb, and the tension in international relations, the spheres of influence created some rules whereby the superpowers knew their limits. Spheres of influence created order in chaos and helped to prevent a major war. Stalin had respected the lines that had been drawn; Khrushchev tried to cross the line, but eventually the system held together. What is more, spheres of influence helped to maintain the pluralist system against a single sovereign, although, as I have argued above, this particular pluralist system was not a strong one in defending freedom. Cold War pluralism did not give states the possibility to do things their way. Keal (1983, 199–200) also argues that not only did the system of spheres of influence maintain peace between the superpowers but hierarchical relationships maintained order within the blocs and spheres of influence shielded the influenced areas from external challenges.

All this is not to idealise the Cold War or to say that Cold War spheres of influence were not that bad after all. I was only eight years old when the Berlin Wall fell, and I cannot possibly understand how people lived and felt during those years. Superpower politics affected millions of people, and Orwell foresaw that spheres of influence entail totalitarianism, violence, war, suppression and manipulation of people. But this should not mean that the concept of sphere of influence has no history, that it is fixed within its Cold War uses. If a sphere of influence expresses a relationship between the influencing and the influenced, and if it affects international order and its rules and institutions, then it is necessary to take a historically and theoretically broader view on spheres of influence than the Cold War alone can offer.

The Cold War, including the Cuban Missile Crisis, constitutes much of our understanding of spheres of influence. Just like the Monroe Doctrine, it is a beacon signalling spheres of influence at work. The events of the era comprise a memory that makes spheres of influence understandable. The Cuban Missile Crisis is a manifestation of, a concrete reference to, what a sphere of influence is and, more specifically, what spheres of influence have meant for the relations between the influencing and influenced powers. The usefulness of the Cold War memory is that it reminds us of the dangers of antagonism and division in the society of states in the age of nuclear weapons. We forget this too easily. But the question remains whether in the end the issue in the Cuban Missile Crisis was spheres of influence rather than nuclear parity. Were spheres of influence reduced to a balance of power in a manner that prevents us from talking any longer about a struggle for spheres of influence? Did the nuclear factor alter the sphere-of-influence logic in a fundamental manner? Was the fear of mutual suicide so overwhelming that it overruled considerations of spheres of influence and made even Khrushchev accept defeat and humiliation by retreating from Cuba? According to Lippmann (1963), nuclear deterrence does not prevent nuclear war. I agree with Lippmann in that as long as there are nuclear weapons, the possibility of a nuclear war *really* exists. Lippmann commented on the missile crisis as follows:

> Had the missiles been put in place, they would have changed seriously the balance of nuclear power in the world. The United States deployed its whole military power, nuclear and conventional, against such an alteration of the status quo. It would do the same, and for the same kind of reason, if the Soviet Union moved its military force against Berlin or against any other point which is critically important to the maintenance of the status quo in the balance of strategic power. (Lippmann 1963)

How much could little Cuba weigh on the scale where the other weight was nuclear war? If Kennedy and Khrushchev understood that nuclear war would become a reality if the missiles were kept in Cuba, they could not have cared for any trivial matters relating to spheres of influence. Khrushchev gave up the dream of nuclear parity; he gave up a balance of power, all for the sake of avoiding war. What drove the Soviet premier to give up the confrontational sphere-of-influence logic must have been the fear of destroying the entire planet, or at least the human race. It is even uncertain whether Khrushchev sought a communist bridgehead in the Caribbean or was planning all along to advance military parity, or even superiority. Even if the conflict began as a competition over spheres of influence, it ended up in a negotiation on nuclear weapons. Even American missiles in Turkey entered the bargain. What was agreed on Cuba, where it all began, was not much: a promise from the United States not to intervene. The United States was left with communist Cuba and with Castro. The Soviet Union was left with humiliation. What the nuclear age brought as an extra for the logic of spheres of influence was that, in addition to – or even instead of – a fear of the spread of an alien ideology, the spread of the power of the Other, or losing the balance of power, great powers now had to take into consideration a dangerous military scenario in which rivalry over spheres of influence could end up in a nuclear war.

I began this research by being critical of the transmission of Cold War thinking on spheres of influence into the present. I was also critical of how the Cold War forms a unitary yet uninformative picture of spheres of influence and dominates the image of Russia's sphere-of-influence policy. Later I came to realise that the problem was not so much conceiving of spheres of influence in Cold War terms but the fact that Cold War spheres of influence had even not been studied. And how could they have been, when no theories on spheres of influence had yet been elaborated? With the knowledge we have today, with archives more and more open, the Cold War could very well be a fruitful source for theorising spheres of influence. I believe the Cold War offers more than a burden of pejorative associations destined to encumber the concept of sphere of influence: it contributes to a theoretical tradition in that it is a part of the history of spheres of influence, the most explicit and familiar phase, but not the only one. Even if rooted in pejorative associations, the Cold War knowledge offers material for the normative discussion we lack and need. Failing to read the Cold War policy of spheres of influence means we will not be able to take a critical view of the contemporary manifestations of spheres of influence either.

Chapter 6
Conclusions

6.1 Framing Sphere of Influence

The continuous use of the concept of sphere of influence in political language, in particular, as a means to shame and blame Russia, testifies to its importance. Yet, the concept in which one finds inscribed the orbit metaphor of territorial influence spilling over state borders has been left unexamined since the end of the Cold War. The historical meaning of the concept of sphere of influence is drawn from the memory of the Cold War, which imbues the concept with pejorative associations. There is a silent agreement on this pejorative pall, which means that IR has settled the normative question without even beginning to discuss it. In order to end the silence on spheres of influence I have tried to contest the concept though historical sources.

When contesting the concept of sphere of influence, the first observation is that spheres of influence are presented either as the ultimate evil or as a potentially useful and even necessary part of international political life. The former view dominates the contemporary understanding of the practice of establishing spheres of influence, while the latter view is found in international theorising on spheres of influence. Little (2007) has observed that there are two views of the balance of power: adversarial and associational. Adversarial balance means the manipulation of distribution of power by the great powers, in their own favour, in an anarchical international order (11–12). The image of an adversarial balance of power, the inherently competitive nature of power, comes from the metaphor of 'weighting scales' (66). Associational balance instead relies on cooperation and a metaphor of an arch, or body, where parts are bound together (66–7). In associational balance, the image of balancing is associated with the institutions of international society (11–12). This refers to a balance of power in an international society which is closer to the solidarist end of Buzan's spectrum. Little's separation of the two metaphorical sources of the balance of power, the scales and the arch/body, also illuminate the two views on the concept of sphere of influence: one dominant, and the other subjugated.

The present pejorative uses of the term 'sphere of influence' could be likened to that which Little calls an adversarial interpretation. It means spheres of influence are inherently endowed with power games, competition and unjust submission of the weaker states. This is the orbit which consists of a central power and its satellites. These very same spheres of influence are also the Cold War spheres of influence. These are Orwell's super-states. Adversarial spheres of influence are linked to an adversarial balance of power, where changes in power relations are dependent on spheres of influence and based on competition and conflicts.

The associational spheres of influence do not exist in the contemporary usage. Yet, they do exist within the literature on international society. A more positive view of spheres of influence addresses the contribution spheres of influence can make to international order by limiting conflicts, and managing both great power and intraregional relations. These would be what Bull (2002, 215) terms 'positive sphere-of-influence agreements' and Keal (1983, 23–4) refers to as 'spheres of responsibility' (see Chapter 3.6). Even closer to the idea of an associational model of spheres of influence is a vision where the small states voluntarily – or because of the pressure created by the system – lose some of their sovereignty to the hands of a great power. The great influencing powers then balance the scales by managing their respective spheres of influence, contributing to global peace and order. The level of cooperation between the central powers is not discussed extensively by any of the scholars, but certain agreements, tacit or formal, should be a part of the deal, in order to make the system of *Großräume* stable.

What determines whether one views spheres of influence as either adversarial or associational, to use Little's terms, is the approach a model of spheres of influence takes on matters of international order and justice. Thus, in my search for the origins and meanings of the concept of sphere of influence, I have identified the dimensions of order and justice as the framework for the inquiry. The relationship between spheres of influence, order and justice explains where the pejorative associations of the concept have originated. A sphere of influence either contributes to international order or it does not, but no conceptualisation of it can avoid questions of international order. This means that if we wish to use the term 'sphere of influence', we should not only reflect on what actions constitute a sphere-of-influence policy, but also address the nature of the international system: a sphere of influence, when viewed historically, defends plurality against solidarist or universalist tendencies. When spheres of influence do not involve an open regional solidarist agenda; as they did for Naumann, Schmitt, Carr and Lippmann; they relate to international order by tacit understandings, stability of possessions, limiting conflicts, sovereignty, great power management and non-intervention/intervention. Even if a sphere of influence is not necessarily confined to a particular region, it most often expresses a regional solution to the demise of the system of states and to the dangers of a world state. Thus, to the initial 'Do spheres of influence contribute to order?', a second question can be added: 'What kind of order do spheres of influence contribute to?'

Justice, the second element that is relevant for our present understanding of spheres of influence, refers here to justice between states. When an analysis of spheres of influence addresses interstate justice, the context is the sovereign equality of states and in particular relations between the great and the small. When it is claimed that a sphere of influence can contribute to international order, or that political unification is a necessity, the argument is that the order-producing effect of a sphere of influence takes priority over the rights of the influenced states. Spheres of influence have not been seen as having a bearing on human justice because there is practically no discussion on the relationship between spheres of influence and the individuals living within them. Indeed, the interconnectedness of intervention and spheres of influence is discussed in terms of the violations against the states that are the objects of intervention, not the human beings affected by it. The focus on sovereignty strengthens the link between spheres of influence and international order as a system of states. On the other hand, the history of spheres of influence also points to a system where sovereign states did not yet exist, the suzerain system; but even more to an international order where the state ceases to function as the principal international actor. This in turn directs our focus to the middle of the pluralist-solidarist spectrum of international society, where spheres of influence could be called regional solidarist projects, *Großräume* or super-states.

The table below summarises the dominant view of the relationship between spheres of influence, order, justice and the nature of the system in the selected historical and conceptual episodes. The first episode consists of the current political imagination on spheres of influence in the post- Cold War order. The English School and the Cold War are grouped as one vision of spheres of influence because the Cold War theoretisations emanate from the School. The conceptualisations of spheres of influence as entities between the nation-state and the world state form the third episode. The entries reflect the answers to the following questions:

1. Do spheres of influence contribute to international *order* among the society of states?
2. Do spheres of influence violate interstate *justice*, that is, do they necessarily violate state sovereignty?
3. Do spheres of influence operate within the limits of the *system* of states?

Table 6.1   Relationship between spheres of influence, order, justice, and the system

	Post-Cold War spheres of influence	**The English School / Cold War spheres of influence**	**Spheres of influence between nation and humanity**
Order	Do not promote order	Promote order and instability	Promote order
Justice	Violation of sovereignty	Violation of sovereignty	Plurality and reciprocity
System	System of states	*Regional solidarism within the system of states*	New *nomos*

Order, justice and system represent elements which bind spheres of influence to international theory and the pejorative uses of the concept. Order connects justice and the system, for it expresses the potential of spheres of influence to resolve or worsen problems within the society of states. Arguments that spheres of influence can contribute to international order and represent regional solidarism act as justifications for the violation of sovereignty which spheres of influence tend to result in. When it comes to international order, at present a sphere of influence is not envisioned as a useful tool of achieving a balance of power but a Cold War relic that represents the power games of the system of states. But when we look into the past, a sphere of influence is conceived of as an arrangement which can promote international order, and even one that can create a new order to replace the system of equal sovereign states. When it comes to justice, it seems that violations of sovereignty are necessarily a part of spheres of influence. The theorists presented here had to take a stance towards sovereignty, admitting that spheres of influence have repercussions for the equality of states. The concerns for injustice presented by the English School theorists are not new; they are embodied in the present regime of truth about spheres of influence. But, if we attempt to contest the concept of sphere of influence, it is necessary to pay close attention to the theorists reflecting on the world wars who argued that justice for the small had to be, and most importantly could be, taken into consideration within spheres of influence. Looking at the above table, these theorists can be seen as promoting the most radical view of spheres of influence. If we ignore Orwell, we get the least pejorative visions of spheres of influence. Next, I present the three factors of order, justice and system in more detail.

6.1.1   International Order

Within the English School, Bull and Keal discussed the contribution spheres of influence could to make to international order. In *The Anarchical Society* (2002), Bull establishes his idea on great power management which is maintained by a balance of power. The spheres of influence of the United States and the Soviet Union are a part of that balancing game and contribute to international order (Bull 2002, 199–204). Keal makes an even stronger case for spheres of influence with a potential to contain and prevent conflicts. The problem with order for Keal (1983, 211) is its instability. If spheres of influence contribute to the stability of international order, it is only very temporary, and as long as spheres of influence are composed essentially of relations among the influencing powers, competition between them entails the prospect for conflict over spheres of influence.

The present understanding of spheres of influence from a pejorative perspective means that there is no discussion on their possible contribution to order. Great power management, humanitarian intervention and the principle of a responsibility to protect are examples of ideas of international influence without outright pejorative senses; in other words, they can be both defended and opposed. Thus, other forms of influence, ones more justified, can be seen as contributing to international order. We lack studies which would examine the order-producing mechanism of spheres of influence during the Cold War and the present alike. If we look at Keal's and Kaufmann's accounts, Cold War spheres of influence are seen as contributing to some kind of order, but the Cuban Missile Crisis and its interpretations demonstrate that this order is rather problematic. Stability could easily turn into a conflict over the limits of spheres of influence, as indeed it did. Spheres of influence were part of the international order that prevented a third world war and maintained bipolarity, but it is altogether another thing to argue that that order was a good one. It was an order which could also have led to a nuclear war. It was an order which was based on hatred, fear, division and competition. This was certainly not the kind of order that was envisioned after the Second World War. For the theorists Naumann, Schmitt, Carr and Lippmann spheres of influence were the salvation of plurality and thus they embodied the promotion of order. Only Orwell imagined the system of super-states as a rather frightening order. Instead, Naumann, Schmitt, Carr and Lippmann all envisioned how a sphere of influence, or whatever they referred to it as, would become the middle way of international political organisation, contributing to a new *nomos*.

6.1.2   *Justice in Spheres of Influence*

In the English School conception pursuing a sphere of influence clearly entailed a violation of sovereignty. But when we look at spheres of influence through the lens of international institutions, the question of whether spheres of influence are inherently unjust is far from settled. Intervention and non-intervention as principles connected to spheres of influence emerge from a jungle of arguments over legality and legitimacy. Most pressing is the justification of humanitarian intervention and its relation to establishing or consolidating a sphere of influence. The English School affinity for great power management and occasional justification of intervention indicates that some sympathy is found for spheres of influence. Still, the only way to justify a sphere of influence is to argue that it contributes to international order – as Keal does. This means that spheres of influence bring regional order but, more importantly, that management of them becomes an ordering principle in the relations of the influencing powers. The inherent injustice of spheres of influence becomes manifest if influence is exerted without the consent of the states subjected to that influence, and this problem of injustice troubled Keal.

The Cold War spheres of influence are deemed unjust by Kaufman and Keal, but these scholars also draw attention to the possible legitimacy and formality of spheres of influence. To read from the Cold War episode, spheres of influence can be built in a manner in which the influenced state accepts its position and is even ready to commit this acceptance to paper. Formality, nevertheless, does not make a sphere of influence necessarily just, if the influenced state is forced into a union with the influencing state. But legitimising influence through such an agreement could be viewed as justified as part of the process of *normalising* spheres of influence as a *de facto* practice of the time. The question arises: what does legitimacy do for the idea of a sphere of influence, and does the establishment of a sphere of influence then turn into integration? The Cold War period offers an interesting possibility to study how much justice a sphere of influence can actually incorporate. Was there consideration of justice or were the small states simply relegated to the role of 'satellites' of the superpowers? Keal (1983, 212) and Kaufman (1976, 11) were of the opinion that there was not much, if any, room for justice.

Injustice also troubled Naumann and Lippmann, who both tried to elaborate on how spheres of influence would turn injustice into a mutually beneficial relationship of protection. They also began their reasoning with the system-level consideration of how to manage international relations in an age of conflict and war; that is, how to create a viable international order. Spheres of influence, Schmitt's and Carr's *Großräume*, Naumann's Mid-Europe and Lippmann's Good Neighbor Policy were the answers. Spheres of influence would create rules and boundaries regarding international influence, establish a new balance of power, and reduce the number of international actors, making the management of international relations simpler in the process. Justice is the issue where the theories relating to the period of the world wars diverge most from those in all the other episodes, because it forms the only conceptualisation where we can find an attempt to overcome the inevitable injustice of influence. Three justifications are presented: the benefits for the influenced, pluralism against universalism and, ultimately, world peace. It was only within the context of the world wars that spheres of influence emerged as regional constellations of the willing. If there was unwillingness, those resisting needed to be converted for the sake of preventing another world war.

In contemporary political discourse spheres of influence are not being justified, either by Western analysts or Russians, for both of whom the term is pejorative. For Western analysts spheres of influence represent a uniquely Russian policy, and for Russian analysts they signal United States' interventionism and export of democracy. This is by no means surprising, because there are as few examples of successful spheres of influence periods in history as there are defenders of the policy. Whether we look at the colonial period, the Cold War or the post-Cold War era we see spheres of influence as the embodiement of injustice in international relations.

6.1.3   System of States or a New Nomos?

Finally we arrive at the relationship between spheres of influence and the nature of international order as a system of states. The world-war-era theorists again make an exception by positing spheres of influence as an aspect of a new *nomos*. Yet, even if there is an explicit idea of a new international order and its constituent regional units, it still hangs on to the idea of sovereignty. This is not because sovereignty as such would be upheld as it was before – these theorists did, in fact, declare the end of sovereignty – but because of the need to explain that regional solidarism would still enable its units to hold on to the power to regulate their internal affairs. In order to sell the idea to those affected, sovereignty was promoted as the means to avoid an image of Orwell's super-state. With the question of sovereignty as the focal point, Naumann, Schmitt, Carr and Lippmann positioned their visions of spheres of influence between nation and humanity. Just as I believe that the English School conception of spheres of influence should be placed in the middle of the pendulum of international society; so, too, should *Großräume,* the Good Neighbor Policy and the super-states, but with the recognition that the international society is composed not of sovereign states, but of regional constellations. In this vision the state has run its course and something new is taking its place. Because this kind of regional solidarism is constructed as a force against the state and the world state, it constructs an idea of a new *nomos*. The explicitness of the argument for a new *nomos* is important, because that argument becomes the justification for spheres of influence. Units larger than states become a ncessity; they become a means to achieve peace when sovereignty has failed.

In the contemporary literature, a sphere of influence is seen as a foreign policy tool strictly confined to the policies of states and not as an entity or a regional constellation in its own right. A sphere of influence is not an instance of integration or regionalism; it is not a progressive, but a regressive and conservative idea of influence. For the English School, spheres of influence are part of the society of states. For Keal (1983, 15) and Kaufman (1976, 11) spheres of influence entail a violation of the sovereignty of the influenced state, but not its complete denial. Nor does Bull (2002) make any reference to the absolute abandoning of sovereignty when discussing spheres of influence in various parts of *The Anarchical Society*. Even though spheres of influence are not the centre of attention for the English School, they clearly emerge in the context of international institutions. Spheres of influence are fixed within the system of states and can be found within the debate on pluralist and solidarist societies. Jackson's concept of regional solidarism becomes an apt description of what a sphere of influence looks like from the English School perspective. Likewise, in Keal's and Kaufmann's analysis of the Cold War, spheres of influence represent regional solidarism which emerges as a bipolar order within a system of states. Thus, they do not discuss the demise of the state itself, unlike Schmitt and others.

In addition to debating spheres of influence from the normative perspective, looking at their inherent injustice and justifications, theorising international order adds substance to the concept of sphere of influence. The history of the concept reveals that spheres of influence can be located in a debate on the nature of international order. This means that spheres of influence could be the answer to the weaknesses of the other two options for an international order: the system of states and the world state. This less pejorative view of spheres of influence is implied in the theorisation on Mid-Europe, *Großräume* and Good Neighbor Policy. I wanted to take the idea even further, by identifying spheres of influence as falling in the middle of the pluralist-solidarist spectrum. The reason why the idea of a sphere of influence sits so well within the pluralist-solidarist/universalist debate is that it contributes to the criticism of the world state and world society of individuals. If we want to situate the concept of sphere of influence both theoretically and historically within the discipline of IR, it is exactly here that it can be found: within the dichotomy of pluralism and solidarism. These traces have gone unnoticed until this research. This makes *sphere of influence*, not necessarily 'an old-style concept', conservative or even pejorative; but a progressive idea in the attempt to imagine a new pluralist order after the system of states. The concept combines that which is seen as good and valuable in pluralism and solidarism alike. To be sure, spheres of influence might not solve the tension between pluralism and solidarism; they might well represent an unimaginable international order, but they can still address the contemporary challenges of international order. Stepping out of the fixed meaning of *sphere of influence* does not mean the acceptance of unjust practices; it means reflecting on a sphere of influence as an idea which encompasses theorisation on international order and justice among states.

6.2   Taking Spheres of Influence Seriously

In this research, the concept of sphere of influence has been reviewed and revised based on its normative history in international theory. I have opened up paths towards the English School, ideas on regional constellations, the Cold War and contemporary studies. Nevertheless, this should be considered only a beginning. Next I will express my thoughts on the concept of sphere of influence in international theory and put forward those questions which I feel merit further investigation.

The English School is clearly a source in which the topic of spheres of influence was not sufficiently explored. It is as if the authors stopped half-way through discussing the role of spheres of influence in international society. I wonder whether, had the English School theorists taken spheres of influence more seriously, we might now have students interested in studying the topic. If the English School overlooked its opportunity to scrutinise spheres of influence, we have overlooked the English School's omission in neglecting spheres of influence. Keal's (1983) study is an interesting case, because it has not been adequately noticed within the discipline and especially not within the English School. Keal is the missing link between the English School and spheres of influence. His study draws on English School concepts and he comes close to writing a conceptual history of spheres of influence. Keal discusses colonialism, the Monroe Doctrine and the Good Neighbor Policy, for example, connecting spheres of influence to other episodes of history than simply the Cold War. However, even Keal's account has its shortcomings: first, it needs updating in the post-Cold War situation; and second, it neither pays attention to the uses of the concept in political parlance, nor does it situate the concept within IR theory. In a word, the English School neglected spheres of influence: the concept and phenomenon were never framed within the institutions of international society. However, the subject of spheres of influence is not wholly lacking in the English School theory if one looks carefully enough. A sphere of influence could very well be a derivate institution of Bull's great power management. As such, it would establish the significance of spheres of influence in history, practice and theory. It would lift spheres of influence from the metaphorical meaning, from the pejorative trap, to a meaningful relationship with other rules and institutions of international society.

The need to theorise the concept of sphere of influence becomes evident when discussing the relationship between spheres of influence and sovereignty, because violations of sovereignty take central stage when attempting to define the concept. Sovereignty is also important for the present understanding of spheres of influence, because when it is seen to be violated, it reinforces the pejorative associations of the particular conception of influence involved. Because sovereignty is such a central concept of IR, by affecting sovereignty, *sphere of influence* becomes a central concept as well. Since modernity, sovereignty and the international have been seen as interdependent (see Bartelson 1995, 189–90). There can be no sovereignty without the international system and no international system without sovereignty. Thus the state has taken centre stage in international political theory. A sphere of influence has the potential to break this canon by foreshadowing an international system that is formed not out of sovereign states but from some sort of 'great-states'. Could spheres of influence ever become the basis of a new international order, a new international law? Or does sovereignty nevertheless persist within a sphere of influence to an extent where it could accommodate the inequality which a sphere of influence entails? Does a sphere of influence only take away the content of sovereignty and leave it formally intact, as Schmitt envisioned?

David Armstrong (1999, 559) writes that despite the changes in international relations over the last 50 years this central fact remains: 'A sovereign state cannot formally be subject to any external jurisdiction except by its own consent' and international law remains the law of states. Thus, for a sphere of influence to have any legitimacy in the present it needs to be a voluntary union of states, which does not involve violations of sovereignty. Likewise, in a forceful unification, which leaves no room to speculate about the sovereignty of the subjects, the new territorial unit is no longer a sphere of influence in its historical sense. On balance, if we dismiss concerns over the loss of sovereignty when considering spheres of influence, we lose that which has for a long time defined the concept. On the other hand, one could turn the attention away from sovereignty by focusing on the consent of the influenced. So, rather than discussing whether a sphere of influence violates sovereignty, we could discuss whether the consent of the influenced determines the appropriate term: where the influenced state resists its position, this qualifies as a sphere of influence; where the influenced state happily agrees to its position of being influenced, the relationship is one of alliance or integration. Here, the pejorative connotations follow the concept of sphere of influence, but the notion of influence would assume different levels of legitimacy.

Watson (2007, 65) sees the current international society as a concert of hegemonial powers where peripheral states are becoming increasingly willing to accept the donors' terms for the aid they need. Watson argues that state independence is becoming limited and nation-states everywhere may come to exercise less than total sovereignty. This trend toward collective hegemony began back with the Concert of Europe in the form of not so much a right as an obligation to intervene in other states (66). Watson asserts that after the collapse of the Soviet Union a concert has formed again (67). But this new concert is less concerned with maintaining the system of separate states than it is with peace and prosperity (79). Watson identifies ideas which belong to the hegemony-suzerainty area of the pendulum (see Chapter 2.3); for example, management of the international system, the privileges and responsibilities of great powers and rich nations, the Concert of Europe, intervention, standards of civilisation, human rights and women's rights, donor and recipient states, strings being attached to aid, derogations of sovereignty, and limits to independence (82). This is actually quite illustrative of the picture that emerges out of the history of *sphere of influence*. We see a movement towards a solidarist international society, but one which retains the special role of great powers and their influence over other states. We see sovereignty and the rule of non-intervention fading, giving room to the solidarist claims to human rights, but we see neither equality of states nor a world government emerging. We see the same pendulum gravitating towards great power management, just as it has been for the past two centuries. If we believe Watson and his pendulum theory we need to start taking the idea of sphere of influence more seriously, for it suggests that a sphere of influence is a fact of contemporary world politics, not merely a metaphor, a discourse or a pejorative term used as a means of shaming nations.

An analysis of the Cold War theorisations on spheres of influence and the Cuban Missile Crisis proves that there is still much to learn when it comes to understanding the phenomenon of spheres of influence. There is also much potential to theorise on spheres of influence with reference to the unique setting of the Cold War. For example, we can ask if the Cuban Missile Crisis is an example of spheres of influence contributing to international order or rather to disorder: was the crisis caused by competition over spheres of influence (causing disorder), or was it caused by a struggle for nuclear parity or some other form of conflict in which respect for spheres of influence prevented the escalation of the crisis (maintaining order)? Moreover, it is possible to study the relationship between institutionalisation and legitimisation of influence during the Cold War. Keal and Kaufman deemed the Cold War spheres of influence unjust but they recognised different forms of influence, with *de jure* influence representing an act of legitimisation. The Cold War idea of a sphere of influence was not pervaded by pejorative connotations to the extent it is today, which made it possible to see a sphere of influence as a formal arrangement that an influenced state can accept. In addition to questions of order and legitimacy, there is room to speculate on how much bipolarity depended on the division of spheres of influence and how much on the nuclear parity. Moreover, one could study if Cold War spheres of influence maintained order inside the blocs and restrained or prevented conflicts. Answering these questions would require empirical studies geared to conceptualising spheres of influence in the Cold War context.

Contesting the concept of sphere of influence helps us to question our beliefs about Russia's attempts to establish a sphere of influence, Cold War style. The first thing to acknowledge is that the term *sphere of influence* can be evoked as a means of 'memory politics'; reviving a certain memory in order to shame a present policy. When used in this way, the term becomes a tool of exclusion and can mobilise political activity. As I have argued, Russian scholars and politicians consider spheres of influence in a pejorative manner just like their Western colleagues. Can we still claim that *sphere of influence* is the concept that explains how the Russians see the drama of great power politics unfolding? And if so, what kind of *sphere of influence* is involved – one following the spirit of Schmitt's *Großräume*, Lippmann's Good Neighbor Policy, a new Soviet Union, or perhaps the super-state that Orwell was so afraid of? Rather than making claims about Russia's sphere of influence, it would be more interesting to ask what kind of *sphere of influence* the country pursues, and how the policy is being justified.

I am not arguing that we should not write and speak about Russia and spheres of influence. On the contrary, we need to discuss the two together, but in a way which contests the concept of sphere of influence and takes into consideration Russian political imaginations. Russian foreign policy experts rarely try to deny the country's interest in influencing its neighbourhood and there is no sign of the country wanting to relinquish its influence in the post-Soviet states. Thus, Russian influence is real, there is no denying that. I would argue that the dream lurking behind the Russian discourses is a *Großraum* in the style of the Good Neighbor Policy, even if the Russians are afraid to say so. The leaders of Russia see their country as a peacemaker in the region, mediating, bringing stability, fighting drug trafficking, and so on, but this still does not translate into an explicit vision of a Good Neighbor Policy. The reason why the Russian experts and politicians cannot verbalise their idea of a sphere of influence is that it represents systematic injustice and is too close to the idea of 'bloc politics'. Russia has chosen to uphold international law and the principle of non-intervention (in speech, at least) – which does not allow spheres of influence – because of the preoccupation with the United States, with its universalist threat and interventionist policies. Even though the Russian policy makers would take advantage of all the normative aspects of spheres of influence (for example, contribution to order and peace), the injustice that is inherent in spheres of influence cannot be articulated aloud, for this question would have to be answered if the Russians began speaking in favour of establishing a sphere of influence. Another reason for depoliticising influence is that there is a great deal of resistance against Russia's foreign policy. Arguments legitimising spheres of influence, or whatever territorial influence is termed, are of little use if the influenced states do not accept their position. Naumann paid great attention to this, and that is why he wanted to make sure that above all, influence would be acceptable for the influenced states. Moreover, considering the erratic progress with regard to democracy and human rights in Russia, there is also a danger of any Good Neighbor Policy coming closer to the Orwellian version of a super-state than that of responsibility. This is what the Western analysts in fact propose when they use the concept of sphere of influence as a pejorative notion to describe Russian foreign policy. What they have in mind is a dichotomy between good and bad influence, Russia's influence falling inevitably in the latter category.

One way to make sense of spheres of influence is to cease thinking about them in terms of absolute dichotomies. Watson offered the pendulum idea, and Buzan the spectrum, for breaking the pattern of thinking about solidarism and pluralism as exclusive choices. If we take Bull's spectrum of primacy and dominance as the two ways to consolidate a sphere of influence, we could see the movement between the two ends, such that primacy represents less of a violation of the rights of the influenced, and dominance involves more of a trampling of those rights. Then we would not have bad and good influence but violations of the rights of the influenced on a different scale. Moreover, if we attach to this 'spectrum of violation' to the consent of the influenced, we have another variable. More consent would make influence closer to primacy and less would take us towards dominance. We would then have two variables to determine whether a sphere of influence constitutes primacy or dominance: violation of (sovereign) rights and consent of the influenced. We can also reason that spheres of influence, when viewed as dominance, represent more of a pluralist international society which is founded upon sovereignty and the non-intervention principle. In a pluralist society spheres of influence could be conceptualised, like Keal and Bull do, as the crucial, even if unjust, elements of a great power management system. At the other end of the spectrum, a system which allows the unpacking of sovereignty could more easily accommodate spheres of influence understood in terms of primacy. Thus, in a solidarist society sovereignty would not define the relations among states as rigidly as within pluralism, and this would leave more space for mutually beneficial asymmetric relations to be formed and institutionalised – such as integration projects led by central power(s). If we wish to keep sphere of influence a notion which represents the tenets of the pluralist society, we could call the spheres of influence of a more solidarist society spheres of responsibility (see table 6.2).

Taking Buzan's spectrum idea, if sovereignty is a social contract, if we cast doubt on the usefulness of the nation-state in principle, and if we imagine concentration of power working together with limitations on sovereignty, we can find the middle of the pluralist-solidarist spectrum. The reason why we need to make sense of the middle of the spectrum is that it can also help us make sense of Russian visions of order and influence without the pejorative burden of the term

Table 6.2   A sphere of influence as dominance and primacy in pluralist and solidarist international societies

Spheres of influence at the pluralist end of international society	*Spheres of responsibility at the solidarist end of international society*
Dominance	Primacy
More violation	Less violation
No consent	Consent

sphere of influence. Ultimately the use of the term *sphere of influence* in relation to Russia boils to the usefulness of shaming and blaming. If we believe there is no need to investigate Russian visions of influence, and that the uncontested concept of sphere of influence is descriptive and useful, then we can stick to the existing regime of truth. I believe in the opposite: the need to constantly renew our political imagination.

6.3 Beyond the Pejorative

The normative problem is the heart and soul of the concept of sphere of influence. Then why is it that, in the present, we lack a discussion on the justice/injustice of spheres of influence? It is because we have ignored the history of spheres of influence and left unexamined the place the concept holds in IR. The Cold War mindset has left the concept of sphere of influence unchallenged; IR has failed to acknowledge that it is a contested concept. It is because the concept of sphere of influence is so strongly normative, that it must be contested. Connolly (1993, 2) writes, 'For to adopt without revision the concepts prevailing in a polity is to accept terms of discourse loaded in favor of established practices'. If one accepts the concept of sphere of influence without revision, one ends up constructing a certain image of Russian foreign policy. In fact, in order to condemn the practice of establishing or consolidating spheres of influence, one must begin by contesting the very concept. Contesting the concept of sphere of influence means problematising the present distinctive features that have rendered it an immutable and emotional metaphor of injustice. As a conclusion to this study I will devote the last words to elaborating the subjugated views on spheres of influence. My purpose is to stimulate discussion on the normative aspects of spheres of influence by bringing to light that part of the intellectual history of sphere of influence which has so far remained hidden and unarticulated.

Sphere of influence is not in essence a pejorative notion; it has been forged into one by the fires of the Cold War. Yet, *sphere of influence* is fundamentally a normative notion, because it has always needed justification. Colonial influence experienced its normative rise and fall, but this never happened to spheres of influence. Spheres of influence emerged as a type of political influence which embodied questions of inequality of power and violation of sovereignty and it has remained just that. The concept of sphere of influence, when contested, signifies a struggle for justification, a struggle for political pluralism and most importantly, a struggle between political reality and the ideal or utopian dream. Spheres of influence express the tension between morality and power politics, something which the pejorative interpretation does not capture.

What makes the concept of sphere of influence so topical is not only its popularity in political language, but its relationship to questions of law, order and justice within the system of states and outside of it. But when I look at the history of the concept of sphere of influence that I have attempted to unravel, the most relevant origins of the concept lie in the period when the globe was devastated by the two world wars. In this context the idea of influence beyond state borders, of regional constellations, is one which attempts to envision international order so as to rescue the world from war caused by nationalism. The origin of the concept, which I believe I have succeeded in ascertaining, was not in justifying oppression, violence and power. The impetus for establishing and consolidating spheres of influence is indeed war, but *preventing war*, that is, managing relations among the great states and preventing major war between them. Even the English School, especially Bull and Keal, envisioned the contribution that spheres of influence and great power management could make to international order. Those who theorised on the fair or just sphere of influence often did it from the perspective of their own nationalistic sentiments, but even so, they considered the world at large, because they knew that a new international order based on spheres of influence could not be forged by force. The project would have to work on a global basis and people would have to benefit from it. The power relation is expressed as 'responsibility' with the argument that this is the only way forward in the process of transforming the international system. But like any idea, when interpreted and put into practice it can suffer in the process and become transformed into something that is the complete antithesis of its initial intention. The Cold War destroyed the ideals of those who theorised on the creation of spheres of influence as an order for world peace. I believe none of them would have wished to see the bloc politics of the Cold War unfolding. The Cold War caused spheres of influence to lose that perhaps small, but still evident, element of compassion.

IR has been moving away from the state-centric perspective in recent years to study not only non-state actors on the international scene but also the effects that international theory has on individuals. For example, the concepts of human security and women's security have been established by moving beyond the traditional security concept dominated by the state. *Sphere of influence*, as I have stated, is an idea about the system of states but, as a theory, it must be viewed also as an attempt to organise international life such that people can live together. This is the eternal dilemma of humankind – how to live together in diversity. Both pluralism and solidarism are answers which international theorists have offered to us. But the history of spheres of influence has somewhat neglected the human perspective. The consideration of justice proceeds at the level of states and thus remains an abstraction. One way to approach justice in the case of spheres of influence, and as something more than a relationship between states, is to ask questions about the nature of the influencing state's regime. This is even more relevant when the dissatisfaction with Russian foreign policy relates to a dissatisfaction with the progress of democracy in the country.

During the Cold War, both the United States and the Soviet Union were recognised as having a sphere of influence, regardless of the differences between their regimes. The capitalists and the communists alike were capable of consolidating spheres of influence. Even though spheres of influence were implemented by different means and meant different things in practice, the same name was given to both superpowers' policies of influence. In sharp contrast, Lippmann thought that the United States would rule its neighbourhood in good will and its hegemony could not be likened to an interventionist sphere-of-influence policy. But what kind of democracy can sphere-of-influence policies represent? The closer we get to a notion of democracy in spheres of influence and the benefits they entail for the states influenced, the further we get from the pejorative associations of the concept, and the closer we step towards ideas on regionalism and integration. Orwell's *Nineteen Eighty-Four* is written from the perspective of the individual, demonstrating what life could be like in a totalitarian super-state, but we are left to wonder what is offered at the other pole – that with better-justified spheres of influence. Even if spheres of influence have been discussed historically more than anything as a matter of interstate justice, one should ultimately judge the justice and legitimation of spheres of influence at the level of the individuals affected. Naumann, Lippmann and Orwell got closest to capturing this perspective, even though none of them theorised how the super-state would, for better or worse, provide for the good life.

Something Carr wrote left an impression on me – something which seemed insignificant at first but which conflicted with the pejorative image of the concept of sphere of influence. Carr (1965, 69) argued that small or medium-sized nation states lack the resources to provide well-being for their people. This was his justification for constructing a *Großraum*. I wonder if it would be possible to transform the questions of interstate justice relating to spheres of influence, that is, the sovereignty dilemma and inequality of states, into a discussion on how spheres of influence affect the people living within them. Does a sphere of influence connect or divide people? What about the security and well-being of the influenced *people* rather than of the influenced state? Sovereignty is a value for a state, not necessarily for its inhabitants. Bringing in human justice to complete the normative discussion on spheres of influence means writing a new history of the phenomenon.

This research began by exploring what has been a pejorative yet uncontested concept but it should end with the words of Carl Schmitt (2003, 39):

> The earth has been promised to the peacemakers. The idea of a new *nomos* of the earth belongs only to them.

References

Allison, Graham and Philip Zelikov. 1999. *Essence of Decision: Explaining the Cuban Missile Crisis*. New York: Longman.

Anderson, Paul. 2006. 'Introduction'. In *Orwell in Tribune: 'As I Please' and Other Writings 1943–7*, edited by Paul Anderson, 1–56. London: Politico Publishing.

Armstrong, David. 1999. 'Law, Justice and the Idea of a World Society'. *International Affairs*, 75 (3): 547–61.

Astrov, Alexander. 2011. 'Great Power Management without Great Powers? The Russian-Georgian War of 2008 and Global Police/Political Order'. In *Great Power (Mis)Management: The Russian-Georgian War and Its Implications for Global Political Order*, edited by Alexander Astrov, 1–23. Farnham, Burlington: Ashgate.

Bartelson, Jens. 1995. *A Genealogy of Sovereignty*. Cambridge: Cambridge University Press.

——. 2009. *Visions of World Community*. Cambridge: Cambridge University Press.

Blouet, Brian W. 2005. 'Halford Mackinder and the Pivotal Heartland'. In *Global Geostrategy. Mackinder and the Defence of the West*, edited by Brian W. Blouet, 1–16. London, New York: Frank Cass.

Bordachev, Timofei. 2008. 'The Limits of Rational Choice'. *Russia in Global Affairs*, 4, <http://eng.globalaffairs.ru>.

Brzezinski, Zbigniew. 1998. *The Grand Chessboard: American Primacy and Its Geostrategic Imperatives*. New York: Basic Books.

——. 2004. *Choice: Global Domination or Global Leadership*. New York: Basic Books.

Bull, Hedley. 1966a. 'Society and Anarchy in International Relations'. In *Diplomatic Investigations. Essays in the Theory of International Politics*, edited by Herbert Butterfield and Martin Wight, 35–50. London: Allen & Unwin.

——. 1966b. 'The Grotian Conception of International Society'. In *Diplomatic Investigations*, edited by Herbert Butterfield and Martin Wight, 51–73. London: George Allen & Unwin Ltd.

——. 1969. 'The Twenty Years' Crisis Thirty Years on'. *International Journal*, 24 (4): 625–38.

——. 1984a. 'Conclusion'. In *Intervention in World Politics*, edited by Hedley Bull, 181–96. Oxford: Clarendon Press.

——. 1984b. 'Introduction'. In *Intervention in World Politics*, edited by Hedley Bull, 1–6. Oxford: Clarendon Press.

——. 2002. *The Anarchical Society. A Study of Order in World Politics*. New York: Palgrave. First published 1977.

Bull, Hedley and Adam Watson. 1985. 'Introduction'. In *The Expansion of International Society*, edited by Hedley Bull and Adam Watson, 1–12. Oxford: Clarendon Press.

Burnham, James. 1941. *The Managerial Revolution: What is Happening in the World*. New York: John Day.

——. 1947. *Struggle for the World*. London: Cape.

Butterfield, Herbert. 1966. 'The Balance of Power'. In *Diplomatic Investigations: Essays in the Theory of International Politics*, edited by Herbert Butterfield and Martin Wight, 132–48. London: Allen & Unwin.

Buzan, Barry. 2004a. *From International to World Society? English School Theory and the Social Structure of Globalisation*. Cambridge: Cambridge University Press.

——. 2004b. *The United States and the Great Powers: World Politics in the Twenty-First Century*. Cambridge: Polity Press.

Buzan, Barry and Ole Waever. 2003. *Regions and Powers: The Structure of International Security*. Cambridge: Cambridge University Press.

Carr, Edward Hallet. 1965. *Nationalism and After*. London: Macmillan. First published 1945.

——. 2001. *The Twenty Years' Crisis 1919–1939: An Introduction to the Study of International Relations*. Houndmills: Palgrave. First published 1939.

Chadwick, French E. 1916. 'Peace Through Worldwide Monroe Doctrine'. *New York Times*, SM4.

Chernyshev, Sergey. 2010. 'Towards a United Eurasia'. *Russia in Global Affairs* 3. <http://eng.globalaffairs.ru>.

Ciută, Felix. 2006. 'What Are We Debating? IR Theory between Empire and the "Responsible" Hegemon'. *International Politics*, 43: 173–96.

Clover, Charles. 1999. 'Dreams of the Eurasian Heartland: The Reemergence of Geopolitics'. *Foreign Affairs*, 78 (2): 9–13.

Cohen, Saul B. 1964. *Geography and Politics in a Divided World*. London: Methuen.

——. 2003. 'Geopolitical Realities and United States Foreign Policy'. *Political Geography*, 22: 1–33.

——. 2005. 'The Eurasian Convergence Zone: Gateway or Shatterbelt?' *Eurasian Geography and Economics*, 46 (1): 1–22.

Colombo, Alessandro. 2007. 'The "Realist Institutionalism" of Schmitt'. In *The International Political Thought of Carl Schmitt: Terror, Liberal War and the Crisis of Global Order*, edited by Luiza Odysseos and Fabio Petito, 21–35. New York, Oxon: Routledge.

Connolly, William E. 1993. *The Terms of Political Discourse*. Oxford, Cambridge: Blackwell.

Coones, Paul. 2005. 'The Heartland in Russian History'. In *Global Geostrategy. Mackinder and the Defence of the West*, edited by Brian W. Blouet, 64–89. London, New York: Frank Cass.

Curzon, Lord. 1907. *Frontiers*. Oxford: Clarendon Press.

Davis, Lynn E. 1974. *The Cold War Begins: Soviet-American Conflict Over Eastern Europe*. Princeton: Princeton University Press.

Der Derian, James. 1987. *On Diplomacy: A Genealogy of Western Estrangement*. Oxford: Basil Blackwell.

Dunne, Tim. 1998. *Inventing International Society: A History of the English School*. London: Macmillan.

Evans, Gareth. 2008. 'The Responsibility to Protect: An Idea Whose Time Has Come … and Gone?' *International Relations*, 22 (3): 283–98.

Foucault, Michel. 1980. 'Two Lectures. Lecture One: 7 January 1976'. In *Power/ Knowledge: Selected Interviews and Other Writings 1972–1977 / Michel Foucault*, edited by Colin Gordon, 78–92. Brighton: The Harvester Press.

Fox, William R.T. 1944. *The Super-Powers: The United States, Britain, and the Soviet Union – Their Responsibility for Peace*. New York: Harcourt, Brace and Company.

Freund, Julien. 1995. 'Schmitt's Political Thought'. *Telos*, 102: 11–42.

Furman, Dmitry. 2006. 'A Silent Cold War'. *Russia in Global Affairs*, 2, <http:// eng.globalaffairs.ru>.

Fursenko, Aleksandr and Timothy Naftali. 1998. *'One Hell of a Gamble': Khrushchev, Castro and Kennedy 1958–1964*. New York, London: W.W. Norton & Company.

Fursenko, Aleksandr and Timothy Naftali. 2006. *Khrushchev's Cold War: The Inside Story of an American Adversary*. New York, London: W.W. Norton & Company.

Gordon, Colin. 1980. 'Afterword'. In *Power/Knowledge: Selected Interviews and Other Writings 1972–1977 / Michel Foucault*, edited by Colin Gordon, 229–61. Brighton: The Harvester Press.

Gray, Colin S. 2005. 'In Defence of the Heartland'. In *Global Geostrategy: Mackinder and the Defence of the West*, edited by Brian W. Blouet, 17–35. London, New York: Frank Cass.

Hardt, Michael and Antonio Negri. 2001. *Empire*. Cambridge, Massachusetts: Harvard University Press.

Harle, Vilho. 2000. *The Enemy with a Thousand Faces: the Tradition of the Other in Western Political Thought and History*. Westport (Conn.): Praeger.

Hedenskog, Jakob. 2005. 'Filling "the gap": Russian security policy towards Belarus, Ukraine and Moldova under Putin'. In *Russia as a Great Power: Dimensions of Security Under Putin*, edited by Jakob Hedenskog, Vilhelm Konnander, Bertil Nygren, Ingmar Oldberg, and Christer Pursiainen, 130–55. London: Routledge.

Heffernan, Michael. 2000. 'Origins of European Geopolitics 1890–1920'. In *Geopolitical Traditions: A Century of Geopolitical Thought*, edited by Klaus Dodds and David Atkinson, 27–51. London: Routledge.

Hoffman, Stanley. 1984. 'The Problem of Intervention'. In *Intervention in World Politics*, edited by Hedley Bull, 7–28. Oxford: Clarendon Press.

Holbraad, Carsten. 1979. *Superpowers and International Conflict*. London, Basingstoke: Macmillan.

Horton, Michael. 2009. *Introducing Covenant Theology*. Michigan: Baker Books.

Huntington, Samuel. 2007. *Clash of Civilizations and the Making of New World Order*. Kindle edition. Simon & Schuster.

Hurrell, Andrew. 2007. 'One World? Many Worlds? The Place of Regions in the Study of International Society'. *International Affairs*, 83 (1): 127–46.

Ignatieff, Michael. 2003. *Empire Lite: Nation Building in Bosnia, Kosovo and Afghanistan*. Vintage Books. Kindle edition.

Jackson, Robert. 2000. *The Global Covenant: Human Conduct in a Word of States*. Oxford: Oxford University Press.

——. 2007. *Sovereignty: Evolution of an Idea*. Cambridge, Malden: Polity Press.

Karaganov, Sergey. 2010. 'Global Zero and Common Sense'. *Russia in Global Affairs*, 2, <http://eng.globalaffairs.ru>.

Kaufman, Edy. 1976. *The Superpowers and Their Spheres of Influence: The United States and the Soviet Union in Eastern Europe and Latin America*. London: Croom Helm.

Keal, Paul. 1983. *Unspoken Rules and Superpower Dominance*. London: Macmillan.

Kennedy, John F. 1961. 'Address Before the American Society of Newspaper Editors'. April 20, <http://www.jfklibrary.org>.

——. 1962. 'Radio and Television Report to the American People on the Soviet Arms Buildup in Cuba'. October 22, <http://www.jfklibrary.org>.

Khrushchev, Nikita. 1962a. 'Chairman Khrushchev's Letter to President Kennedy, October 23'. Accessed 24.8.2012, <http://www.pbs.org/wgbh/americanexperience/features/primary-resources/jfk-renounce/>.

——. 1962b. 'Letter From Chairman Khrushchev's to President Kennedy, October 24.' Accessed 2.11.2013. <http://history.state.gov/historicaldocuments/frus1961-63v06/d63>.

——. 1962c. 'Telegram From the Embassy in the Soviet Union to the Department of State, October 26.' Kennedy-Khrushchev exchanges. Accessed 2.11.2013. <http://history.state.gov/historicaldocuments/frus1961-63v06/d65>.

——. 1962d. 'Letter From Chairman Khrushchev, to President Kennedy, October 27.' Accessed 2.11.2013. <http://history.state.gov/historicaldocuments/frus1961-63v06/d66>.

Kimball, Warren F. 1991. *The Juggler: Franklin Roosevelt as Wartime Statesman*. Princeton: Princeton University Press.

Kosachev, Kostantin. 2007. 'Russia and the West: Where the Differences Lie'. *Russia in Global Affairs*, 4, <http://eng.globalaffairs.ru>.

Kremeniuk, Viktor. 2008. 'U.S. Foreign Policy in a Presidential Election Year'. *International Affairs: A Russian Journal of World Politics and Diplomacy*, 5: 39–48. Eastview.

Laffey, Mark and Jutta Weldes. 2008. 'Decolonizing the Cuban Missile Crisis'. *International Studies Quarterly*, 52: 555–77.

Lavrov, Sergei. 2007. 'The Present and the Future'. *Russia in Global Affairs*, 2, <http://eng.globalaffairs.ru>.

——. 2008. 'Russia and the World in the 21st Century'. *Russia in Global Affairs* 3, <http://eng.globalaffairs.ru>.

——. 2009. 'Diplomacy Today: Subject and Method'. *International Affairs: A Russian Journal of World Politics and Diplomacy*, 6: 1–10. Eastview.

——. 2010. 'The Euro-Atlantic Region: Equal Security for All'. *Russia in Global Affairs* 2, <http://eng.globalaffairs.ru>.

Leonard, Mark and Nicu Popescu. 2007. 'A Power Audit of EU-Russia Relations'. Policy Paper. Accessed 14.1.2012, <http://http://ecfr.eu/page/-/documents/ECFR-EU-Russia-power-audit.pdf>.

Lindley, M. F. 1926. *The Acquisition and Government of Backward Territory in International Law*. London: Longmans, Green & Co.

Linklater, Andrei and Hidemi Suganami. 2006. *The English School of International Relations: A Contemporary Reassessment*. Cambridge: Cambridge University.

Lippmann, Walter. 1940. *Some Notes on War and Peace*. New York: Macmillan.

——. 1945. *U.S. War Aims*. Boston: Little, Brown and Company.

——. 1963. 'Cuba and the Nuclear Risk'. *The Atlantic Monthly*. February.

Little, Richard. 2002. 'International System, International Society and World Society: A Re-evaluation of the English School'. In *International Society and the Development of International Relations Theory*, edited by B.A. Roberson, 59–79. London, New York: Continuum.

——. 2007. *The Balance of Power in International Relations: Metaphors, Myths and Models*. Cambridge: Cambridge University Press.

Lo, Bobo. 2002. *Russian Foreign Policy in the Post-Soviet Era: Reality, Illusion and Mythmaking*. Houndmills New York: Palgrave Macmillan.

Lukin, Alexander. 2008. 'From a Post-Soviet to a Russian Foreign Policy'. *Russia in Global Affairs*, 4, <http://eng.globalaffairs.ru>.

Luoma-aho, Mika. 2000. 'Carl Schmitt and the Transformation of the Political Subject'. *The European Legacy*, 5 (5): 703–16.

——. 2007. 'Geopolitics and Grosspolitics: From Carl Chmitt to E. H Carr and James Burnham'. In *The International Political Thought of Carl Schmitt: Terror, Liberal War and the Crisis of Global Order*, edited by Louiza Odysseos and Fabio Petito, 36–55. Oxon: Routledge.

Mackinder, H.J. 1996. *Democratic Ideals and Reality. A Study in the Politics of Reconstruction*. Washington, DC: National Defense University Press. First published 1919.

——. 2004. 'The Geographical Pivot of History'. *The Geographical Journal*, 170 (4): 298–321. First published 1904.

Markedonov, Sergei. 2007. 'The Paradoxes of Russia's Georgia Policy'. *Russia in Global Affairs*, 2, <http://eng.globalaffairs.ru>.

——. 2008. 'Regional Conflicts Reloaded'. *Russia in Global Affairs*, 4, <http://eng.globalaffairs.ru>.

Mearsheimer, John J. 2001. *The Tragedy of Great Power Politics*. New York, London: W. W. Norton & Company.

Minaev, Maxim. 2010. 'Punching Above One's Weight'. *Russia in Global Affairs*, 4, <http://eng.globalaffairs.ru>.

Monroe, James. 1823. 'Annual Message to Congress 12 February (Monroe Doctrine)'. Accessed 12.1.2012, <http://www.ushistory.org/documents/monroe.htm>.

Morgenthau, Hans. J. 1993. *Politics Among Nations*. New York: McGraw-Hill, Inc.

Naumann, Friedrich. 1917. *Central Europe*. Translated by Christabel M. Meredith. New York: Borzoi Books, Alfred A. Knopf. First published 1915.

Neumann, Iver B. 1999. *Uses of the Other: 'The East' in European Identity Formation*. Manchester: Manchester University Press.

——. 2008. 'Discourse Analysis'. In *Qualitative Methods in International Relations: A Pluralist Guide*, edited by Audie Klotz and Deepa Prakash, 61–77. New York: Palgrave Macmillan.

——. 2011. 'Entry Into International Society Reconceptualised: The Case of Russia'. *Review of International Studies*, 37 (2): 463–84.

Newsinger, John. 1999. *Orwell's Politics*. Houndmills, Basingstoke, Hampshire: Macmillan Press.

Nikolaev, Sergei. 2009. 'Russia-Central Asia: Toward Prosperity and Security'. *International Affairs: A Russian Journal of World Politics and Diplomacy*, 4: 26–34. Eastview.

Nye, Joseph. 2004. *Soft Power: The Means To Success In World Politics*. New York: Public Affairs.

Odysseos, Louiza and Fabio Petito. 2007. 'Introduction: The International Political Thought of Carl Schmitt'. *The International Political Thought of Carl Schmitt: Terror, Liberal War and the Crisis of Global Order*, edited by Louiza Odysseos and Fabio Petito, 1–17. New York, Oxon: Routledge.

Orwell, George. 1946. 'James Burnham and the Managerial Revolution'. *New English Weekly*. May. Accessed 12.1.2012, <http://www.k-1.com/Orwell/site/work/essays/burnham.html>.

——. 2000. 'Nineteen Eighty-Four'. In *George Orwell: The Complete Novels*, 743–925. London: Penguin Books. First published 1949.

——. 2006a. 'As I Please 7'. In *Orwell in Tribune: 'As I Please' and Other Writings 1943–7*, edited by Paul Anderson, 83–6. London: Politico's Publishing. First published 1944.

——. 2006b. 'As I Please 57'. In *Orwell in Tribune: 'As I Please' and Other Writings 1943–7*, edited by Paul Anderson, 238–41. London: Politico's Publishing. First published 1945.

——. 2006c. 'You and the Atom Bomb'. In *Orwell in Tribune: 'As I Please' and Other Writings 1943–7*, edited by Paul Anderson, 247–49. London: Politico's Publishing. First published 1945.

Ò Tuathail, Gearóid. 1996. *Critical Geopolitics: The Politics of Writing Global Space*. London: Routledge.

——. 1998. 'Introduction: Thinking Critically About Geopolitics'. In *The Geopolitics Reader*, edited by Gearóid Ó Tuathail, Simon Dalby, and Paul Routledge, 1–12. London: Routledge.

Papkova, Irina. 2011. 'Great Power Misalignment: The United States and the Russo-Georgian Conflict'. In *Great Power (Mis)Management: The Russian-Georgian War and Its Implications for Global Political Order*, 43–58. Farnham, Burlington: Ashgate.

Popescu, Nicu. 2006. 'Russia's Soft Power Ambitions'. CEPS Policy Brief, <http://aei.pitt.edu/11715/1/1388.pdf> (accessed 5.5.2012).

Popescu, Nicu and Andrew Wilson. 2009. 'The Limits of Enlargement-Lite: European and Russian Power in the Troubled Neighbourhood'. Policy Paper. European Council on Foreign Relations. Accessed 14.1.2012, <http://http:// ecfr.eu/page/-/documents/ECFR_ENP_report.pdf>.

Prozorov, Sergei. 2011. 'From Katechon to Intrigant: The Breakdown of the Post-Soviet Nomos'. In *Great Power (Mis)Management: The Russian-Georgian War and Its Implications for Global Political Order*, edited by Alexander Astrov, 25–42. Farnham, Burlington: Ashgate.

Putin, Vladimir. 2006. 'There Are More Benefits to be Gained through Friendship with Modern Russia'. *International Affairs: A Russian Journal of World Politics and Diplomacy*, 4: 1–7. Eastview.

——. 2011. 'A New Integration Project for Eurasia: The Future in the Making'. Article Published in the Newspaper *Izvestia*. Accessed 1.12.2011, <http:// premier.gov.ru/eng/events/news/16622/>.

Roberson, B.A. 2002. *International Society and the Development of International Relations Theory*. London, New York: Continuum.

Roosevelt, Theodore. 1904. 'Annual Message to Congress (Corollary to the Monroe Doctrine)'. Accessed 20.8.2012, <http://www.ourdocuments.gov/doc. php?doc=56>.

Rotblat, Joseph. 2007. 'Appendix 3: The Nobel Lecture'. In *A Quest for Global Peace: Rotblat and Ikeda on War, Ethics and the Nuclear Threat*, edited by Joseph Rotblat and Daisaku Ikeda, 129–36. London, New York: I.B. Tauris.

Round Discussion. 2010. 'BRIC as a New Form of Multilateral Diplomacy'. *International Affairs: A Russian Journal of World Politics and Diplomacy*, 2: 97–112. Eastview.

Routledge, Paul. 1998. 'Introduction'. In *The Geopolitics Reader*, edited by Gearóid Ó Tuathail, Simon Dalby, and Paul Routledge, 245–55. London: Routledge.

Rutherford, Geddes W. 1926. 'Sphere of Influence: An Aspect of Semi-Suzerainty'. *The American Journal of International Law*, 20 (2): 300–325.

Sakwa, Richard. 2011. 'Russia and Europe: Whose Society?'. *Journal of European Integration*, 33 (2): 197–214.

Schmitt, Carl. 2003. *The Nomos of the Earth in the International Law of the Jus Publicum Europaeum*. Translated by Ulmen, G.L. New York: Telos. First published 1950.

Spykman, Nicholas John. 1944. *The Geography of the Peace*. New York: Harcourt, Brace and Company.

Steel, Ronald. 1999. *Walter Lippmann and the American Century*. New Brunswick, New Jersey: Transaction Publishers.

Suganami, Hideki. 2010. 'The English School in a Nutshell'. *Ritsumeikan Annual Review of International Studies*, 9: 15–28.

SVOP. 2007. 'The World Around Russia: 2017: An Outlook for the Midterm Future'. The Council on Foreign and Defence Policy, State University – Higher School of Economics, Rio-Center. Accessed 12.9.2012, <http://cceis.hse.ru/data/2010/12/19/1208309423/2017_eng_reader.pdf>.

Taubman, William. 2005. *Khrushchev: The Man and His Era*. London: Simon & Schuster UK Ltd.

Trenin, Dimitri. 2002. *The End of Eurasia: Russia on the Border Between Geopolitics and Globalization*. Washington, DC: Carnegie Endowment for International Peace.

——. 2009. 'Russia's Spheres of Interest, Not Influence'. *The Washington Quarterly*, 32 (4): 3–22.

Tsygankov, Andrei P. 2010. *Russia's Foreign Policy: Change and Continuity in National Identity*. Lanham, Boulder, New York, Toronto, Plymouth: Rowman & Littlefield Publishers.

Ulmen, G.L. 2003. 'Translator's Introduction'. In *The Nomos of the Earth in the International Law of the Jus Publicum Europaeum*, by Carl Schmitt, 9–34. New York: Telos.

Vigezzi, Brunello. 2005. *The British Committee on the Theory of International Politics 1954–1985: The Rediscovery of History*. Milan: Edizioni Unicopli.

Vincent, R.J. 1974. *Nonintervention and International Order*. Princeton, New Jersey: Princeton University Press.

——. 1990. 'Order in International Politics'. In *Order and Violence: Hedley Bull and International Relations*, edited by J.D.B. Miller and R.J. Vincent, 38–64. Oxford: Clarendon Press.

Walker, R.B.J. 1995. *Inside/Outside: International Relations as Political Theory*. Cambridge: Cambridge University Press.

Waltz, Kenneth. 1979. *Theory of International Politics*. New York: McGraw-Hill.

Watson, Adam. 1985a. 'European International Society and Its Expansion'. In *The Expansion of International Society*, edited by Hedley Bull and Adam Watson, 13–32. Oxford: Clarendon Press.

——. 1985b. 'New States in the Americas'. In *The Expansion of International Society*, edited by Hedley Bull and Adam Watson, 127–42. Oxford: Clarendon Press.

——. 1992. *Evolution of International Society*. London: Routledge.

——. 2002. 'The Practice Outruns the Theory'. In *International Society and the Development of International Relations Theory*, edited by B.A. Roberson,145–55. London, New York: Continuum.

——. 2007. *Hegemony & History*. Oxon, New York: Routledge.

Wendt, Alexander. 1992. 'Anarchy is What States Make of it: The Social Construction of Power Politics'. *International Organization*, 46: 391–425.

Wight, Martin. 1966a. 'The Balance of Power'. In *Diplomatic Investigations: Essays in the Theory of International Politics*, edited by Herbert Butterfield and Martin Wight, 149–75. London: Allen & Unwin.

——. 1966b. 'Western Values in International Relations'. In *Diplomatic Investigations: Essays in the Theory of International Politics*, edited by Herbert Butterfield and Martin Wight, 89–131. London: Allen & Unwin.

——. 1977. *Systems of States*. Leicester: Leicester University Press.

——. 1995. *Power Politics*, edited by Hedley Bull and Carsten Holbraad. Leicester: Leicester University Press. First published 1946.

Wilhelmsen, Julie and Geir Flikke. 2005. 'Evidence of Russia's Bush Doctrine in the CIS'. *European Security*, 14 (3): 387–417.

Williams, John. 2005. 'Pluralism, Solidarism and the Emergence of World Society in English School Theory'. *International Relations*, 19 (1): 19–38.

Windsor, Philip. 1984. 'Superpower Intervention'. In *Intervention in World Politics*, edited by Hedley Bull, 45–66. Oxford: Clarendon Press.

Wolff, Larry. 1994. *Inventing Eastern Europe: The Map of Civilization on the Mind of the Enlightenment*. Stanford, California: Stanford University Press.

Index